Lisbon

Footprint

Caroline Lascom

Contents

Listings

About the author

Caroline Lascom graduated from the University of Manchester with a degree in Latin American studies. After stints at BBC magazines in London and Evans and Novak in Washington DC, she finally traded the suit for the sarong and got back to her Latin roots. An intended two-week stop over in Lisbon en route to Brazil soon turned into a year living in Bairro Alto, teaching English and getting under the skin of Europe's most laid-back city. After a few years travelling around Central and South America and working as a freelance writer and translator in Barcelona she joined the Footprint editorial team in Bath. As well as returning to Lisbon whenever possible she is also the co-author of Footprint Havana.

Acknowledgements

Many thanks to everyone who helped out with the research of this guide. Thanks to Carlos Ferreira for his kind hospitality, to Sebastião in Sintra for his companionship, place to write and use of his horses, to indefatigable Alcântara clubbers José and João Filho and Bairro Altistas Angelina and Gusmão. Thanks to Maria Gonçalves for all her gastronomic tips and cultural nuggets. Thanks also to António at Opus Gay for all his guidance and everyone at Frágil, Lux and Stasha.

Very special thanks to my family for all their support and to Adrian for the photos and excellent company.

Thanks to everyone at Footprint, especially Sarah Thorowgood and Claire Boobbyer. Thanks also to Stephanie Lambe and to Rachel Fielding for commissioning me.

Arriving in Lisbon is like hurling yourself into a medieval portal. Weaved into precipitous hills, the Alfama is where Lisbon began, a bewildering medina of jumbled houses, cobblestone streets, vertiginous alleyways, and *becos,* barely wide enough for the passing of a fat goat. Beneath the castellated mass of the iconic Castelo de São Jorge, serpentine streets rise and fall to countless *miradouros* where suddenly, with surreal drama, a hazy mirage of architectural marvels rises gloriously from honeycombed red roof-tops.

In the valley below Lisbon unfurls like an amphitheatre along the River Tagus, casting its spell of antiquity. Arthritic trams chug up ludicrous gradients, zigzagging before a concertina of squat dwellings where gypsy-eyed boys leap-frog over chunks of Roman walls. Washing is strewn like origami from gritty *tascas* encrusted with lustrous 16th-century *azulejos* tiles. Alongside hole-in-the-wall grocers, where smelly sheaves of codfish hang from the rafters, a pristine baroque cupola soars above an arboreous Renaissance park.

Brave Old World

Belém was the Cape Canaveral of the 15th century, the launch pad for Vasco da Gama's epic endeavours which would see the Portuguese flag waving on five continents. In an ecstasy of maritime glory, megalomanic monarchs enshrined their victories in stone, bequeathing an architectural confection that went by the name of Manueline. Whimsical monasteries and turreted castles infused with oriental mystique sprung up along the banks of the Tagus, where fantastical creatures and exotic peoples were paraded by returning adventurers. Portuguese pride reached its zenith, buoyed by hopes of eternal glory. In 21st-century Lisbon, along the shaggy streets of the Alfama and Bairro Alto, black-shawled divas sing out the soliloquys of Portugal's national song, the fado, a requiem for Portugal's 15th-century glory days, and a coping mechanism for cosmic historical woes of promise unfulfilled.

Back seat drivers

With its back to Europe, and its soul circa 1498, scrupulously low-key Lisbon has long taken a back seat while its western neighbours strutted their stuff. During nearly 50 years of solitude, Salazar smothered Lisbon in a conservative mantle, and his legacy of fascist-style behemoths now erupt across the city like gatecrashers at a medieval party. But, with gear crunching acceleration, Lisbon has emerged from its cocoon.

The party started with Expo 98 when from the drawing board of Alpha architects, Siza Vieira and Santiago Calatrava, came glitzy Parque das Nações, where shimmering steel pavilions look like billowing waves, apartment buildings like ocean liners and metro stations like space pods. And it's not all physical; the Portuguese *movida* has gone stratospheric. Gilded *Lisboetas* emerge from glitzy riverside warehouse conversions, flanked by crumbling walls still emblazoned with 1970s revolutionary murals. Along the tribal streets of boho Bairro Alto, achingly hip scenesters emerge from Barbarella fashion boutiques, sleek bars, über clubs and style emporiums.

At a glance

Baixa and Rossio

Straight-to-the-point, square and spare, Lisbon's downtown, the Baixa, is the city's commercial nexus, a grid of uniform blocks and thrusting thoroughfares. Built in the wake of the 1755 earthquake (see p39), it was an ideal forged by the bombastic Marquês de Pombal. Pedestrianized Rua Augusta is the Rambla-esque central promenade which funnels south to handsome Praça do Comércio, Lisbon's Whitehall and medieval city gateway fanning majestically onto the River Tagus. Baixa's main square is effervescent Rossio, the city's central reference point, where banks bump up against art nouveau cafés, baroque churches, hole-in-the-wall *ginginha* bars and neoclassical theatres.

Bairro Alto

Bairro Alto has always been Lisbon's Latin quarter, described by Portugal's great contemporary novelist José Saramago as "exalted in name and location, but low in its way of life". Essentially a residential district, by day a tribal peace prevails. From crumbling buildings splattered with shocking pink bougainvillea and festooned with washing, community life ticks over nonchalantly in play schools, antiquarian bookstores, grocers and barbers. But by night, attitude and angst unite for creative revelry. Lisbon's cool emerge from bubble-gum boutiques and record shops stacked to the rafters with vinyl. Skirting the district's outer edge, Rua da Misericordia leaves behind Bairro Alto's raffish charms. A clutch of antique shops, a lavish baroque church and languid botanical gardens usher in Príncipe Real, gay, aloof and hip, the old town incarnation of style Lisbon.

Chiado

Gentrified, fashionable Chiado is Lisbon's cultural heartland and retail playground, where Hermés, Cartier and Ana Salazar rub

Ten of the best

Best

1 **Mosteiro dos Jerónimos** The most beautiful example of the Manueline style, the embodiment of Portuguese maritime glory, p83.

2 **Alfama** Where Lisbon began, a medieval medina of serpentine streets lined with pastel-clad Moorish houses rolled out like a tapestry onto Lisbon's highest hill, p63.

3 **Sintra** Romantic, blissful Eden of lush mountains, ravines nestled with Moorish castles, fairy-tale palaces and eerie monasteries, p105.

4 **Museu Calouste Gulbenkian** Dizzying collection of Lalique jewellery, Oriental art, Egyptian antiquities and 20th-century European masterpieces, p90.

5 **Antiga Pastelaria de Belém** Pay homage at the temple of the greatest purveyor of *pastéis de nata* in Portugal; 10,000 people a day can't be wrong, p152.

6 **Convento e Museu Arqueológico do Carmo** Destroyed by the earthquake, this surreal convent with skeletal arches and a nave overgrown with grass exudes ethereal mystique, p54.

7 **Lux** Saunter through the sleek bar, cruise out onto the breezy terrace, order a cocktail, and lap up the stunning sea views and beautiful people, p166.

8 **Design Museum** A fantastic collection of 20th-century design icons, from French art nouveau furniture to Arnie Jacobsen chairs and Philippe Starck cheese graters, p85.

9 **Tram 28** A hair-raising tram ride through the backstreets and vertiginous alleyways of Old Europe, p72.

10 **Bairro Alto bar hop** A bacchanalian kernal of the stylish, salacious, eccentric and jazzy, seared with fiesty cocktails and coated in sticky rough wine, p160.

shoulders with dusty antiquarian bookshops, contemporary art museums, and sumptuous rococo theatres. During the 19th century, Chiado provided the backdrop for literary musings, political intrigue and revolutionary fervour. The area was devastated by fire in 1988, and while it remains a place of grace and taste, an enchanted district within an advancing metropolis, the arrival of a new department store and a more cosmopolitan vibe infected the prevailing literary romanticism. Today, bouffanted ladies meet for afternoon tea, footballers wives amass consumer durables and media darlings and tourists camp out on the terraces of turn-of-the century art nouveau cafés.

Avenida da Liberdade and around

The spine of the city, the Avenida, forges north from Praça dos Restauradores in the Baixa to the manicured lawns of the Parque Eduardo VII. Along the mile long, seven-lane, traffic-clogged nightmare spans an architectural pastiche of art deco, art nouveau and modernist buildings, a parade ground for Lisbon's upwardly mobile denizens. Infused with more than a whiff of urban angst, it also harbours seedy nooks of low-level prostitution but spreading furtively to the east and west, a clutch of stellar museums, smokey jazz bars, dingy *tascas* and Renaissance parks are worthy of off-base exploration.

Alfama, Castelo and around

Unfolding like a medieval diorama beneath the mystical Castelo de São Jorge, the Alfama is Lisbon's spiritual heart. An old Moorish quarter where ribbons of alleyways coil into blind alleys, where steep *travessas* and crooked alcoves reveal timeless vistas, and where old world rituals and customs unfold like an old Pathé newsreel. Stooping old *varinhas* (fish wives) shrouded in black, tout the catch of the day, while tour groups parade before an awesome spectacle of lavish baroque churches, gasping at melting sunsets and cooing at public fountains where locals still wash their clothes.

São Bento, Estrela and Lapa

Descending west, Chiado's backyard is the earthy neighbourhood of São Bento. Hardly easy on the eye, it is a web of ramshackle steets punctuated with sticky *tascas*, and closet-sized shops stuffed with everything from Victorian bras to African voodoo dolls. São Bento gives way to Estrela – smarter, smug and with a preppy vigour ensuring a healthy line up of arty cafés, bars and bookshops. To the south, grungy riverside Alcântara plays hosts to some of the best club nights in the city. Estrela's lush park has a coquettish vibe: students flirt in dreamy rose gardens and craggy old men while away the hours playing *boules* and reading *La Bola*. Further west, streets climb to haughty Lapa, a hushed and flushed district where ambassadors, presidents and pop stars sejourn, serviced by palatial hotels, tantalized by some of the finest Portuguese cuisine and soothed by immaculately coiffered foliage.

Belém and the western waterfront

Stretching along the Tagus, Belém is Portugal's imperial triumphs made stone. From where Vasco da Gama set sail, a panoply of marvels reveal the historical and psychological DNA of the city – the sensational Mosteiro dos Jerónimos, the epitome of the Manueline style, with stone like whipped cream, and the oriental mystique of Lisbon's poster child the Torre de Belém. But Belém is not all curl and swirl and a shrine to glories past, the cutting edge Design Museum parades a reverential display of pop art icons and gadgets and salivating *Lisboetas* flock to the *Antiga Pastelaria de Belém*, the cathedral to Lisbon's famed custard tart, the *pastel de nata*. Beyond museums and imperial endeavour, Belém is a living, breathing suburb of candy-coloured houses, manicured gardens and seaside walkways.

Northern Lisbon and the Gulbenkian

The wide boulevards between Praça Marquês de Pombal and Campo Grande form the *Estados Novos*, the frontier, where medieval Lisbon crosses into a brave new world of conspicous consumption and throughly modern malaise. This network of prosaic single-minded throughfares, flanked by fascist-style behemoths, banal office blocks and shopping malls, doesn't exactly invite tourist attention, but for rainy days and Sundays, there is a clutch of impressive museums, and child-friendly activities, and Lisbon's premier attraction, the unassailable Museu Calouste Gulbenkian. Football pilgrims pay homage at the hallowed turf of *Benfica* and *Sporting*, with two, newly spruced stadiums unveiled for Euro 2004.

Parque das Nações

To the northeast, suburban sprawl gives way to sleek modernism at Parque das Nações, site of Expo 98, homage to Vasco da Gama and a startling contrast to the old city's souk-like streets. This one-time urban wasteland has metamorphosized into a cosmic landscape with a feathery-steel metro station that looks like it is about to take flight, zen gardens and breezy walkways, a glitzy shopping centre, modernist public art spaces and an array of family attractions.

Around Lisbon

Less than an hour by train from central Lisbon, Sintra is unmissable. Nestling in an arcadia of velveteen hills are Moorish palaces, eerie ruined castles, hobbit hermitages and arguably the greatest act of architectural blasphemy in Portugal, the Palácio da Pena. The rugged Atlantic beaches of Cascais and Estoril, cast in the role of the Portuguese Riviera, are just over half an hour away by train. While spruced and moneyed Cascais clings tentatively to its charming old fishing heritage, Estoril, immortalized in spy novels and Bond movies, was the enclave of playboys and exiled monarchs. The sublime baroque palace of Mafra, symbol of Portugal's opulence after the discovery of diamonds in Brazil, is close to the gusty surfing beaches of Ericeira, and Queluz, Lisbon's

Versailles, oozing French grandeur and Portuguese eclecticism.

Trip planner

With burning summers and a mild winter climate, Lisbon is a good year-round destination. From November to March, swirling Atlantic winds and heavy downpours can soon dampen outdoor exploration plans but with excellent museums, the child-friendly Parque das Nações, warming port wine, hearty Alentejo cuisine and cafés galore, pulling down the hatches for a while can be pleasurable nonetheless. June is non-stop jubilation, when Lisbon celebrates the People's Saints. Festivities climax with the festival of Saint Anthony on the June 12-13, a great time to visit when not suprisingly prices are at a premium and pre-booking accommodation is recommended. Many museums close on Mondays, while on Sunday, many are free.

A weekend (2-4 days)

While Lisbon's main sights are clustered within easy reach, with seven ludicrous hills to negotiate, attempting to fit in too many on foot, especially in summer, can be a draining experience.

A weekend trip will allow plenty of time to take snap shots of the main sights of central Lisbon, the old town, Belém and even Parque das Nações, and still give you time for relaxed close encounters with the Moorish quarters of Alfama and Graça, as well as a muse round the art nouveau coffee shops or designer labels of chi chi Chiado. Bohemian Bairro Alto and the western waterfront can be saved for nocturnal hedonistic pleasures – expanding your repertoire of Portuguese gastro classics, sharpened with punchy caipirinhas.

Kick-start the day in Rossio, the city's downtown centre, with a turbo-charged *bica* (espresso) and *pastel de nata* at one of the area's iconic cafés, like *Café Suiça*, before strolling down pedestrianized Rua Augusta to Praça do Comercio, where the unofficial tourist Tram 28 departs for a magical helter-skelter ride around the city. Inevitable free-wheeling around Lisbon's old town begins with the imposing cathedral, culminating at the Castelo de

São Jorge, where from its ramparts the city's past, present and future is revealed.

Unhurried wanderings around neighbourhoods of the Alfama, Graça and Santa Cruz, yield earthy charms. Coiling alleyways reveal majestic church towers and pristine domed basilicas erupting into a jumbled skyline and leave time to marvel at the scarlet sunset from the *miradouro* of Graça. If it is Tuesday or Saturday, have a nose round Feira da Ladra flea market, which you can follow up with a soulful lunch at the Mercado de Santa Clara restaurant. For high art, there is a treasure trove of artefacts at the Museum of Decorative Arts or save your cultural feast for a minimum half-day pilgrimage to Lisbon's premier site, the awesome Museu Calouste Gulbenkian, 10 minutes by metro from Rossio.

It would be a sin to dedicate anything less than one day to Belém, a 25-minute tram ride from Praça do Comercio, steeped in the exoticism and glory of Portugal's maritime past. The sublime Mosteiro dos Jerónimos is a Manueline confection good enough to eat and a mere stone's throw from the temple to Lisbon's divine *pastel de nata*, the *Antiga Pastelaria de Belém*. The universal favourite is the Design Museum, saluted as one of the best of its kind in Europe.

To leave out heavenly Sintra, Byron's "glorious Eden", from any trip to Portugal would be a huge mistake. Here you can visit hysterical Bavarian castles and mystical Moorish palaces, surrounded by jagged peaks, covered in lush greenery and pinnacles rising like fingers, or gorge yourself on *queijadas de Sintra* and gallop through the mountains on horseback.

One week or more

A week will allow you time to linger in the city's most atmospheric quarters and target the crème de la crème of Lisbon's museums. Priceless porcelain, 18th-century French furniture and enigmatic Portuguese landscape paintings are displayed against a sumptous art nouveau backdrop in the Casa António Gonçalves. In Lapa, the acknowledged masterpieces of 15th-century Portuguese art are displayed at the Museum of Ancient Art. Chiado's Contemporary Art Museum flaunts Portugal's most dynamic naturalist artists of the 19th century, in a more postmodern setting. The eerie Convento do Carmo houses a mind-boggling display of artefacts from Peruvian mummies to classical antiquities.

The wonderful display of *azulejo* tiles at the Tile Museum, a 15-minute bus ride from Restauradores, is one of the city's best museums, while the Fado Museum will prepare you for more informed appreciation of the nuances and history of the national song and its iconic goddess, Amália. Northern exposure will be minimal with time constraints, but just 20 minutes by metro from Rossio, a half-day dedicated to the glitzy Expo site Parque das Nações unmasks Lisbon's futuristic alter ego. With its modernist landscape, wonderous aquarium, child-friendly parks, and soothing riverside walkways, it's a perfect antidote to the old town alleys and vertigo-inducing hills.

Make time for serious city sleuthing in the medina of Alfama's medieval streets. Get away from the crowds and uncover Lisbon's African and Brazilian soul in raffish Mouraria and São Bento, or for more refined pursuits, amble the manicured streets of haughty Lapa.

Lisbon's panoramic beauty is best appreciated from the sea and the commuter ferry ride across the river to Cacilhas and the Rio-esque statue of Cristo Rey reveals Lisbon's antiquarian splendour from atop the Golden Gate clone of Ponte 25 de Abril.

By night, you can spend more time bar-hopping in Bairro Alto, become more familiar with fado in Alfama, dance to hip-swaying African *mornas* in São Bento or test your street cred at cool warehouse conversions, like *Bico de Sapato*.

Less than an hour's train ride from the city you can bask on the beaches of Cascais, explore its backstreets and its fishing village past. The 18th-century convent-palace of Mafra is a baroque masterpiece, the symbol of Portugal's glorious hey day, while the lofty Palácio de Queluz is often refered to as Portugal's 'mini Versailles'.

Contemporary Lisbon

On the western fringes of Europe, with its face to the Atlantic and its toes dipped in Africa, Lisbon has always done things its own way with more than a whiff of graceful solemnity. Arriving in the city it certainly feels as though this 'Old' European capital has skipped a century or two. While Paris flaunts its chic and Barcelona revels in architectural aplomb, understated Lisbon seems to have relished being on the sidelines, perennially cast in the role of Spain's poor relation. But it's this defining nonchalance that hypnotizes both artful *flâneurs* and lazy hedonists. Nothing quite sums up Lisbon's quirky, phlegmatic status like the bloodless revolution of 1974. So laid back were the revolutionaries that while making their final advance on the capital they stopped their tanks at a red traffic light.

For all its apparent lackadaisical charm, 21st-century Lisbon is in the throes of another revolution, and it's a far cry from the despairing metropolis of Wim Wenders' 1988 movie, *Lisbon Story*. At every turn it appears the city is blazing a trail. It all began with Expo 98 and the construction of its Calatrava-designed stage, charismatic Parque das Nações, where sun glimmers on steel and creative brio meets post-modern vision. Lisbon's got a new swagger and celebrity status but most significant of all for *Lisboetas* is that their city, which always sought solace from the sea, has once again turned towards the water. From where Vasco da Gama set sail for India, glitzy cruise ships loll alongside sleek warehouses, furnished with a style to rival London or Milan. And all just in time to host its next big party – Euro 2004.

Viewed from any of Lisbon's high-altitude *miradouros*, the city spreads out below in an architectural pastiche, a juxtaposition of modernism and traditionalism, taste and tack, the monstrous and the magnificent. While art deco curves and art nouveau swirls rub harmoniously against one another, if you whisper the word 'Amoreiras' most *Lisboetas* will flinch unequivocally. The work of polemical architect Tomás Taveira, this chunky, brash, shopping centre thrust its way incongruously onto the skyline in the 1980s, heralding the dawn of a new and conspicuous consumption.

Having been labelled in the 15th century as the greatest empire of its time and then denigrated in the 20th as Europe's underachieving Third World nation, it's not surprising that the Portuguese psyche has taken a battering. Ravaged by earthquake, razed by fire and cocooned in the padded cell of nearly half a century's worth of dictatorship, Portugal has long been experiencing an identity crisis. But the current centre-right government, with Jose Manuel Durão Barrosa at the helm, has recently been relishing its growing stature on the world stage. In 1999 Portugal was saluted internationally for its smooth handover of the former colony Macau to China and its role in the reconstruction of an independent East Timor. With a bolstered sense of pride, 2003 has seen Portugal keenly embracing its role in President Bush's 'New' Europe. In the aftermath of the recent Gulf War, Barrosa committed some 150 national guard troops and aid provisions to the reconstruction of Iraq, a policy which proved controversial at home but obviously scored points with the US.

Despite an acute funding crisis and the legacy of a totalitarian regime, a throbbing creativity pulsates through the city's artistic communities. From contemporary architecture and the performing arts to fashion and experimental music, Lisbon's hotbed of creative talent is gaining international recognition. Young, irreverent Bairro Alto fashion designers are showing their collections on the catwalks of London, Paris and Milan and contemporary artists like Paula Rego, the first artist-in-residence at London's National Gallery in 1990, are exhibited in galleries worldwide. And celebrity culture, epitomized by the unassailable popularity of Portugal's *Big Brother*, is nevertheless berated by older generations as the most potent symbol of declining traditional values and polluted sense of national identity. In coffee shops across the city you'll still hear *Lisboetas* longing for the days of Salazar when fado, football and Fátima were the unifying national obsessions.

Rossio, the bustling heart of downtown Baixa
Rebuilt following the great earthquake in 1755, the neoclassical Teatro Nacional de Dona Maria II, baroque marble fountains and undulating mosaic paving of Praca dom Pedro IV contrast with the thrusting towers of Salazar's 20th-century Estados Novos to the north.

If, as the saying goes, hemlines follow the economy, things are definitely on the up. Since joining the EU in 1988, and bidding *adeus* to the escudo in 2000, Portugal has received millions of dollars in aid from EU grants. The catch 22 has been that as a result of Portugal's increased financial buoyancy it no longer qualifies for EU subsidies and in 2001 the public deficit spiralled to 4.1% of GDP. Keeping up with the *Joãos* was big in the 90s. Debt went through the roof as gadget-crazy *Lisboetas* yearning for desirable consumer durables, most notably mobile phones and cars, went on a spending frenzy. But since 2002, Barroso's government has pushed through unpopular measures, including a rise in sales tax, which has helped cut the public deficit forecasts for 2004 to an estimated 2.8% of GDP.

However, Lisbon's soaring Euro-capital kudos belies bleaker undercurrents. In graceless suburbs breeze-block housing breeds a subculture of crime, violence and HIV. Portugal has the highest rate of HIV infection in the EU and is the only nation where rates of infection are on the rise. Most worrying of all, the highly drug-resistant HIV subtype G, which was previously thought to exist only in Africa, was recently discovered in Portugal. Racism also remains an acute problem and Portugal's vast immigrant population came under the spotlight in October 2003, when *Time* magazine's cover story entitled "When the Meninas came to town", depicted medieval, traditional Bragança in Northern Portugal as "Europe's new red light district", following an investigation into the influx of Brazilian prostitutes to the area. The story was a bombshell for Lisbon's Euro 2004 PR campaign.

Lisbon's allure has always been its intimacy, its secrets yielded to the errant wanderer. While the city's medieval kernels still intrigue, its time-honoured rituals enchant and its architectural glories mesmerize, 21st-century Lisbon is laced with a dynamism which has redrawn the skyline, improved infrastructure and provided the city with a much-needed ego boost. While the city embarks on a road less travelled, *Lisboetas* are shedding their vintage woes and melancholy slough and facing up to the challenges of the future.

Lisbon is economically accessible from London and regional UK airports, with scheduled flights from as little as £100. In October 2003, new low cost airline *Now* added Lisbon to its proposed schedule for 2004, and other budget airlines are expected to follow suit. Other options including travelling by *Eurostar* and *TGV* down to Spain and connecting with sleepers to Lisbon, as well as the 40-odd-hour *Eurolines* coach services, work out much more expensive and are impractical for a short visit.

With seven muscle-aching hills to negotiate, labyrinthine streets and medina *becos* and *travessas*, getting around Lisbon, especially in the blaze of summer, can be a physically demanding experience, but one that is graciously aided by trundling trams, Gothic Eiffel-esque elevators and an efficient bus and train network. Lisbon's clean, efficient and artful underground is a pleasure to use, though generally, when nosing around the centre and old town quarters, your feet are all you'll need. An excellent train network links Lisbon to the Atlantic beaches and Sintra in less than 45 minutes.

Getting there

Air

From UK and Europe The national airline is **TAP Air Portugal** which flies daily from Heathrow and Gatwick (two hours 20 minutes). Prices are highest between June 20 and August 14, at Christmas and during school holidays, costing upwards of £118, including taxes, for a restricted return ticket, and exceeding £400 for a flexible ticket. From Manchester, TAP code shares routes with **PGA, Portugália Airlines**. There is one daily flight at 1855, costing upwards of £160. There are three daily direct **British Airways** flights with competitive prices and frequent special offers, upwards of £113 including taxes, from London airports, rising to £186 from Manchester. Other continental airlines such as **Air France**, **Iberia**, **KLM**, **Lufthansa** and **Swissair** offer scheduled services via the carrier's European hub city, but they tend to be more expensive, with added taxes and often inconvenient waiting periods. From January 2004, **Now** airlines intends to begin routes from Luton with fixed fares from £65 one way, regardless of when you book. If you have a week or more, and time permits, a cheaper, flexible alternative from Manchester is the **Monarch** scheduled flight to Faro, with fares starting at £47, one-way, midweek, advanced booking. From Faro, convenient bus and train services run direct to Lisbon, see below (around four hours) and you have the benefit of creating open-jaw tickets.

From North America There are daily direct flights from New York JFK with **TAP Air Portugal**, and Newark with **Continental** (6¾ hours) and **British Airways** fly to Lisbon from JFK via London. Low season winter fares (September to April, except peak December 15 to January 2 period), can be as low as US$350 plus taxes (around US$100), flying mid-week, with September and October being the cheapest months. During summer, peak fares start at US$650, plus taxes. Cheapest fares are limited to a 30-day

→ Airlines and agents

Air France, T 0845 0845 111, www.airfrance.com
Airline network, T 0870 241 00 11
www.airline-network.co.uk
Alitalia, T 0874 5448 259, www.alitalia.it
American Airlines, T 1 800 433 7300,
www.aa.com (USA)
British Airways, T 0870 8509850, www.ba.com
Cathay Pacific, T 020 8834 8888,
www.cathaypacific.com
Continental Airlines, T 1 800 525 0280,
www.continental.com (USA)
Dial-A-Flight, T0870 333 4488, www.dialaflight.com
Expedia, T 0870 0500808, www.expedia.com
Iberia, T 0845 601 2854, www.iberia.com
KLM, T 0870 5074 074. www.klm.com
LastMinute, www.lastminute.com
Lufthansa, T 0845 7737 747, www.lufthansa.com
Monarch, T 0870 0 40 63 00, www.flymonarch.com
Now, T 0845 4589737, www.now-airlines.com
PGA, Portugália Airlines, T 087 075 500 21,
www.pga.pt
Qantas, T 1 300 650 729, www.quantas.co.au (AU)
Singapore Airlines, T 618 820 30 800,
www.singaporeair.com (AU)
STA Travel, T 0870 1600 599, www.sta-travel.com
TAP Air Portugal, T 08456 010 932,
www.tap-airportugal.co.uk
Travelocity, T 0870 876 3876, www.travelocity.com
Trailfinders, T 020 7937 1234, www.trailfinders.com
Virgin Atlantic, T 01293 450 150, www.fly.virgin.com

maximum stay, booking up to 14 days in advance. From Toronto **British Airways** flies to Lisbon via London, (9½ hours, plus transfer) with peak season fares starting at CAN$1,700.

From Australia and New Zealand   There are no direct flights to Lisbon from Australia or New Zealand; you have to change at least twice. Gateway cities include Singapore and Kuala Lumpur. Airlines that fly to European cities from Australia and New Zealand include: **Alitalia**, **British Airways**, **Lufthansa**, **Malaysian Airlines**, **Qantas**, **Singapore Airlines** and **Virgin Atlantic**. Low season prices start from A$1,700 rising to A$2,500. A cheaper alternative is to fly to London or Madrid and reconnect from there. Flight time from Sydney is 22½ hours, plus transfers.

Getting to and from the airport   Lisbon's **Portela airport** (LIS), **T** 21 841 3700, www.ana-aeroportos.pt, is 6½ km from the city centre. Facilities include a duty-free shop, informative tourist information office (0600-2400), car hire agencies (including **Auto Jardim**, **Avis**, **Eurodollar**, **Europcar** and **Hertz**), 24-hour restaurants, cafés, ATMs, bureaux de change and left luggage. The **AeroBus** is the cheapest and most convenient way to reach the city centre, departing every 20 minutes (0700-2100) making 10 stops en route, including Saldanha, Marquês de Pombal, Praça dos Restauradores, and arriving in the city centre (Rossio) in around 20-25 minutes, before terminating at Cais do Sodré railway terminal. A ticket costs € 2.35 (free for **TAP Air Portugal** passengers) and is valid on the **Carris** transport network for the remainder of that day. If you are arriving late, and are on a budget, **local buses** 5, 8, 22, 44 and 83 operate 0600-2130 to Praça dos Restauradores and Cais do Sodré, and bus 45 runs until 0115 from outside the terminal. There are **taxi** ranks, immediately outside the terminal exit available 24 hours a day. A taxi to the city centre should cost €12-15 (each piece of additional luggage is €1.50 extra) but the price of the fare is often at the whim of an unscrupulous driver. Always try and fix a fare as there have been many reports of fares at 50% inflated value.

Road

Car Driving in Lisbon, and in Portugal for that matter, is a hair-raising experience. With incessant honking, constant rear-ending, a toxic riot of fumes, and unbridled road rage, it's certainly not for the faint hearted. If you are taking your own vehicle into Portugal, contact the very helpful **Automóvel Club de Portugal** (ACP), Portugal's national motoring association, Rua Rosa Araujo 24, **T** 21 318 0100 (emergency breakdown **T** 21 942 9103), www.acp.pt, who will provide advice to motorists if you are a member of a European organization with a reciprocal agreement. Speed limits are 120 kph (74 mph) on motorways, 90 kph (56 mph) outside built-up areas and 50 kph (30 mph) in towns. Motorways, indicated by the prefix "A"; (*auto-estradas*) have been greatly improved although on most routes tolls apply (*portagens*). International Driving Permits and national driving licences, a Green Card, third-party insurance and a warning triangle are compulsory.

Driving times to Lisbon From Porto – 3¼ hours; Faro and the Algarve – four hours 20 minutes (longer on summer weekends); and Madrid – eight hours 55 minutes.

Bus/coach **Eurolines UK Ltd**, **T** 08705-143219, www.eurolines.co.uk runs daily services at 2100 from London Victoria, with a change in Paris (arriving 0645, leaving 1230) and arriving Lisbon at 1230, the following day; a total journey time of 42 hours. Prices for a single journey, £94/peak £98, return £145/peak £151. Peak season is July 4-September 7, and December 17- January 4. There are no financial benefits and with a mere reclining seat to ease the discomfort, the novelty factor is unlikely to get you beyond the Channel Tunnel. *Eurolines* also connects with Spanish cities including, Madrid, Barcelona and Seville. International and regional buses arrive at the **Arco do Cego bus station**, on Avenida João

Cristóstomo, north of Marquês de Pombal, in Saldanha.

Within Portugal, **Rede Expressos**, www.rede-expressos.pt is the principal bus operator, running regional and international services to Faro, Évora, Porto and Seville. There are 10 services daily from Faro to Lisbon, the 1300 (arrives 1700) and 1630 (arrives 1945), €15, providing a good connection with *Monarch* scheduled flights from Manchester, that leave 0730 (arrives 1040).

Train

The national rail company is **Caminhos de Ferro Portugueses** (CP) **T** 21 343 3748, www.cp.pt There are four railway stations in the capital: **Santa Apolónia** for long-distance and international routes and north- and west-bound suburban destinations. **Cais do Sodré** serves the Atlantic beaches of Cascais and Estoril, and Sintra, Mafra and Queluz, there are frequent services from **Rossio**. The **Barreiro** station, on the south bank of the River Tagus, serves the Algarve and the south. Commuter ferries link Barreiro, included in the price of the ticket, with the ferry terminal at Cais do Sodré, Estação Fluvial, without doubt the most stunning panoramic initiation to the city.

Eurostar, **T** 870 6000 0796, www.eurostar.com is the quickest and most pleasurable surface route to Lisbon. Trains depart Waterloo at 1023, arriving Paris Gare du Nord, at 1417. The **TGV** service leaves Paris Gare Montparnasse at 1515, and shuttles down to the Spanish border at Irún, arriving 2132. From there a comfortable a/c sleeper, Portuguese **Sud Expresso**, leaves at 2200 and takes you onto Lisbon, arriving at Santa Apolónia station next morning at 1053. In total the fare will probably exceed £260 making this a considerably more expensive and time consuming option.

Intercity trains (*intercidade*) connect all of Portugal's major cities to either Lisbon or Porto. For routes north to Porto, the fastest, most comfortable, and most expensive (still very cheap by UK standards) service is run by **Alfa**. Intercity services to Faro take between 3½ and four hours. Overnight trains operate from Madrid

(10 hours) and Paris (18½ hours). You should book train tickets in advance (internet bookings accepted) or arrive at least 30 minutes before the journey. Weekend services are usually jammed.

Getting around

Bus

Sights to the west of Baixa, Chiado, Lapa, Belém, Ajuda and further along Doca de Jardim de tabaco, are covered by an efficient network of orange buses run by the **Carris** (**T** 21 361 30 00, www.carris.pt). A *simple* (one-way) ticket costs €1, or see passes and pre-pay fares box, next page. There is a good system of night buses, although taxis provide the most convenient and safest means of getting home after late-night clubbing.

Car

Unless you have arrived by car, driving in the city is to be avoided. All the main sites are easily accessible on foot or by public transport and attempting to negotiate reckless traffic, precarious construction, complicated one-way systems and the slender alleys of the older parts of the city, can be horrendous. Traffic jams during rush hour are particularly bad on the Ponte 25 de Abril. There are many central underground car parks including at Praça dos Restauradores and Largo de Camões; average charges per day €8-10. Many hotels provide private parking for guests, often at extra charge.

Metro

Lisbon's metro is fast, efficient and, beyond the expected rush-hour congestion, a pleasure to use. For a map of the underground, see the inside of the back cover. Artistic projects in many underground stations, including themed tiled and sculptural works, initiated by Maria Keil, and landmark architecture by Santiago Calatrava (Oriente Metro) provides a colourful insight into Portugal's contemporary artists. Sights

Passes

Bright yellow **Carris** booths will provide maps of transport routes and other tourist information. The most helpful is just to the right of *Café Suiça* facing the castle, on Praça da Figueira, or at the foot of the Elevador de Santa Justa. On-board fares are €1; two pre-paid journeys, €1; a one-day pass on buses and trams, €2.35; a three-day pass €5.65. Tourist passes allow unlimited journeys on the bus, tram (including *Elevadores*) and metro: one day, €2.75; four days €9.95; seven days €14.10. You will need to show identification. If you are staying for one month or more, the most convenient and cost effective option is the monthly pass, which costs €21.50. To obtain this you will need to provide passport photos.

which are most efficiently reached by metro are those to the north and west of the old city. There are four metro lines. The **Linha Oriente** (red), **Linha Caravela** (green), **Linha Girasol** (yellow) and **Linha Gaviota** (blue). Further extensions, are scheduled for completion in 2004. The metro runs from 0600-0130, trains run every couple of minutes during peak periods, every 5-7 minutes at off-peak times. With the exception of Oriente and Campo Grande (approximately 20 minutes including change of line) most journeys will be no more than around 10 minutes. Tickets can be purchased from the ticket booths, or from the machines in the entrance to each station (*estação*).

Taxi

Taxis in Lisbon tend to be inexpensive compared to other European capital cities. An average trip from Rossio to the northern reaches of the city, the Gulbenkian for example, should be no more than around €5. Taxi drivers are renowned for clocking up additional charges, especially for bags, and anything that requires

→ Travel extras

Tipping In expensive, tourist-orientated restaurants, a 10-15% tip is the norm (but watch out for an already included service charge). In cheaper restaurants, bars and cafés it is normal to round up the bill, although remember that wages are low, so give according to the level of service you receive. Unscrupulous taxi drivers often add on their own little extras so, again, discretion is advised.

Safety Although Lisbon is not a dangerous city you should always exercise caution and be aware of pickpockets and bag snatchers, particulary late at night in Bairro Alto, the Alfama and the area around Praça da Alegria. Northeast of the Avenida da Liberdade, Anjos and Intendente are notorious red light districts best avoided day and night. Car crime is particulary on the rise; never leave valuables in your car, or even locked in the boot.

the trunk being opened (they are officially entitled to charge 50 per cent extra of the value of the journey fare if your luggage exceeds 20 kg, which is obviously gauged by the driver to his advantage). Make sure that the meter is switched on, and always try to get an estimated cost before you get into the taxi (fares are higher after 2200 – from Alcântara and Doca de Santo Amaro, expect to pay around €7 back to Rossio at around 0500). There are taxi ranks close to the Baixa-Chiado Metro station and Largo de Camões, or call **Radio Taxis, T** 21 79 27 56; an additional €0.74 call out charge is levied. For getting to/from the airport see p25.

Train

There are frequent train services, approximately every 15 minutes from Rossio to Sintra (45 minutes) and every 15-20 minutes from Cais do Sodré along the coast to Cascais, stopping at Estoril and other small suburban beach towns (35 minutes). Trains are comfortable, air-conditioned and run like clockwork from 0500-

Kinetic kicks

Lisbon's vintage trams are the best way to get around the city. Trundling up hills and weaving in and out of alleyways, these ancient marvels which cover some 72 km of track have been in operation since 1901. With their original wood pannelling, grumpy drivers, sparking fuses and kids hanging on for dear life at the back, it's a memorable experience. Get on at the front, pay €1 or show your pass, squeeze on and hold tight.

For just one euro, instead of €13, take unofficial tourist **Tram 28** which runs from Largo Martim Moniz in the Baixa to Prazeres, stopping at: Avenida Almirante Reis; Largo da Graça; Castelo de São Jorge; Rua da Voz do Operário; Mosteiro de São Vicente de Fora; Feira da Ladra; Sé; Baixa; Chiado; Largo do Camões; Calçada do Combro; São Bento; Assembleia da República; Basilica da Estrela.

0230 daily. If you go clubbing in Alcântara, the last/first train back to Cais do Sodré, with an onward cab to your hotel, is the most economical and safest route home.

Tram

A helter-skelter ride on one of Lisbon's ancient emblematic trams is the most enjoyable way to get around Lisbon. A good induction and excercise in orientation is to take Tram 28, see p72, which operates as Lisbon's unofficial tourist tram. One single journey, *tarifa en bordo,* costs €1. It is much more cost-effective to buy a travel pass, see above, or buy tickets in advance from the *Carris* booths. Get on at the front of the tram, buy a ticket from the driver, or show your pass, punch your ticket, then exit at the rear. The brand spanking new super tram, number 15, runs from Praça da Figueira to Belém and then on to Ajuda Palace. Buy your ticket from the machines in the centre of the tram, and hold on to it for inspection.

Walking

Most of the main sights of the Baixa, Bairro Alto, Chiado and
Alfama, can be reached on foot. From Rossio up to the castle is a
good 30-minute uphill amble. From Rossio to Marquês Pombal, a
25-minute stroll. Rossio to Lapa, via Estrela, takes 45 minutes. Tram
28 is never too far away to hop on and hop off at will, and
countless *miradouros*, with liquid refreshment and stunning views,
help alleviate weary muscles.

Tours and tourist information

Tours

Bus and tram **Carristur**, Rua 1° de Maio, 103, **T** 21 361 30 10, runs
four open-top bus and tram tours, beginning in Praça do
Comércio:

Expresso Oriente Open-top bus tour with taped audio system,
which includes Parque das Nações, Parque Eduardo VII, Bairro Alto,
Príncipe Real, Museu Nacional do Azulejo, Casa dos Bicos and Campo
Pequeno Bullring. You are able to get on and off at any of the stops
along the route throughout the day, and use your ticket on the Carris
network; 1030-1730, March to October, November to February 1130,
1330, 1530, €13, children €6.50, Lisbon Card, €9.75.

Tagus tour Belém, Estrela, Gulbenkian, Amoreiras, Eduardo VII;
approximately every half an hour, from 0915-2130, (1715 October to
March), adults €13, children €6.50, Lisbon Card, €9.75.

Hills Tramcar Covers the same route as Tram 28 but without the
welcome addition of local hoi polloi. It covers Alfama, Chiado,
Lapa, Bica, Sé, Elevador de Santa Justa; Martim Moniz;
approximately every half hour, 0900-1900 June to September,
0900-1800 October to May. €16, children €8, Lisbon Card €12.

Discoveries Tramcar Alfama, Mouraria, Belém, Sé, Santos and
Cais da Rocha (1½ hours). Leaves from Praça do Comércio 1130,
1430, 1630 and from Belém 1250, 1550, 1750. Adult €16, children
€8, Lisbon Card €12.

Lisbon Card

If you plan on using the Carris public transport network a great deal and visiting lots of museums, it's worth investing in the Lisbon Card, available from 'Ask Me Lisbon' tourist offices, listed below, and at the tourist information office at the airport. The card is available for 24, 48 and 72 hours, and allows free access on the transport network as well as discounts at 27 museums and monuments. Before you buy, it's worth checking the list of sites where discounts apply as many are of rather niche appeal and some of the key museums, for example the Gulbenkian and the Contemporary Art Museum in Chiado, are free on Sundays anyway. There are also shopping and restaurant discount cards; lists of participating establishments are available from the tourist office. For the Parque das Nações discount card see pxxx.

24 hours adults €11.25, children €4.50
48 hours adults €18.50 children €6.25
72 hours adults €23.50 children €9.00

There's a **two-day pass**, T 96 629 85 58 for further information, which includes unlimited travel on all four sightseeing tours listed above, AeroBus, and regular Carris network including night services; €40 adult, €20 children, family ticket €60.

Bus tours around Lisbon   The **Sintra Mystery and Romanticism** trip, T 96 629 85 58, is a four-hour whistlestop tour to Palácio de Queluz, Vila de Sintra, Monsterrate, Colares, Cabo de Roca, Boca de Inferno, and Cascais and Estoril. Buses leave at 1400 daily from Praça do Comércio. Adults €40, children €20, family €60.

River cruises   Between 1 March and 31 October **Transtejo**, T 21 885 56 30, www.transtejo.pt   operates leisurely sightseeing cruises along the Tagus, taking in the Basilica da Estrela, Palácio da Ajuda, Torre de Belém, Cristo Rey, and then Castelo de São Jorge, Panteão Nacional, and Igreja de São Vicente sweeping north to Parque das Nações. You can stop off in Belém and Parque das Nações and return on later cruises. Boats depart from Cais do Embarque, Praça do Comércio at 1100 and 1500, stopping at Parque das Nações at 1145 and 1545, and at Belém at 1300 and 1700. Adults €15, children and seniors €8, with Lisbon Card €12. Drinks and light snacks are included.

Sidecar tour company Create you own tour, wherever, whenever with this slightly mad company. Be driven around Lisbon's criss crossing streets in a 1947 side car with the wind in your hair, or go the Cuban way and cruise along the coast to Cascais in an ageing Chevy. Endless possibilities, **T** 351 96 396 51 05, www.sidecartouring.co.pt

Tourist information

Lisbon's main tourist offices, **Ask me Lisbon**, are in Praça do Comércio, which also includes café, an excellent restaurant, shops and internet access, and in Palácio Foz, Praça dos Restauradores. They can be very busy and staff can be brusque. More specialist information on sports, the arts, and other specialist subjects, are tucked away in filing cabinets, as well as guides to the palaces and museums in the city and surrounding areas. For transport information, head for the yellow booths on Praça da Figueira and at the foot of the Elevador de Santa Justa. During the summer, yellow tour office kiosks also spring up across the city. There is convenient one at the bottom end of Rua Augusta, close to the Arco de Vitória.

Baixa and Rossio

*Downtown Lisbon is pure theatre; the commercial heart and
microcosm of the city. Set against a prosaic backdrop of banks,
budget hotels and generic brand names, the Baixa's central square,*
Rossio*, and its more antiquarian side-kick* **Praça da Figueira***,
provide some of the best free entertainment in the city. All Lisbon's
masses seem to drift across Rossio's undulating mosaic paving. More
nonchalant, Praça da Figueira reveals time-defying rituals and giant
yuccas hang from the rafters of hole-in-the-wall grocers.*

Southbound from Rossio, **Rua Augusta** *is the main pedestrian
thoroughfare, lined with touristy pavement cafés, international chain
stores and leather emporiums, populated by quirky puppeteers, buskers
and gilded and ghostly human statues. This climaxes with the over-
arching splendour of the* **Arco de Vitória***, gateway to* **Praça do
Comércio***, designed to out-pomp the most regal of Europe's squares.*

▸▸ *See Sleeping p122, Eating and drinking p136, Bars and clubs p159*

Sights

★ Rossio (Praça Dom Pedro IV)
Map 2, C8 , p248

Surrounded by whizzing traffic, all roads seem to lead to Rossio.
Designed by Carlos Mardel and Eugénio dos Santos, it was formally
known as Praça Dom Pedro IV, and is Lisbon's most vibrant square.
Former site of a Roman Hippodrome and the setting for bullfights
and the burning of heretics during the Middle Ages, Rossio now
hosts a spectacle of a different kind. The epicentre of downtown life,
here you can buy lottery tickets, a bunny rabbit, change money, pay
homage to the Big Mac alongside Lisbon's international youth or
muse with the avant garde over shuddering *bicas* (strong espressos)
in art deco coffee shops, like the iconic **Café Nicola** or **Pastelaria
Suíça**, see p138 and p139.

The neoclassical **Teatro Nacional de Dona Maria II**, built in 1846 by Fortunato Lodi, occupies the north side of the square. Surmounted by a sculpture of Portuguese playwright Gil Vicente, it provides a lofty grandeur to Rossio's populist frisson. During the 18th century this was the site of the Palace of the Inquisition, where in 1761 the sentences of the *auto da fés* were meted out. In the centre of the square stands the 27-m high **statue of Dom Pedro IV**, the emperor of Brazil before ascending the Portuguese crown in 1826. The marble pedestal features figures representing Justice, Strength, Prudence and Temperence. Legend has it that the statue, sculpted in France by Elias Robert in 1870, was not in fact Dom Pedro at all, but Emperor Maximilian of Mexico. It is claimed the statue was making a stopover in Lisbon, en route from France to Mexico, when the news broke that Maximilian had been assassinated. Due to an uncanny likeness, it was decided that the statue of Maximilian would serve as Dom Pedro and a deal was brokered.

To the northwest stands the interlocking horseshoe arches of **Rossio station**. Designed in 1887, this neo-Manueline confection characterized a late 19th-century nostalgia for the period of the Discoveries, when Portuguese maritime power reached its zenith.

● *Pass though the arched gateway on Rossio to Rua dos Sapateiros to see one of Lisbon's remaining examples of art nouveau, the old movie house, the Animatógrafo, which is now a sleazy strip club.*

Praça da Figueira
Map 3, C/D1, p250

Adjacent to Rossio, Praça da Figueira retains more endearing old world charm. Alongside ornate seed shops, fish hang in giant salted sheaves from old-fashioned shops and lottery sellers, hash peddlers and backpackers mill around budget *pensãos*. A pivotal transport nexus, the square was given a nip and tuck in time for Expo 98. Well on the tourist trail, **Pastelaria Suiça** joins the two squares – the outdoor terrace is one of the best vantage points to survey the

The Great Earthquake

"And the earthquake became flesh in Pombal, its son"

In the 18th century, Lisbon was at the cusp of greatness, one of the most important cultural and political centres of the day. Then on 1 November 1755, at 0930, Lisbon was struck by an earthquake, killing tens of thousands (estimates range from 40,000 in Lisbon to 250,000 worldwide) in less than 10 minutes, and reducing the city's commercial heartland to rubble. Shudders were felt across North Africa, and tremours were felt in France, Switzerland and Northern Italy. Before this fateful day, downtown Lisbon had been a maze of coiling streets and cramped alleys. The destruction spared nothing; in lavish baroque churches across the city, the congregations gathered for All Saint's Day were buried alive when marble domes and roofs collapsed. Nobles and peasants, children and the elderly were sucked into the bowls of the Baixa as roads opened up and swallowed the city in terrifying gulps. In its wake, a huge tidal wave estimated to be 50 ft high, engulfed Lisbon. Those who were not buried in the detritus were swept out to sea.

Commemorating All Saint's Day, every altar in every church and every chapel was set alight with candles and lanterns which set everything ablaze, creating a hellish spectacle. The effects of the earthquake stretched way beyond the city's physical destruction. Religious beliefs were called into question as the devout began to ponder whether the conflagration was the result of an angry God retaliating for Lisbon's sins. But they were hard pressed to explain why one city was destroyed while others like Paris or Madrid, just as 'sinful', were spared. Depictions of the earthquake have been evoked in art and literature, including Voltaire's *Candide*, whose beliefs in the laws of nature had been profoundly altered by the earthquake.

Praça da Figueira
Shoe shiners and lottery ticket sellers compete for trade in the piquant squares of downtown Baixa.

action against the spectacular backdrop of the castle. The **statue of Dom João I**, usually mobbed by irreverent pigeons, forms the nevertheless dignified centrepiece. On the south side, the charmingly old-fashioned **Confeitaria Nacional** was considered to be one of Europe's most elegant salons when it opened in 1829, its saliva-inducing window displays now include fine pastries, cakes smothered in cream and shiny brioches the size of beach balls.

Northeast of Praça da Figueira, **Praça Martim Moniz** – an ugly urban wasteland where the city gates once stood – honours the eponymous knight who, during the sacking of Lisbon in 1147, tied himself to the castle gateway so that Dom Afonso Henríques' crusaders could take the city from the Moors.

Baixa district
Map 3, D-F 1-2, p250

While hardly a beauty, Baixa oozes life, its old world poetry injected with modern fizz. **Rua Augusta** is the main tourist parade ground and the inevitable starting point for a stroll. Alongside the golden arabesque swirls of art nouveau store fronts, knots of grizzled old men read the papers hung at corner kiosks and tourists settle in at premium-rate pavement cafés watching a carousel of buskers, street artists and the ubiquitous Peruvian pan pipers.

In the 19th century, Baixa was Lisbon's commercial heart, with streets named according to their trades – Rua dos Sapateiros, the shoemakers' street, Rua da Prata, silversmiths' street, and Rua Augusta, August Street, was for the wool and silk merchants.

Beneath the Banco Comércial Português, the **Núcleo Arqueológico**, *Rua dos Correeiros, 9, T 21 321 7000, Thu 1500-1700, Sat 1000-1200, 1500-1700, free, guided tours only (available in English if you call to arrange a visit in advance),* displays artefacts from the first to the 18th century, uncovered during renovation work on the bank and subsequent excavation.

A feat of kinetic eccentricity, the Gothic Eiffel-esque **Elevador de Santa Justa**, *Rua de Santa Justa, Oct-Apr 0900-1900, May-Sep 0830-2230, €1,* is one of Lisbon's most iconic and memorable images. Designed by an apostle of Eiffel, Raoul Mesnier du Ponsard, who also designed Lisbon's other three remaining *elevadores,* it was inaugurated in 1902. Originally powered by steam, the 45-m vertical wrought-iron structure was built to link the Baixa with Largo do Carmo, via a 25-m walkway. Ongoing building works mean that the walkway's exit, leading to Chiado, is closed but from the café panoramic views reveal the city below.

● *On Rua Aurea, at number 82, is the Banco de Totta e Açores, an act of architectural insurrection built by the prestigious architect Ventura Terra in 1905. Its classical style defies the trite constructions that characterized Baixa Pombalina.*

Lisbon

★ Street cars of desire

Best

- •Elevador da Lavra, p46
- •Tram 28, p72
- •Elevador da Bica, p49
- •Elevador da Glória, p49

Praça do Comércio
Map 3, I2, p251

Often described as Lisbon's reception room, Praça do Comércio is to Lisbon what Place de la Concorde is to Paris and what Plaza Mayor is to Madrid. Formally known as Terreiro do Paço, after the sumptous royal palace – Palácio do Ribeira – which stood here until the earthquake of 1755, the city's most dignified square fans gloriously onto the River Tagus and now houses Lisbon's main tourist office and one of the city's gastronomic highlights, see p136.

Praça do Comércio was Pombal's attempt to stage a coup in architectural symbolism, the culmination of an enlightened despot's vision for a model city. The square's showpiece is the bronze equestrian statue of the king **Dom José I**. Cast in 1774, it was the work of renowned sculptor Machado de Castro. The statue is flanked by classic 18th-century three-storey pastel-yellow buildings, designed by Eugénio dos Santos, now occupied by administrative offices. On the north side of the square, nestling beneath the arcaded colonnades, is one of Lisbon's most famous literary landmarks, **Café Martinho do Arcado**, see p137, which first opened in 1782. Fernando Pessoa, see p53, its most celebrated

! The fate of the monarchy was sealed in this square. The royal family, returning home from the Alentejo in 1908, were crossing the square in their gilded carriage, when King Carlos and heir apparant, Crown Prince Luís, were assassinated.

Elevador da Bica
The vintage Elevador da Bica tram slices through the streets of Santa Catarina in Bairro Alto.

patron, is claimed to have penned *Mensagem* at one of the original wooden tables. Two of Portugal's other literary legends, Almeida Garret and Eça de Queirós also came here to muse during the belle époque before heading to the Avenida da Liberdade for a customary stroll on Lisbon's chi chi boulevard.

● *Around the corner, on Praça do Muncipio, the Câmara Municipal (City Hall), built in 1974 and attibuted to Eugénio dos Santos, was considered by Fernando Pessoa to be Lisbon's most beautiful building. The façade was erected after the earthquake.*

Largo de São Domingos and around
Map 2, C8, p248

The **Igreja de São Domingos** stands on the site of the Convento de São Domingos where, between the 16th and 19th century, the sentences of the Inquisition were gruesomely carried out. Originally founded in 1242 by Don Sancho II, it was virtually destroyed by the earthquake in 1755. Today, all that remains of the original construction are the vestry and the high altar, which had been restored in 1748 by Ludovice of Mafra fame, see p115. The church was rebuilt by Manuel Caetano de Sousa, who reconstructed the portal using the royal chapel and balcony that had been salvaged from the Paço da Ribeira. This is one of the Baixa's most combustible corners, the social hub of the African community, and where crinkled men clutching Duralex glasses of sticky cherry liqueur spill out onto the square from closet-sized *ginginha* bars, see p159.

To the northwest runs the pedestrianized **Rua das Portas de Santo Antão**, famous for its fish and seafood restaurants where waiters brandish multi-lingual menus, gigantic lobsters peer through the windows of 1950s restaurants and coffee shops provide late-night sustenance. During the Middle Ages, this district was famous for its debauchery. By the 15th century, Rua Jardim do Regedor was known as Rua da Mancebia (Concubinage Street). In the 19th century, it became the Lisbon's racey cabaret district, its

All about Amália

The undisputed queen of fado, Amália Rodrigues was an icon, the soul of the nation and an international legend, who for more than half a century entranced the masses with her spellbinding voice and heartfelt lyrics. When she died in 1999, aged 79, there were three days of national mourning. Thousands lined the route to Cemiterio dos Prazeres – where she was buried until 2001 when she was moved to the National Pantheon – weeping uncontrollably and singing her songs, in scenes likened to the death of Princess Diana.

A woman of gravity and charisma, she rewrote the rules, broke new ground and defied the purists with her Miles Davis-style improvisations and daring. Choosing to work with avant garde composers and looking beyond the traditional themes of fado, she was the first *fadista* to don the black clothes of mourning. Throughout her life Amália remained an enigma, she never sold out, never became a brand – you wouldn't find her on the front of *Hola* – she was a diva in the true sense of the word. She kept her private life private and let her music reveal her soul. A ravishing beauty, men worshipped her but she remained happily married for 36 years to César Seabra, an engineer. Truly relentless, between 1950 and 1995, she would perform on average four times a month. In 1952, before Portugal had TV, Amália became the first person from Portugal ever to appear on television, a guest on *Coke Time with Eddie Fisher*. Constantly surrounded by loyal poets, musicians and producers from London to New York to Paris, gregarious Amália would often host parties when the revelry would continue until early morning, and the indefatigable diva would still be singing.

Moulin Rouge, echoed in the imposing **Coliseu dos Recreios**. Designed by Goulard in 1888, with a tall classical façade, topped by a metallic dome, it provides an incongruous grandeur to this narrow prosaic street of Pombaline severity. Originally built to house a circus, it is now a major concert venue, see p180. At number 58, the **Casa de Alentejo**, built in the 17th century, was the site of Maxim's casino before it became a cultural centre for the Alentejo community in 1932. It's worth dropping in for the fine regional dishes, see p137, as well as for its Moorish serenity.

From the Largo da Anunciada, the **Elevador da Lavra**, reaches up to the Torel district. Opened in 1884, it was the world's first ever funicular and originally powered by water.

● *The steep incline above leads up to Rua de São José where locals feast on* balcalhão *and Brazilian* telenovelas *in cheap* tascas.

Praça dos Restauradores
Map 2, B7, p248

The 'Restorer's Square' commemorates Portugal's regaining of independence from Spain in 1640 with a soaring obelisk. Grabbing attention alongside the square is one of Lisbon's architectural icons, the **Eden Cinema**, a voluptuous art deco marvel, built in 1929. Unfortunately, only the stunning staircase was ever classified, the rest of the building having been sacrilegiously converted into an aparthotel. (Its lavish interior masqueraded as a Russian hotel in the Wim Wender's movie *Until the End of the World*.) Alongside, the lofty **Palácio Foz**, built in 1755, was the work of Francisco Xavier Fabri. It was bought by the Marquês de Foz in 1886 when it received the first of many facelifts. The ballroom features outstanding paintings by Columbano Bordalo Pinheiro (1857-1929). The palace, rather prosaically, now houses the second of Lisbon's main tourist offices.

From behind the Hotel Eden, the **Elevador da Glória** defies one of Lisbon's steepest gradients, chugging cartoon-style to the stunning **Miradouro de São Pedro de Alcântara**.

Bairro Alto

At 2200 the nocturnal nerve centre of Bairro Alto wakes from siestaed languor for the dedicated pursuit of pleasure. In Lisbon's 'High Town', centuries overlap along labyrinthine alleyways where peeling doorways reveal sleek bars, gritty tascas and fado houses. Seductive Brazilian samba mingles with deep techno and black-shawled divas sing out the nation's woes while the aroma of grilled sardines wafts above balconies strewn with washing and lined with blazing geraniums.

*Old world charm is juxtaposed with the baroque magnificence of the Jesuit **Igreja de São Roque** and the exotic gardens of the **Jardim Botânico** in the gay epicentre of stylish **Príncipe Real**. Connecting the Baixa with Bairro Alto, the **Elevador da Glória** chugs up one of the city's gradients to the stunning **Miradouro de São Pedro de Alcântara** with sweeping views of the Castelo de São Jorge. Just a stone's throw away is the palatial **Instituto do Vinho do Porto**, surrounded by dusty bookstores and antique emporiums.*

▸▸ *See Sleeping p125, Eating and drinking p145, Bars and clubs p165*

 ## Sights

Museu e Igreja de São Roque
Largo Trindade Coelho, **T** 21 323 53 81. *1000-1700, closed Mon. Museum €1.50, free Sun. Map 2, D6, p248*

The humble façade of the 16th-century Jesuit church of São Roque belies its baroque interior, characteristic of the flamboyant reign of King João V (1706-50), whose credit rating was immeasurably bolstered by the discovery of diamonds in Brazil in 1728. Known as *O Magnífico* for his weekly endowments to the city's needy, his cultural patronage was unprecedented (as were his trysts with the nuns of Odivelos convent, producing three bastard heirs).

The chapels, decorated in precious marbles, amethyst and ivory, with ceilings lavishly painted in *trompe l'oeils*, are overwhelming.

There are paintings by Florentine masters and Mudéjar *azulejo* tiles from Seville. But far and away the extraordinary highlight is the **Capela de São João Baptista**, an elaborate blending of gilt bronze, jade and lapis lazuli. The chapel was executed in Rome by Vanvitteli and Niccoló Salve, upon the orders of King João V, and was blessed by Pope Benedict XIV in 1744 before being transported to Lisbon and erected in São Roque in 1749. Next door, the **Museu de Arte Sacra** houses a collection of 16th- and 17th-century European sacred art, as well as an assortment of gold and silver religious artefacts, vestements and altar frontals.

Príncipe Real and around
Map 2, A2, p248

Rua Dom Pedro V, a street studded with all things antiquarian, bakeries like opera houses and restaurants with confessional-style cubicles, leads to Praça do Príncipe Real. Laid out in 1960, it is a shady oasis of swooping palms, tropical shrubs and cascading fountains, encircled by pastel-painted 19th-century mansions. By day, the square is the sleepy preserve of flat-capped old men playing cards. By night, it is a busy meeting place and popular gay cruising area. Heading south towards the river, Rua do Século leads back to Bairro Alto, while heading down Travessa da Palmeira, a detour along narrow streets lined with town houses and des res apartments leads to arty **Praça das Flores**, another charming, leafy, less touristed square with a French feel.

Continuing along Rua da Escola Politécnica, the **Jardim Botânico**, *Mon-Fri 0900-1800, Sat 0900-1330, €1.50 (another entrance on Rua da Alegria)*, laid out in 1873, was considered one of the marvels of Southern Europe. As one one Swiss botanist, Robert Choclat, frothed, the gardens of Provence and Liguria were "nothing more than barren heaths besides this exuberant subtropical vegetation". It is a deliriously romantic setting, with over 18,000 botanical species from around the world. It is also one of the most calming spots in the city.

Miradouro de São Pedro de Alcântara and around
Rua de São Pedro de Alcântara. *Map 2, B5, p248*

From the Calçada da Glória, the arthritic **Elevador da Glória**, *0700-1255,* is the most entertaining way to reach Bairro Alto from the Baixa. The clunking tram deposits passengers at the sweeping *miradouro* of São Pedro de Alcântara. The view from the small tranquil garden is perhaps the best in the city, with the terracotta rooftops of the old city spreading out below Castelo de São Jorge. Just opposite is the **Instituto do Vinho do Porto**, the lavish former Palácio Ludovice, and a rather fusty setting from which to become more familiar with the national tipple, see p163. Continuing up the hill, at Rua São Pedro de Alcântara, 71, is **Biblarte**, an antiquarian bookstore and historical meeting place for Lisbon's literati. The shop was once owned by Russian Jew Eliezer Kaminesky, who was a close friend of Fernando Pessoa. The bookstore contains many valuable incunabula, as well as a first edition of *The Lusiads*, valued at €15,000, a bargain due to some missing pages.

Miradouro de Santa Catarina and around
Map 2, G3, p249

Elevador da Bica, chugs from Rua dos Cordoeiros to Calçada do Combro. Turning left, Rua M Saldanha leads to the Miradouro de Santa Catarina, dominated by the statue of **Adamaster**, the writhing mythical sea monster, from Luís de Camões epic *The Lusiads*. There are more wistful panoramas across the Tagus, usually set to the strumming of a guitar and the lively chatter from the medley of characters who cluster around the terrace café.

Docile Santa Catarina has some of the most endearing streets in the city, with crumbling pastel-painted houses, draped in laundry and shrouded with medieval mystery, anachronistically flanked by some of the hippest bars in the city, like *WIP*, see p164. One of the loveliest streets to explore is **Travessa da Laranjeira**.

Chiado

*To the west, straddling one of Lisbon's seven hills, gentrified Chiado is the city's literary soul. Old world elegance and time-honoured rituals remain. Along haughty **Rua Garrett**, studded with high fashion boutiques and art nouveau jewellery stores, dapper old gents still parade their sartorial elegance and Chiado's gilded ladies out for afternoon tea still eminate Parisian style and grace. The literary legacy of cryptic genius Fernando Pessoa, still hangs in the air, his spirit immortalized in stone at **Café A Brasileira**. Devastated by fire in 1988, Chiado has been born again from the drawing board of Portugal's architect supremo, Àlvaro da Sieza Vieira, and in 21st-century Chiado Soho-style wrought-iron architecture is delightfully juxtaposed with the rococo elegance of the **Teatro Nacional de Sao Carlos**.*

*Where 19th-century bakeries flank hip minimalist bars, Calçada do Sacramento leads to the peaceful enclave of **Largo do Carmo**, site of one of the most enigmatic buildings in the city, the cadaverous **Convento do Carmo**. Heading along Rua Serpa Pinto, towards the river, the **Museu do Chiado**, is one of the finest exhibition spaces for Portugal's 19th- and 20th-century artists.*

▸▸ *See Sleeping p124, Eating and drinking p139, Bars and clubs p160*

 ## Sights

Rua Garrett
Map 2, F7, p248

Throughout the 19th century, Chiado's bourgeoisie imitated Parisian refinement. Elegantly bouffonted *Tias* (a lady of Chiado) paraded on **Rua Garrett**, patronizing exclusive boutiques, nibbling on delicate pastries in elegant turn-of-the-century salons, like **Pastelaria Bérnard**, see p148, and feasting on culture at the **Teatro de São Carlos**. While 21st-century Chiado makes a decent stab at cosmopolitan chic, *Tios* (Chiado residents) bemoan the district's shifting demographics, its literary mythology diluted by trite generic branding. Alongside dainty art nouveau glove shops and wood-panelled 19th-century pharmacies, thrusts the international department store **Armázens do Chiado**, with its soulless fast food eateries. A stone's throw from the queen of Portuguese design, **Ana Salazar**, stands the doyen of disposable fashion *H&M*, and wonderful **Livraria Betrand**, the oldest bookstore in the city, fights the trade-stealing might of *Fnac*.

● *From Rua Garrett, head up to Rua da Trindade, 30. The building's façades is smothered in* azulejo *tile panels; the work of 18th-century tile master Ferreira das Tabuletas who was also responsible for the allegorical panels in the old beer hall, Cervejaria Trindade (1863), see page 146. There is a small café serving snacks with views of the nearby Teatro de Trindade.*

Largo de Chiado and around
Map 2, F6, p248

Café A Brasileira is one of Lisbon's enduring literary landmarks, the setting for *tertulías literárias*, lively discussion groups in which debate would often culminate in chair throwing, cup smashing and brawls. During the First World War, it was the backdrop for political intrigue, as Portugal provided a neutral enclave for European spies. During the Salazar years, *Café A Brasileira* was a hotbed of revolutionary fervour and fell under the watchful eye of the PIDE, Salazar's secret police. Most famously, it was the haunt of the enigmatic poet Fernando Pessoa, see box p53, whose literary mysticism still seems to hover over the city. A bronze statue of the man resides on the terrace, the work of sculptor Lagoa Henriques. Mobbed by tourists, it seems ironic that such a private man should now be such a public spectacle. Behind the café's art nouveau façade the interior is a work of Renaissance-style theatricality, with splendid gilt carvings and narcissistic mirrors floor to ceiling.

Just opposite *Café A Brasileira*, Rua Serpa Pinto leads to the creamy clean façade of **Teatro Nacional de São Carlos**, *Rua Serpa Pinto, 9, **T** 21 346 84 08*. Built in 1792 by José da Costa e Silva, it was one of Lisbon's first neoclassical buildings, inspired by La Scala in Milan. To see the stunning rococo interior, you have to buy a ticket to one of the performances, see p178.

Marking the boundary between chi chi Chiado and boho Bairro Alto, **Praça Luís de Camões** is a hub for late-night taxis and site of an underground car park. Taking centre stage is a grandiose statue of the poet Luís de Camões, cast in 1867, by the renowned Vítor Bastos. Such a prosaic setting seems unbefitting of Portugal's national hero and most revered poet, who penned the epic *As lusiadas* (*The Lusiads*), a tribute to Portuguese maritime glory.

Cais do Sodré
Map 2, J5, p249

Heading towards the River Tagus from Largo de Camões, Rua do Alecrim, punctuated by antique shops, old beer halls and suave restaurants, leads to Cais do Sodré train station which connects Lisbon with Cascais and the seaside resorts. Opposite the station, capped by a large Moorish-style dome, is the recently renovated **Mercado da Ribeira**, Lisbon's earthier answer to Barcelona's La Bouqería. From 0600, it is an eye-popping medley of slippery octopus with bloated bags of ink, bloody entrails, coiling innards and a kaleidoscopic bounty of fruit and vegetables. On the second floor is the tamer, more polished and tourist-orientated **Loja de Artesanato**, *Mon-Thu 0900-2000, Fri/Sat 0900-2100, collectors' fair on Sun 0700-1500*, which sells port, nuts, honey and olive oil at

! In Brazil, Chiado is symbolic of historic Lisbon. In October 1988, following the devastating fire, Brazilian President José Saremy visited the district and in the 1950s President Kubitshek visited Café A Brasileira, where he drank a *bica*, ate a *pastel de nata*, and signed his name on the marble counter.

▶ Enigma

"Tedium is absent only from landscapes that don't exist, from books I'll never read. Life, for me, is a somnolence that never reaches the brain. This I keep free, so that I can be sad there." *The Book of Disquietude*.

Refered to by many *Lisboetas* simply as "the poet", Fernando Pessoa (1888-1935) is the most revered figure of Portuguese literature. Eccentric, cryptic and understated, he was the very embodiment of the city where he lived and died. Pessoa was easily recognisable wandering Lisbon's streets, always neatly be-suited with a signature bow tie, trimmed moustache and gold-rimmed spectacles. His image is immortalized in bronze, outside *Café A Brasileira*.

Pessoa means 'person' and he used various pseudonyms, or heteronyms, to reveal different aspects of his personality. The poet Alberto Caeiro, was "The Master for himself". The *Book of Disquiet* was attributed to "demi-heteronym" Bernardo Soares, an accounts clerk who Pessoa referred to as "a mutilation of my personality". His meditations on love have been vaunted for their luminosity, inspired by his relationship with a 19-year-old office worker Ophelia Queiroz in 1919.

Pessoa was intensely patriotic and his writings became a means of exhaulting Portugal. Until the last year of his life, he published only a few poems, vestiges of prose and a slender file of pamphlets and manifestos. His finest work of all was his poem *Mensagem* (Message), published in 1934, which aims to address Portugal's destiny.

inflated prices and a twee assortment of regional handicrafts.

● *Exiting to the rear of the market, take a diversion to medieval Lisbon. Rua dos Remolares is a raffish rough-hewn street of old cobblers, bakeries and hole-in-the-wall cafés where salt-ravaged fisherman sell tackle on street corners, fishwives gossip and dogs run amok.*

Santuário do Cristo Rey and Ponte 25 de Abril

T 21 275 10 00. *0900-1800. The commuter ferry leaves for Cacilhas every 20 mins. Map 1, H4, p246*

For less than a euro, the Cais do Sodré commuter ferry across the river to Cacilhas provides exhiliarating views of Lisbon spreading along the banks of the Tagus, the city's architectural DNA. The decision to construct a kind of mini-Corcovado was made in 1940, when eminent Portuguese bishops met in Fátima and voted to erect a statue overlooking the capital in case Portugal should suffer the same pummelling as war-torn Europe. The concept was the brainchild of Cardinal Cerejeira, who had visited Rio de Janeiro in 1934 and wept with joy at the majesty of Corcovado. It was completed in 1959 and financed by public donations. The sanctuary, a riot of religious kitsch, was built as a symbol of national gratitude. You can take the lift to the top of the statue for unrivalled 360° views of Lisbon, which draws in the Costa Caparica and Sintra and spectacular perspectives of Ponte 25 de Abril. Erected in 1966 the bridge was conceived as an overt imitation to the Golden San Franscisco icon. Never one for modesty, Salazar christened the bridge, Ponte Salazar. When democracy was restored in 1974, it was renamed Ponte 25 de Abril. There is a small bar at the foot of the statue, but little else to detain in the area.

★ Convento e Museu Arqueológico do Carmo

Largo do Carmo, **T** 21 347 86 29. €3. *Tue-Sun 1000-1700, free Sun, Map 2, E7, p248*

The extraordinary Convento do Carmo was constructed between 1389 and 1423 and was one of the largest churches in Lisbon. It was built during the reign of King Dom João I by Nuno Álvares Pereira, a military commander who was instrumental in Portugal's victory at the battle of Aljubarrota in 1385, which secured Independence from Spain. The convent was destroyed by the

★ Convento do Carmo

The 15th-century Carmelite convent is one of Lisbon's most mysterious sites and serves as a poignant remainder of the unsparing devastation of the 1755 earthquake.

earthquake in 1755, when the roof caved in on the congregation who had come to worship on All Saints Day. All that remains of the original construction is the main chapel. Reconstruction work of the Gothic vaults was never completed, leaving an eerie skeletal frame. It is a truly ethereal place where feral cats loiter, grass sprouts surreally from what was the nave and weeds writhe over altar pieces. The convent now houses the Museu Arqueológico do Carmo, established in 1834 to house religious artefacts from across Portugal that were in danger of being destroyed following the abolition of the religious orders. An order decreed by new the constitutional monarchy which resulted from the defeat of Dom Manuel I following the Civil War.

The first of a series of rooms is dedicated to medieval sculpture, including the 14th-century tomb of Fernanado Sanches, with its intricate carved depiction of a wild boar hunt. Alongside is the 14th-century tomb of King Fernando I, decorated with finely sculpted relief scenes from the life of St Francis of Assisi. The 18th-century tomb of Queen Maria Ana of Austria is the work of Machado de Castro, the master behind the equestrian statue of Dom João I, in Praça do Comércio. There is a collection of pre-Columbian artefacts, including rather agonized-looking mummies from 16th-century Peru and lustrous 16th-century *azulejo* tile panels depicting the Passion of Christ. There are also fragments of Visigothic architectural sculptures, and funerary stones and plaques that date to the 11th-century Moorish period. The final exhibits concern the Lower and Middle palaeolithic periods and a range of artefacts that relate to the discovery of a late Neolithic settlement (3,500-1,500 BC), including tools, vases, necklaces of teeth, bone and shells which look like they could have been made yesterday.

● *It is best to arrive at 1000, before the crowds engulf this peaceful enigmatic site and when skeletal arches cast sinister bat wing shadows against the convent walls. Have breakfast at the nearby* Panificacão do Chiado, *see p147, then wait in the peaceful Largo do Carmo for first entry.*

★ Museu do Chiado

Rua Serpa Pinto, 4, **T** 21 343 21 48. *Tue 1400-1800, Wed-Sun 1000-1800, €3, free on Sun 1000-1400. Guided visits for temporary exhibits available.* Map 2, H7, p249

Chiado's contemporary art museum, opened in 1994, houses an impressive collection which focuses exclusively on the period from 1850-1960 and includes the works of great Portuguese masters from the Romantics to the surrealists and modernists. The building itself, designed by French architect Jean Michel Wilmott, is a postmodern masterpiece of industrial glass and steel walkways and exposed brickwork, harmoniously carved from the original 17th-century Convento de São Francisco.

The most engaging exhibits feature the works of the *Grupo de Leão*, Lisbon's avant garde circle of 19th-century painters who would muse and booze in the cafés of Chiado and the Baixa, *Café A Brasileira* and *Nicola*. The spirit of the group is captured in one of the museum's showpieces, the self-portrait by Columbano Bordelo Pinheiro (1857-1929), famous for his biting satires. The painting features José Malhoa (1855-1933), whose sensual and haunting landscapes are also displayed. Malhoa was most renowned for his poignant *O Fado*, the visual embodiment of the national song.

From José de Almada Negreiros (1893-1970), the master of Portuguese modernism, there are two art deco diptychs, entitled *Bar de Marinheiro* (1929) and *Jazz* (1929). There are works by Portugal's most celebrated sculptors, *A Viuva* (The Widow) by Antonio Teixeira Lopes (1866-1942) cast in carerra marble and the neoclassical allegories of Antonio Soeres dos Reis (1847-89) including *A Riqueza* (1877). A small collection of French sculpture climaxes with Rodin's *The Bronze Age* (1876-77). Originally titled *The Wounded Warrior*, it depicts with uncharacteristic realism a naked young man clasping a spear. So lifelike was the masterpiece that Rodin was accused of taking a cast from the model and debate raged for years. There is a small courtyard café and bookshop.

Avenida da Liberdade and around

This elegant tree-lined boulevard (inaugurated in 1886) is to the city what the Champs-Elysées is to Paris. It quickly became a show ground of bourgeois tastes and tendencies, a place where Lisbon's artists and aristocrats would saunter, until the expansion of the city and the creation of the Estados Novas in the early 20th century usurped its elitist pretensions. Beginning at **Praça dos Restauradores***, it's an unabashed paean to consumerism, catering to Lisbon's upwardly mobile denizens with designer shopping, airline offices, plush hotels, elegant restaurants, charming art nouveau cafés, a clutch of stellar museums and the* **Cinemateca***, Lisbon's national film theatre.*

Wandering off the main thoroughfare, streets pirouette into leafy squares and spidery alleyways, revealing more of Lisbon's magical realism. Gravity-defying elevadores *lead to Renaissance splendours, statues to miracle-working doctors and jazz bars. The raffish quarters of Anjos and Intendente, red-light districts, are best avoided.*

▸▸ *See Sleeping p126, Eating and drinking p148*

 Sights

Along the Avenida
Map 6, p254

The Avenida has always been Lisbon's front room, an architectural time line climbing northwards to the lush expanses of Parque Eduardo VII. At number 180 the dome of the old egg-yolk yellow **Tivoli cinema**, constructed in 1920 with Parisian elegance by Raul Lino, stands delightfully juxtaposed to the vanguard Bauhaus **Hotel Vitória**, at number 168, designed by Cassiano Branco. At number 266, the **Diário de Notícias** building bears the hallmark of one of the most influential Portuguese architects of the 20th century, Porfírio Pardal Monteiro, while at 185, the **Tivoli Lisboa** hotel symbolized the dawn of 1950s modernist tendencies.

Halfway along the Avenida, behind *Tivoli Lisboa*, cinema lovers should visit the **Cinemateca Portuguesa**, *Rua Barata Salgueiro, 39, T 21 359 62 00, www.cinemateca.pt, free*, housed in a lovely restored pastel-pink mansion. Small exhibits of late 19th-century camera equipment are displayed around the grand central staircase which leads to a rather over-the-top art nouveau tiled courtyard. See also p171.

Despite the weekday urban malaise of constant traffic, single minded retail frenzy, and a low-level red light district, on Sundays the Avenida retains its haughty French aura with old men reading papers on shady benches and well-heeled families and laissez faire tourists relaxing on the terraces of ornate cafés.

Jardim de Torel and around
Map 6, G9, p255

The **Elevador da Lavra** finishes its steep ascent on Rua Câmera Pestana in the district of Torel, an aloof neighbourhood of shady, tree-lined avenues flanked with neo-Renaissance mansions, fronted with manicured lawns. Turning left onto Travessa do Torel, a gate opens out onto the Jardim de Torel, a Pre-Raphaelite Eden where towering palms seem to hang from the hillside, framing one of Lisbon's least visited and most breathtaking *miradoures*. Rua de Júlio de Andrade, leads to **Campo dos Mártires da Patria**, a large concrete square with a small pond and café overshadowed by university faculty buildings. In the centre of the square stands the statue of Portuguese doctor Sousa Martins, eerily surrounded by gravestones, candles, photographs and flowers. 'Miraculous Martins' (1843-1897), revered for his unremitting dedication to saving the lives of poor children, committed suicide when he discovered that he was dying of tuberculosis. Relatives of the sick and needy come in droves to pray for his saintly intervention.

● *To explore some of the least-touristed and most charming backstreets with their tile-encrusted houses festooned with laundry and bright bougainvillea, head south along Calçada de Santa Ana towards Largo de São Domingos. A plaque on Rua de Martim Vaz marks the birthplace of Amália Rodrigues, see p45.*

★ Casa-Museu da Fundação Medeiros e Almeida

Rua Rosa Araújo, 41, **T** 21 354 78 92. *Mon-Sat 1300-1730, closed Sun. €5. Good multi-lingual information, very helpful, knowledgeable staff. Metro Rotunda, Marquês de Pombal. Map 6, E4, p254*

One of Lisbon's most underrated museums, the former private residence of António Medeiros e Almeida, houses an outstanding collection of 17th- to 20th-century fine arts. The priceless artefacts, displayed in 25 rooms, range from porcelain, furniture and ceramics to silverware, paintings and sculpture. There are portraits by George Romney (1734-1802), landscapes by Thomas Gainsborough (1727-88) and scenes of Lisbon by Portuguese artist Carlos Botelho (1899-1982). Of most interest is the collection of 18th- and 19th-century furniture, including the works of François Linke – the most influential and celebrated furniture maker of the late 19th century – a Louis XIV-style cabinet with strong art nouveau influences and a long case clock in rosewood with ormolu mounts and glass marble. Look out for the 18th-century Louis XV commode by master cabinet maker Pierre Roussel (1723-82), in laquered oak, marble and bronze, which was taken from the Palais Rose in Paris – the Gestapo headquarters in France – to Germany by Goering where it was sold to an art dealer.

In the Sala das Pratas (Silver Room), there is a dinner service engraved with 'N' said to have belonged to Napoleon Bonaparte and gleaming Regency period silverware by Paul Storr (1792-1838). The Sala do Lago (Lake Room) contains marble and gilded bronze 18th-century wall fountains from the Palace of Versailles and 18th-century *azulejo* tile panels. The Sala dos Relógios (Clock Room) has an ornate long case clock by Thomas Tompion (1639-1713), one of the most important English clock makers of the 17th-18th century. Priceless porcelain from the Han dynasty

(206 BC) and rare pieces from the Qing dynasty (18th century) are displayed in the Sala das Porcelanas (Porcelain Room).

Praça das Amoreiras
Metro Rato. Map 6, G1, p254

A five-minute walk along Rua das Amoreiras from the chaotic traffic fuelled nexus of Largo Rato, leads to Praça das Amoreiras (Mulberry Square). This delightful square, framed by the arches of the **Aquaducto das Águas Livres**, is decorated with crumbling *azulejo* tiles, its chunky pillars propping up cavorting teenagers. an An amazing feat of engineering, which even withstood the 1755 earthquake, it stretches 68 km, partly underground, and took 20 years to build (finally completed in 1729). The *amoreiras* were planted by the Marquês de Pombal and during the 18th century the square was home to a silk factory. The **Mãe d'Água** water reservoir was built in 1834 to collect water for the public fountains in the city.

Fundação Arpad Szenes-Vieira da Silva
Praça das Amoreiras, 58, **T** 21 388 00 44, fasvs@fasvs.pt *1200-2000, closed Tue and public holidays. 1000-1800 Sun. €2.50.*
Map 1, E6 p246

This small, often overlooked gallery exhibits the work of two of Portugal's most renowned artists: Maria Helena Vieira da Silva (1908-92) and Hungarian Arpad Szenes (1897-1985). Born in Lisbon, Vieira da Silva moved to Paris in 1928 where she studied sculpture in the studio of Bourdelle. She met Szenes, who was already an acclaimed painter and member of the Second School of Paris and they married in 1930. Exhibiting for the first time in Paris in 1933, Vieira da Silva was soon at the vanguard of European art, creating a buzz with her innovative techniques.

   The exhibition begins with two self portraits of the artists, which reveal their different styles and personalities – the dark colours and severe lines of introspective Vieira da Silva and the colourful liberated strokes of the extrovert Szenes. Vieira da Silva concentrated on expressionist urban themes, brooding grey cityscapes which evoke a claustrophobic, mechanized world. The death of her father as a child had affected her greatly and the artist's feelings of confronting a closed door, which only death could open, is a recurring theme. *Le Bataille des Rouges et des Bleus* (1953) and *Le Cataclysme* (1954) are two of the collection's highlights.

By contrast, Szenes luminous landscapes, including the ethereal *Etude Mer* (1979) and *Gaviotas* (1977), exude calmness and a sense of well being. In the old building there are examples of Szenes' lesser-known works from the 1930s, including *Enfant au-cerf-volant* (1935) which reveals his earlier surrealist tendencies and in particular the influence of Miró.

The upper floors of the gallery are often used for temporary exhibitions featuring artists who were profoundly influential on Vieira da Silva, including, in 2003, a retrospective of Marc Chagall.

Parque Eduardo VII and Praça Marquês de Pombal

Parque Eduardo VII, **T** 21 388 22 78. *Oct-Mar 0900-1630, Apr-Sep 0900-1730. Estufas €1.50. Map 6, B2/3, p254*

At the top of the Avenida, Praça Marquês de Pombal is surrounded by Lisbon's worst traffic headache. In the centre of the square towers the eponymous autocrat, bombastically admiring his handiwork – downtown Lisbon. Spreading behind the square is Lisbon's largest park, named after English king, Edward VII, who visited Lisbon in 1903. The park's northern reaches are the best place to begin exploring, where a viewing platform framed by austere columns and a 1997 sculpture by João Cutileiro celebrating the 1974 revolution, provides sweeping views.

Surrounding the formally laid out garden of topiary and tamed foliage, hilly verges and tree-lined pathways meander among shady glades and picnic areas. The highlight of the park, on the western side, is the **Estufa Quente e Fria**, (Hot and Cold greenhouse), a verdant grotto under an oriental bamboo roof.

On the opposite side of the park is the Pavilhão dos Deportes, renamed the **Pavilhão Carlos Lopes** in honour of one of the figureheads of Portuguese and world athletics. It's worth a look for its beautiful façade encrusted with a profusion of *azulejo* tile panels. Just north is the **Restaurante Botequim do Rei**, whose terrace café, serving drinks and light meals, is a lovely place to relax.

● *Head west along Rua Joaquim António de Aguiar for one of the purported architectural truimphs of Portuguese modernism. In 1991, on Rua Castilho, 40, acclaimed architect Henrique Chicó fused the original turn-of-the-century building with a soaring glass high-rise.*

Alfama, Castelo and around

Frederico de Brito "Our Lips meet easily across the narrow street".

*Like a miniature candy-coloured cubist city, whipped up by a cyclone and tossed over Lisbon's highest hills, **Alfama** is a maze of zig zagging streets. Dominating the skyline is the iconic **Castelo de São Jorge** and spreading within its walls the ancient district of **Santa Cruz**, a rough-hewn medina conjuring up images of crusading knights and buried treasure.*

*Trams feel like time capsules to a medieval world, scaling ancient steets to the **Miradouros de Santa Catarina** and **Largo Portas de Sol** where the city reveals itself in all its follies and glories breathtakingly below. The pristine baroque **Panteão Nacional de Santa Engrácia** and the twin bell towers of the **Igreja de São Vicente da Fora** rise amidst clusters of squat houses stacked one on top of the other. Surrounded by seafood restaurants, tour group orientated fado houses and neighbourhood grocers, the **Casa do Fado e da Guitarra Portuguesa** tells the history of the national song, while a short bus ride away set in the tranquil Madre de Deus Convent the **Museu Nacional do Azulejo** houses the finest collection of blue and white azulejo tiles*

*in the country. For more authentic exposure to the Portugal's art forms,
wander around earthy **Mouraria**, the cradle of fado, or the animated
streets of **Graça**, where fragments of lustrous16th-century azulejos
peel from the façades of ramshackle dwellings.*

▶▶ *See Sleeping p129, Eating and drinking p149, Bars and clubs p166*

◉ Sights

★ Alfama
Map 4, H1, p252

Facing the cathedral, bearing left along Rua da Rosa leads up to the
castle while taking the right fork leads along Rua Cruzes da Sé to Rua
de São João de Praça and **Praça de São Miguel**, the heart of
Lisbon's most captivating district. Alfama is furtive ground for
timeless exploration and getting lost is par for the course. *Becos*
(blind alleyways) reveal a bewitching world of supernatural rituals
and medieval customs, where women still haul their washing to
public fountains and late at night the brooding sound of fado seems
to come from every nook and cranny. But this is a newly spruced
brand of antiquity (the advent of mass tourism has brought
gentrification to the area). Whitewashed houses are picturesquely
framed by a sudden riot of *azulejos* and a blaze of geraniums,
upmarket restaurants and fado houses make it a tour group mecca.

The **Igreja da São Miguel** is the epicentre of the All Saint's
festival where, every June, Alfama erupts with pleasures pagan and
divine for the *Marchas Populares*, an unbridled celebration of
Lisbon's popular saints, Anthony, John and Paul, all intrinsic to the
city's religious traditions, see Festivals p183.

Rua da São Pedro is one of the most animated streets where
craggy old fisherman and *varinhas* (fishwives), still proffer the
catch of the day. **Largo do Chafariz** is the tourist hub where
steep stepped streets meander to your own private *miradouros*
where the shimmering River Tagus is framed by a latticework of

★ **Alfama**
*The twin bell tower s of the Igreja de São Vicente da Fora and the
white dome of the Panteão Nacional de Santa Engrácia rise above
Alfama's medieval streets.*

terracotta rooftops, lone palms and wayward bougainvillea. Most
of Alfama's shops and tourist restaurants are clustered in this area.

'Alfama' comes from the Arabic word *alhaman* meaning
'springs', and refers to the hot spring on **Chafariz del Rei**, Rua
Cais de Santarém. This is the site for the oldest public fountain in
the city, built by royal decree during the reign of Don Afonso II in
the 12th century. An official decree in 1551 regulated the water
supply according to sex, race and position. Further up from the
square on **Beco do Mexias** women congregate and can still be
seen doing their washing in public fountains. On **Rua da
Regueira**, the former royal palace, the Palácio de Limoeiro,
became the mint before its reincarnation a prison in the 15th
century. Along **Beco do Carneiro** houses are stacked 4 ft apart,
nestled with sticky floored taverns and chaotic corner grocers.

Rua da Judiaria marks the area where Lisbon's Jewish population fled during the bloody Spanish Inquisition.

East from the square onto **Rua dos Remédios** leads to Calçada de Cascão and the soaring white dome of the national pantheon.

Panteão Nacional de Santa Engrácia
Map 4, F3, p252

The iconic dome of the National Pantheon of Santa Engrácia rises majestically over the jumbled mazes of Alfama. Built in 1682, it is a magnificent example of Portuguese baroque which, at the time, created a stir for its innovative design and craftsmanship. It was to be an epic of Sistine Chapel proportions for one architect João Antunes, a humble stonemason who was appointed Royal architect and was considered the greatest architect of his time. When Antunes died in 1712, it didn't take long for his peers to question his craftsmanship and debate raged as to whether the church would be able to support the weight of the cupola. In the 18th century work was halted and the dome was never built. With the dissolution of the religious orders in 1834, the church became first an arsenal and then a clothing factory. In 1916, when it was chosen as the National Pantheon, construction work of the dome resumed and it was finally completed in 1966. Like its Spanish counterpart, the Sagrada Família in Barcelona, the church has come to symbolize projects that were never to be completed. In the Portuguese lexicon, the popular expression, an "obra de Santa Engrácia" refers to a work which takes an eternity.

Inside the pantheon four rooms provide the final resting place for important literary, political and artistic figures, including Almeida

! One of fado's most legendary figures was Maria Severa, a notorious prostitute and the daughter of a gypsy. When she died, age 26, fado singers began to shroud themselves in black to mourn her death. This tradition continues today.

Garrett and Guerra Junquiero. The body of adored *fadista* Amália Rodriguez (see p45), who died on 6 October 1999, was moved here on July 8 2001. The cenotaph honours an impressive roll call of Portugal's greatest heros from Afonso de Albuquerque (1445-1515), who made Goa the capital of the Portuguese Empire in the Orient, to Vasco da Gama (circa 1469-1524), and Luís de Camões (1524/25-1580), Portugal's renowned poet, the embodiment of the aesthetic and literary ideals of the Renaissance. His epic poem *As Lusiads* praised the Portuguese discoveries and greatest feats in Portuguese history. There are 181 steps (or a lift to the left of the entrance) to the gallery at the top of the dome, where you can survey all that is Lisbon from Ponte 25 de Abril to the west to Ponte Vasco da Gama to the east.

Feira da Ladra

Campo de Santa Clara. *Tue and Sat 0700-1830. Map 4, E3, p252*

The district of Santa Clara, encircling the domed pantheon, is the setting for the twice weekly 'Thieves Fair', where a mishmash of pseudo-antiques, mismatched socks, screws, illuminated Jesus statues and knock-off mobile phones are paraded to a cacophonous soundtrack of hard-nosed sales banter and Euro-pop CDs. The stalls, which climb the hill towards the Mercado de Santa Clara, conform to more capitalist protocol with labelled prices and more tourist-orientated handicrafts, fado CDs and denim mania. Nearby, a great spot for lunch is the Mercado de Santa Clara, see p150.

Igreja e Mosteiro de São Vicente da Fora

Igreja de São Vicente da Fora, **T** 21 882 44 00. *Tue-Sun 0900-1230, 1500-1800. Church free, cloisters €2.50. Map 4, F1/2, p252*

The original church of São Vicente was built upon the order of King Afonso Henríques, following his triumphant conquest of Lisbon in 1147, in honour of Lisbon's patron Saint. Its name – 'Saint

Vincent from the outside' (*de fora*) – testifies to its original location outside of the city walls. In 1580, newly enthroned King Felipe II of Spain (Felipe I of Portugal), ordered that a church be built as an act of one-upmanship, to assert the power of the Spanish dynastic vision, "I inherited it, I bought it, and I conquered it" was his ruling mantra. The chosen architects were the Italian Renaissance master Filipe Terzi and King Felipe's royal architect, Juan Herrerra, who was responsible for the sublime El Escorial on the outskirts of Madrid, but many important masters and architects contributed including Baltazar Alves and João Nunes Tinoco.

A visit to the **cloisters** is the main highlight, accessed through the fanciful arcaded courtyard with its tinkling water fountains. Eighteenth-century *azulejo* tile panels illustrating La Fontaine's fables provide a beguiling contrast to the classical austerity of the monastery. The former refectory now houses the **pantheon of the House of Bragança**, Portugal's ruling dynasty between 1640-1910, including the remains of Catherine of Bragança (1638-1705), wife of Charles II of England. The first actual burial here, in 1907, was King João IV, swiftly followed just a year later by King Carlos. The remains of Portugal's last king, Dom Manuel II, who died in exile in Brazil in 1932, lies here. The café serves light snacks but its major draw is the views across the Alfama and the Tagus.

Casa do Fado e da Guitarra Portuguesa

Largo do Chafariz de Dentro, 1, **T** 21 882 34 70, **F** 21 882 34 78. *1000-1300, 1400-1600, closed Jan 1, May 1, Dec 25. €2.50. Map 4, H1, p252*

A pristine pastel-pink mansion is home to the Museum of Fado and the Portuguese Guitar. It presents the origins of fado, the haunting and lyrical expression of Arab fatalism and the embodiment of *saudade*, an untranslatable term relating to the Portuguese nostalgia for glories past, see box p175. The greatest fado legend of them all, and national heroine, was Amália, see box p45, who transcended the barriers of culture and language to become a true symbol of national identity.

Audio-visual presentations including wax dummies, dioramas, multi-lingual information panels and push button fado music, trace the development of fado within a cultural and social context. Fado's influence on other artistic spheres is chronicled, from the role of fado in Portuguese cinema to the rise of the fado house, and the impact of fascism and censorship. You can surf various tracks from a selection of classic fado CDs, which provides a good initiation into the various styles of fado, and sample taste testers for CD buying – there is a good selection available in the shop. The final exhibits chart the development of the hand-crafted Portuguese *guitarra*, which developed from the Italian cittern and evolved into the English guitar. Exhibits also probe the life of virtuoso performer Carlos Peredes, the innovative and world-renowned composer. There is a museum café serving drinks and snacks, and a good bookshop.

Casa dos Bicos
Rua dos Bacalhoeiros, **T** 21 888 48 27.   *Map 3, H4 p251*

Built in the early 16th century by Braz de Albuquerque, the 'house of spikes' is thought to have been modelled on one of two possible Italian palaces, the Palazzo dei Diamanti in Ferrara or the Palazzo Berilacqua in Bologna, both with façades of raised pyramids. The son of Afonso de Albuquerque, Viceroy of India, Braz is thought to have felt the slenderness of his palace rather inferior in comparison to those of his noble neighbours, so he decided to compensate by

! English King Charles II hit the jackpot when Catherine of Bragança was sent to England with a unprecedented £3,000 dowry when a French suitor could not be found for her. Catherine is also credited with having introduced the great afternoon tea ritual to Portugal.

encrusting a raised diamond pattern onto the façade and endowing the upper two floors with the exuberant arched windows characterstic of the Manueline period. The upper two floors were destroyed by the earthquake in 1755 and were only rebuilt in the 1980s.

● *Close by, on Rua dos Bacalheiros (Codfishman's Street), walking in the direction of Praça do Comércio past the various tourist shops, there are many cheap restaurants serving satisfying grilled fish dishes.*

Doca do Jardim do Tabaco
Map 4, F4, p252

This dockland development close to Santa Apolónia railway station has metamorphosized from a seedy industrial landscape of decrepit warehouses into one of the most painfully hip spots in Lisbon, with sleek nightclubs and high-class eateries, see p149 and p166.

Sé
Largo da Sé, **T** 21 887 66 28. *Cathedral: Tue-Sat 0900-1900, Mon, Sun, public and religious holidays 0900-1700. Free. Cloister: May-Sep Tue-Sat 1000-1830, Mon 1000-1700; Oct-Apr Mon-Sat 1000-1700, closed Sun, public and religious holidays. €1. Map 3, G4, p251*

Lisbon's cathedral was built in 1147 on the site of a mosque by Dom Afonso Henríques in triumphant symbolism following the Moorish defeat. Not surprisingly, considering the crusading climate of the time, the cathedral is a built like a Norman fortress, with a muscular western façade of Romanesque and Gothic design, with two crenelleted, buttressed lateral towers separated by a rose window. French architect Mestre Roberto was inspired by the Romanesque Sé Velha in Coimbra. Of largely symbolic appeal, it is claimed Saint Anthony of Padua was baptized here in 1195.

When Afonso IV ascended the throne in the mid-14th century, a Gothic building frenzy ensued and the king had lofty ambitions to make the cathedral the royal pantheon. The chancel was enlarged and surrounded by an elegant ambulatory of nine Gothic chapels, containing *retablos* and tombs. Following the earthquake in 1755, sections of the south tower subsided and the chancel and royal tombs were completely destroyed. Continuous restoration projects have rendered the once-lavish interior sombre, with little light relief. Having said that, the chapel of Bartolomeu Joanes (1324) contains a baroque Christmas crib by Machado de Castro, and with rather fanciful terracotta figurines it borders on the kitsch. The *retablo* of Saint Vincent, the work of João Antunes, was extravagantly created during the reign of Dom Pedro II (between 1693 and 1712) using inlaid marbles and gilded wood.

Most interesting is the **cloister**, completed in 1325, which houses artefacts unearthed during excavation works that began in 1990, including fifth-century BC Phoenician ceramics, part of a Roman draining system and ceramics, animal bones and fish scales dating back to the Moorish occupation.

Museu do Teatro Romano

Pátio do Aljube, 5, **T** 21 751 32 00, **F** 21 757 18 58, museudacidade@mail.telepac.pt *Free. Map 3, F4, p250*

The Roman theatre, originally built in the first century BC by Emperor Augustus, was rebuilt in AD 57, during the time of Nero, to become one of the most important buildings of Olisipo (the name given to Lisbon by the Romans). The Roman Theatre Museum presents the theatre's history from when it was used as a stage for public events from the fourth century until it was abandoned in the Middle Ages. In the 18th century, following the great earthquake, it was unearthed during the reconstruction of Lisbon but was buried again due to the rules laid down by urban planners of the time. It was inspired by the Roman theatre in Mérida, the best preserved Roman theatre on the Iberian Peninsula.

Igreja-Museu de Santo António

Largo de Santo António à Sé, **T** 21 886 04 47. *0800-1930.   Museum Tue-Sun 1000-1300, 1400-1800.   Map 3, G4, p251*

Adjacent to the cathedral, the baroque church of Saint Anthony was built on the site where Lisbon's patron saint, Anthony of Padua, is said to have been born. Canonized in 1232, charismatic Saint Anthony, the most beloved of Lisbon's popular saints, was truly a saint for all seasons. Protector of the city, advocate of tormented souls in purgatory, patron saint of marriage and of family homes, his persuasive powers gave him cult status. "Saint Anthony, Saint Anthony, find me a husband", remains one of the most popular prayers. It is now traditional for the newly betrothed to visit the church and leave flowers as a gift for him on their wedding day.

Only the crypt remains of the original church, designed by Mateus Vicente in the 18th century, which was destroyed by the earthquake. The museum, next door, has a collection of iconography relating to the saint.

Largo das Portas do Sol and Miradouro de Santa Luzia

Map 3, E6, p250

Heading up Rua da Sé onto Rua da Rosa, edged with dusty antique shops and tourist pit stops, streets fan out into warrens of tiny *becos* (blind alleys) and coiling *travessas* one medieval pile on top of another. This is the route of the unofficial tourist Tram 28.

Lisbon's dazzling vistas are the most memorable images of the city and the Miradouro de Santa Luzia is one of the most romantic. Under vine-draped pergolas lovers swoon, old men philosophize and play cards and a Gulf Stream of tourists gasp and coo at the views across the Tagus. The tiled scenes on the outer walls of the Igreja de Santa Luzia depict Martim Moniz, Lisbon's famous knight and martyr, who tied himself to the castle gate in order that Afonso Henríques' crusaders could take Lisbon from the Moors.

The narrow, cobblestone streets of Rua de Chão da Feira lead up to the castle and its unashamedly touristy prelude of brash souvenir shops and suited waiters brandishing laminated menus.

Alternatively, climb Rua de São Tomé, where tourists flock, and justifiably so, to another stunning *miradouro*. The Largo das Portas do Sol, or the 'Gate of the Sun', was named after the city gates which stood here and the views are truly spectacular. To the north the pristine white towers of the Igreja de São Vicente de Fora and the dome of Igreja de Santa Engrácia, soar from above Alfama.

Fundacão Ricardo Espiritú Santo Silva

Largo Portas do Sol, 2, **T** 21 881 46 00, www.fress.press.pt/ing
1000-1700, closed Mon. €5. Map 3, E6, p250

The Decorative Arts Museum, housed in the reconstructed salons and living rooms of the 17th-century Azurara palace, is one of the most important and valuable collections in the country. It was bequeathed to the state by Ricardo Espiritú Santo Silva, a wealthy banker who bought the palace in 1947 and ranges from priceless porcelain from the Qing Dynasty to 16th-century Franco-Flemish tapestries, fine examples of Namban Art and magnificent pieces of Indo-Portuguese art, made from exotic woods and decorated with carved figures inspired by Hinduism.

The collection's highlights reveal how the enlightened period of the discoveries displaced the fantastical ponderings of the medieval imagination. There is a 17th-century Indian Mogul writing desk made from teak, ebony and ivory and engraved with creatures and the symbol of the Tree of Life. There are extraordinary 15th-century salvars and painfully fragile porcelain from the Ming Dynasty which bears the armillary sphere of King Manuel I.

In the Dom José I room, the multi-functional table is considered one of the finest items of 18th-century furniture and a statement on the wit and whimsy which characterized the period. Made from rosewood, inlaid with tulipwood and ivory, the alternating tabletops can be leafed through like a book: chequers and chess – gambling had become the favourite pastime of the aristocracy – tea table, side table and a dressing table. One of the major crowd pleasers is the travel set made by goldsmith Tomás Correia in Lisbon in 1720 containing 33 utensils used for daily grooming and the preparation of a light meal. There is a charming courtyard café and the devoted and knowledgeable staff are keen to inform.

Castelo de São Jorge
Map 3, C4, p250

Dominating Lisbon's skyline, the dramatic Castelo de São Jorge stands where Lisbon first began. A Roman castrum, Visigothic stronghold and Moorish fortress, it was finally taken in 1147 by King Afonso Henríques following a bloody four-month siege. The castle was named after the warrior Saint George, of ancient Cappadoccia, who became the unifying force for the thousands of Northern European crusaders who had been diverted en route to Palestine to aide Afonso in his quest. A statue of the jubilant warrior stands to the left of the main entrance. The multimedia show **Olissipónia**, is constructed on the site which was formerly the old Moorish palace, the **Paço de Alcáçova**, before becoming the official residence of the Portuguese monarchs until the 17th century. It is believed that it was here that King Manuel I heralded the return of Vasco da Gama following his first successful voyage to India. A portable headset commentary provides a whirlwind tour through Lisbon's history.

After a long period of neglect, Salazar restored the castle in 1938 as tourist attraction and its sprawling ramparts and parapets are something of a Disneyfied anticlimax. Still, the 10 connecting towers provide vertigo-inducing vistas of the city below, best appreciated at dusk, when the palpable aura of a medieval epic descends.

From the top of the Tower of Ulysses the **Câmera Escura** periscope, *daily Jun-Oct 1000-1830, Nov-May 1730 €2 reflects 360°* images of Lisbon, with a multi-lingual commentary.

Mouraria
Map 3, A-C4, p250

When Afonso Henríques sacked Lisbon in 1147, the Moors created a ghetto outside the walls named Mouraria, a commercial riverside district which today remains steeped in the memory of conquest. Historically, it has shared a bittersweet rivalry with it's more easy-on-the-eye neighbour, Alfama. While it may be low on tourist magnets, it's an intriguing earthy place. A combustible melting pot; African clubs and shops unfurl to the modern concrete mass of the Mouraria shopping centre, where African hairdressers rub shoulders with Indian and Chinese food stores and all manner of Brazilian kitsch and knock-off gold in between.

Mouraria has always been associated with fado. **Casa de Severa** on Largo da Severa, 2, was home to Maria Severa (see p66), who died aged 26 in 1846. Amália's song *There's a celebration in Mouraria* evokes the daily lives of its residents. It describes when, on the day of the procession of Our Lady of Health, during bouts of religious fervour, "even Rosa Maria...from Rua do Capelão seems virtuous".

Graça
Map 4, p252

From Largo Portas do Sol, Rua de São Tomé leads to the Calçada de Graça, where, just off to the west, the **Miradouro de Graça** provides more breathtaking views over Lisbon. The terrace café is more popular with *Lisboetas* than tourists – especially on Sundays – enjoying ritualistic strong *bicas*, buttery *torradas* and the weekend edition of *Diário de Notícias*.

Tram 28 deposits passengers on the **Largo de Graça**, the area's social hub which goes about its business with lackadaisical charm. Northeast from the **Convento Nossa Senhora da Graça** stretches scrupulously prosaic Rua da Graça punctuated by lively cafés, *pastelarias* and closet-sized shops selling all manner of bric-a-brac from gold watches to children's toys, ironing boards and religious kitsch.

In the late 19th and early 20th century, the growing workforce of sea traders were housed in Victorian-style tenements in Graça. One such housing project, **Vila Bertha**, stands on Travessa da Pereira. Built in 1908, by Joaquim Francisco Tojal, it has an almost Dickensian quality. Named after the architect's daughter, it is embellished with art nouveau wrought-iron motifs, which came to characterize the bourgeois homes of shop workers lining Graça's quaint mews avenues.

Museu Nacional do Azulejo

Rua de Madre de Deus, **T** 21 814 77 47 *Tue 1400-1800, Wed-Sun 1000-1800. Closed Mon and public holidays. €2.24, free Sun until 1400. Map 1, E9, p247*

Housed in the serene Convento de Madre de Deus, the Tile Museum provides an engaging introduction to the origins of the distinctive Portuguese blue-and-white *azulejo* tiles. It's worth a visit to appreciate the church of Madre de Deus alone. Founded in 1509 and reconstructed following the earthquake in 1755, it forms an integral part of the museum. The interior is overwhelming in its opulence, every inch of the extravagant baroque chapel covered with heady 16th-century paintings by Flemish masters, cooling *azulejos* and lofty statues.

The seemingly endless collection of tiles spans from the 13th to the 20th centuries and also includes informative displays outlining the production process and the evolution of the traditional Portuguese *azulejo* from its Moorish origins. There are 13th-century Mudéjar tiles from Seville decorated with traditional Islamic geometric forms, many already demonstrating Renaissance flourishes, flowers, leaves and imitations of patterned textiles.

São Bento, Estrela and Lapa

*Lisbon's western suburbs, a intriguing juxtapostion of the shaggy, the preppy and the posh, are usually glimpsed from the window of Tram 28. The hard-pressed district of São Bento, an old slave enclave, is stained with the bloody imprint of colonial rule. Action centres on rough-hewn **Rua do Poço dos Negros**, a pile of houses, propped up with scaffolding which unfurl into a web of stepped passageways and which is transformed by night into an enclave of raw African piquancy. The district is dominated by the neoclassical **Palácio da Assembléia da República**, Lisbon's parliament building standing astride **Avenida Carlos I**, the turf of hob-nobbing politicos.*

*Estrela is dominated by the glistening dome of the marble-clad basilica, a mini-Mafra, plonked amid a tangle of prissy residential streets which skirt the serene oasis of the **Jardim da Estrela**.*

*Lisbon's ambassadors, visiting glitterati, footballers and presidents camp out in well-to-do Lapa. Along **Rua da Lapa** and **Rua do Sacramento**, stately mansions crowned with pediments and pillars, flank palatial hotels, romantic villas encased with the frip and whimsy of art nouveau and some of the finest gourmet restaurants in the city.*

▸▸ *See Sleeping p130, Eating and drinking p151.*

 Lisbon

◉ Sights

Basilica da Estrela
Largo da Estrela, *0800-1300, 1500-2000. Free. Tram 25 or 28 from Praça da Figueira. Map 5, C1, p253*

The Estrela basilica is one of Lisbon's most important 18th-century religious monuments and most eye-catching landmarks; its majestic white dome crouches surreally around every corner of Estrela's jumbled backstreets. It was built between 1770 and 1790 by Queen Maria, who was fulfilling a vow to God that she would build a church if she gave birth to a son and heir. Poignantly, the queen did produce an heir but the child died of small pox, aged two, before the church was completed. The two bell towers and elegant rococo dome, marked a return to the flamboyance of the reign of Dom João's superfluous fluffery, which Pombal had intended to nip in the bud. The classical triangular pediment points to the heavens above a graceful battalion of columns and ornate statues, dominating the church entrance. The baroque style is reminiscent of the convent of Mafra, see p116, the work of Mateus, Vicente Ludovice's disciple, who was also from the School of Mafra. The interior is decorated with pink and black marble, and paintings by Pompeu Botoni and Pedro Alexandrino. Queen Maria's tomb is in the transept.

● *An imposing presence, Lisbon's parliament building, Palácio da Assembléia da República on Rua de São Bento, thrusts rather incongruously but with neoclassical ceremonial splendour into São Bento. Built in 1598 as the Mosteiro de São Bento, come the liberal revolution of 1820 and the abolition of the religious orders, it became the capital's political nerve centre.*

Jardim da Estrela
Largo da Estrela. *0700-2400. Tram 25 or 28 from Praça da Figueira. Map 5, B2, p253*

Facing the Basilica da Estrela is Lisbon's oldest and loveliest garden. A romantic idyll, with winding pathways lined with poplars, palms and clumps of satisfyingly untamed vegetation. A lazy Pre-Raphaelite ambience prevails as students take breaks at open-air cafés, men nod off with crumpled newspapers in hand and elderly ladies are enchanted by the rose gardens. It's a lovely place for a picnic and for kids to explore.

● *Just behind the gardens, on Rua de São Jorge, Henry Fielding, aged 47, was buried in the English cemetery. He died here in 1754, before completing* The Journal of a Voyage to Lisbon.

Tiles of the unexpected

Encrusted across seemingly every flat surface in the city, from grotty *tascas* to art nouveau mansions, blue and white *azulejo* tiles are Portugal's most distinctive decorative art form. The name *azulejo* comes from the Arab word *al azulaycha* meaning 'polished little stone', and the art of tile making was one of the lasting consequences of the Arab presence in Iberia. Techniques came to Portugal from Seville, the centre of the tile industry, which employed the archaic ridged tile techniques *cuerda seca* and *arista* until the mid-16th century. Over time tile motifs evolved from geometric Moorish designs into European plant and animal themes which gradually progressed from Gothic to the pure Renaissance style.

In the 16th century, *azulejos* were originally used to tile important buildings. By the 18th century they were being used to cover entire façades – Portugal found it hard to cast off its Moorish taste for excess.

One of Portugal's finest tile is at Sintra National Palace where in the 15th century, Dom Manuel I, in a blaze of maritime glory, set his heart on turning the palace into a faithful imitation of Seville's Alcázar, see p107. *Azulejo* decoration accompanied King Manuel's court to Queluz Palace, where a water canal 115 m long was smothered with 50,000 *azulejos*, see p117. In the 18th century, at the height of the baroque, Ferreira das Tabuletas created some of the finest allegorial panels in the city, including those which adorn the *Cervejaria Trindade*, see p146.

As well as providing architectural window dressing, Lisbon's tiles also reveal the city's history. The crusading knights of the Reconquista are detailed at the Miradouro de Santa Luzia, see p72, and also at the Mosteiro de São Vicente de Fora see p67. At the Museu do Azulejo, a rare panoramic image of the city prior to the earthquake reveals the extent of the devastation.

Casa-Museu Fernando Pessoa
Rua Coelho da Rocha 16-18, **T** 21 396 81 90,
cfpessoa@mail.telepac.pt *Mon-Fri 1000-1800, Thu 1300-2000. Free.
Bus 9, 20, 38, Tram 25, 28. Map 1, F5, p246*

Portugal's beloved and elliptical poet lived here between 1920 and 1935. Languishing in a state of near ruin, it was acquired by the local council who set about restoring it. All that remains of the original construction is the building's façade and the staircase that leads up to the inner sanctum, Pessoa's bedroom.

The house now serves more as a cultural centre for the promotion of poetry than as a museum, and it has been ambitiously attempting to acquire Pessoa's entire literary legacy. Alongside the the poet's own personal library, there are some 1,200 of Pessoa's hand-written notebooks, grappling with such themes as the occult and philosophy, as well as a collection of Portuguese and international poetry.

The highlight of a visit is the portrait of Pessoa, ever the sartorial dignitary, painted in 1954 by Portugal's great modernist artist Almada Negreiros, a great friend of the poet. There is also a study for *Mensagem*, the only work that was published during his lifetime, which tells the story in verse of the history of Portugal. Experts of Pessoa's work have determined that *Mensagem* does not mean 'message' but rather is an amalgam of three Latin words meaning, 'the spirit makes the universe turn'.

Just by the main entrance to the house, Pessoa engraved his own horoscope in stone. He was obsessed by astrology and made a horoscope for everything. He almost discovered the date of his death but the inaccuracy of the hour of his birth apparently misled him by a few months. On the wall of Pessoa's room is the only portrait of Pessoa painted during his lifetime by Spaniard, Rodriguez Castañe. There is the chest of drawers on which Pessoa claimed to have written the book, in the pseudonym, or heteronym, of Alberto Caiero, *O Guardador de Rabanhos*, in one night.

★ **Literary cafés**

Best

- Café A Brasileira, p147
- Martinho de Arcadas, p137
- Café Nicola, p138
- Ler devagar, p191

Museu Nacional de Arte Antiga

Rua das Janelas Verdes, **T** 21 39 12 800. *Wed-Sun 1000-1245, 1400-1800. Tue 1400-1800. €3. Tram E25 from Praça do Comercio. Map 1, G5, p246*

The National Museum of Ancient Art, also known as the Museu das Janelas Verdes, is housed in the former 17th-century palace of Dom Francisco de Távora, Count of Alvor. Alongside the Gulbenkian, this exceptional museum contains the most important collection of 14th-20th century Portuguese art in the country, including paintings, sculpture and decorative arts. The Saint Albert Carmelite convent formed part of the palace and the dazzling baroque chapel, with its profusion of *azulejo* tiles and gilded wood, has been preserved and can also be visited.

Originally created in 1884, the museum was intended to house the great works of art, appropriated by the state from convents and monasteries across Portugal when religious orders were abolished in 1834. Displayed over three floors, European art is well represented and there is an enlightening display of decorative arts from Portugal's colonies. There is an impressive collection of 16th-century masterpieces from the Portuguese school: Francisco Henríques, Gregório Lopes, and 17th-century artists, including Domingos António de Sequeira (1768-1834) and Josefa de Obidos.

In room 57, is one of the collection's unquestionable highlights; the rather blood-curdling, narrative triptych of the *Temptation of Saint Anthony*, attributed to Hieronymus Bosch.

On the third floor, room 11, and hailed as Portugual's most important work of art, is the narrative polyptych of the *Veneration of Saint Vincent* by Nuno Gonçalves, royal painter at the court of Afonso V in the 15th century, and clearly of Flemish influence. Of great historical interest, the six panels in violet and white shades, characteristic of Gonçalves, portray the 58 notable Portuguese figures of the second half of the 15th century. King Afonso V, Queen Isabel, merchants, sailors, explorers and clerics show their devotion to their patron saint, within the context of the crusades of the Avis Dynasty. The artist makes a cameo appearance and Prince Henry the Navigator is thought to feature (the figure wearing a dark hat with a serpentine moustache), this being particularly revealing as no authenticated portrait of the discover has ever been unearthed.

Further crowd pleasers are the two 16th-century Japanese screens, impressive examples of Namban art and rare 18th-century silverware by French silversmiths Thomas and François Germain. There are important Flemish tapestries by Dürer, including the portrait of São Jerónimo, in room 57 floor 1 and works by Holbein.

Belém and the western waterfront

Not surprisingly, tourists flock to the suburb of Belém which, spreading west along the banks of the inky blue Tagus, is a tremendous heap of 15th- and 16th-century Manueline marvels, built to celebrate Vasco da Gama's discovery of the sea route to India. The **Mosteiro dos Jerónimos** *astounds with its sublime cloister where fantastical sea creatures and maritime emblems writhe in milky stone and the* **Torre de Belém**, *the purest form of Manueline style, looks more like a chess piece washed ashore than a defensive fortification. But, while Belém certainly enshrines glories past, it doesn't keep visitors at a distance. It's one of the loveliest places in the city with child-friendly activities and 21st-century toys.*

Chino-clad boys amble across breezy riverside walkways where six-packed rollerbladers and cyclists glide and where super-sleek yachts are moored and primary coloured fishing boats boats bob along the Tagus. Kites fly and frisbies spin across expansive parks and manicured lawns where museum-weary kids let off steam. The **Design Museum** *is a homage to Starck, Eames and all 20th-century design icons. And, no visit to Belém is complete without paying your respects at the shrine to the* pastel de nata, **Antiga Pastelaria**.

▸▸ *See Eating and drinking p152, Bars and clubs p167*

Sights

★ Mosteiro dos Jerónimos

Praça do Império, **T** 21 362 00 34/48. *Tue-Sun 1000-1700. Church free, cloisters €3, free Sun. Map 1, G12, p247*

Without doubt, the iconic Jerónimos monastery is Lisbon's most stunning monument. A UNESCO World Heritage Site since 1984 and a triumph of the age of discoveries, it is a beautiful example of the Manueline style. Portugal's transition from Gothic to Renaissance, Manueline style was characterized by exotic naturalist motifs intricately carved into the creamy stone – crustaceans, ropes, shells and fish, combined with armillary spheres and other royal emblems.

Dom Manuel I ordered the monastery to be built in 1502, to honour Vasco da Gama's discovery of the sea route to India and in appreciation of the Virgin Mary for their safe return. Dollops of cash were apportioned from the *Vintena da Pimenta* (5% of the receipts from the spices and riches from Africa and the East). The monks of the Order of St Jerome (Hieronymite monks) lived in the monastery and it was their duty to pray for the soul of the king and the explorers who sailed from Restelo Beach. For 100 years, Portugal would dominate the sea route to India, bringing the monarchy immense fortune and exotic creatures: elephants, leopards and rhinoceros, which roamed around Lisbon.

The first phase of construction was undertaken by Diogo do Boitaca (1460-1528) and was characterized by Gothic naturalism.

Perenially engulfed by tourists, the delectable **south-facing portal**, is the work of Spanish Renaissance master João Castilho. In the centre is Prince Henry the Navigator and low reliefs evoking scenes from the life of Saint Jerome. Dominating the composition is the serene image of the Virgin. Buttresses, flanked by statuary niches, soar above to form pinnacles resembling whipped cream.

The **west portal** was the work of French sculptor Nicolau de Chanterène, credited with introducing Renaissance art to Portugal, and evokes the profound sense of mysticism which characterized the outward-looking period of the Discoveries. Scenes in the upper niches relate to the birth of Christ, while to the left two lateral niches evoke King Manuel I, his wife Queen Dona Maria I and their patron saints John the Baptist and Saint Jerome.

Through the western portal, the **church of Santa Maria** is unbearably beautiful. Six intricately carved columns, like plaited golden hair, fan organically into the vaulted ceiling which, without any supporting arches, almost appears to be floating in mid-air. In the entrance to the church are the tombs of Luís de Camões, author of Portugal's national epic *As Lusíadas* and, appropriately enough, Vasco da Gama. In the cloisters, a serene pink marble tomb is the final resting place of Fernando Pessoa. The two-tiered, intricately carved **cloister** is the most fêted of its kind in Europe.

● *The monastery is busy all year round but it should be avoided on Sundays. The cloisters are best visited late afternoon, when the stone carvings are bathed in soft dappled light.*

Museu da Marinha

Praça do Império, **T** 21 362 00 19, museumar@mail.telepac.pt *Oct-May Tue-Sun 1000-1700, Jun-Sep 1000-1800.* €3. *Map 1, G11, p247*

In the western wing of the Mosteiro dos Jerónimos, the Maritime Museum, with a colossal 17,000 items, is a glorified presentation of Portugal's maritime history. The Discoveries Room contains chronological displays of replica models from the first fleet of the *caravela Latina* to Vasco da Gama's 1498 flag ship, in which he discovered the Indian sea route, a 1793 frigate and a 44-gun ship, built in Lisbon to form part of a squadron that transported King Don João VI to Brazil in 1807, to escape Napoleon's onslaught. One of the most interesting models is the *Madre de Deus* nau, built in 1589, which sailed twice to India before it was seized by the English in 1592. So taken were the Brits with its magnificence that it was put on display in Dartmouth.

Upstairs, the Royal Barges Pavilion contains original 18th-century barges and fishing vessels. The highlight is the royal barge built in 1780 during the reign of Queen Maria I, a lavishly gilded vessel which remained operational for some 177 years and transported a roll call of famous passengers, including Kaiser Wilhelm II of Germany and Queen Elizabeth II of England.

Among the nautical sundries, there is a 1645 terrestrial globe made in the workshop of Willem Jansz Blaeu (1571-1658), the most famous globe maker of them all. Sundials, telescopes, spice jars and furnishings brought from the East are displayed upstairs in the Orient Room, including a Samurai sword (the carved rings represent the number of victims beheaded). The museum also houses the world's largest collection of astrolabes, the nautical instruments which made Portugal one of the forerunners of European maritime exploration. There is also an intricately carved sculpture of the Archangel Saint Rafael which was carried on board the São Rafael, part of Vasco da Gama's 1497 fleet and don't miss the Santa Cruz seaplane, which made the first South Atlantic air crossing in 1922.

★ Design Museum
Centro Cultural de Belém, Praça do Império, **T** 21 361 29 34.
1100-2000. €3. Map 1, G11, p147

The exceptional Design Museum opened to universal acclaim in 1999 and is considered to be one of the best exhibition spaces of its kind in the world. The vision of media mogul Francisco Capelo who, at the tender age of 45, donated his collection of over 11,000 items to the state, presents a reverential cornucopia of iconic 20th-century design. There are one-off designs in addition to mass-produced objects from Phillipe Starck kettles, colanders and 'Dr. No' armchairs to Charles and Ray Eames' 60s chaise longues.

Engaging exhibits are organized chronologically and present the social transformations that have influenced the development of taste, technique and function; from the 1930s Wall Street crash, which resulted in an aesthetic streamlining characterized by Bauhaus, to the Cuban Missile crisis and Vietnam war, from which arose pop art irreverence and radical anti-design movements. Set against a 1970s context of post-war patriotism and pluralism, there are classic Vener Panton bean bags, plastic orange "cheese" table and chairs and a 'Big Flower Pot' hanging lamp. From the 1950s post-war period of prosperity and optimism, the work of the Scandinavian organic modernists sits alongside George Nelson's 'Marshmellow' sofa, Arne Jacobsen's Egg chair and Paul Henningsen's 1958 "Artichoke" hanging lamp.

Torre de Belém

Avenida de Brasília, **T** 21 362 00 34/38. *1000-1700, closed Mon and public holidays. Map 1, H10, p247*

Belém's tower is the poster child of Lisbon. A dazzling fairy-tale confection, the exotic iconography and maritime imagery reveals Portugal's 16th-century obsession with the Orient. It was built in 1515-21, during the reign of Dom Manuel I, by architect and Manueline Master Francisco Arruda, to defend the Tagus estuary. The tower was originally positioned on an island off the north bank of the Tagus, opposite the beach at Restelo, until the river silted following the earthquake of 1755. Suffused with a mystical aura, the Moorish domed turrets are similar to those used in fortifications in Morocco where Arruda had previously worked. You can climb up to the top of the tower for panoramic views across the estuary.

Padrão de Descobrimentos

Av de Brasília, **T** 21 303 19 50. *Daily 0900-1700, closed Mon and public holidays.* €3. *Map 1, H12, p247*

Reached by an underpass, the Monolithic Discoveries monument stands some 170 ft tall in the shape of a ship's prow. It was built in 1960 by Salazar to commemorate the 500th anniversary of the death of Henry the Navigator. Rather ironically, within the space of a year of the monument's inauguration, Portugal's imperial power was well and truly ruptured when Goa was lost to India. Henry is the monument's major protaganist standing alongside other legendary Portuguese explorers and crusaders, including Vasco da Gama, in a rather cold freize. You can take the lift up to the top of the monument for magnificent views over the Tagus.

Torre de Belém

The image that has graced a thousand tourist brochures. The Torre de Belém is the purest example of the Manueline style and a potent symbol of Portuguese imperial grandeur.

Palácio Nacional de Ajuda

Caláçada da Ajuda, **T** 21 36 37 095. *Daily except Wed, 1000-1700. Sun and holidays 1000-1400. 'Tours' depart every half hour, except lunchtime; 1200-1400. On Fri mornings tours given by vounteers are conducted in English on request. €3, free Sun until 1400 and public holidays. Map 1, G2, p246*

Nestling on a hilltop overlooking Lisbon, amongst an Eden of palms and aromatic pines, the neoclassical Ajuda Palace was the residence of the Portuguese royal family during the reign of Luís (1861-89) and is a depository for a dizzying collection of decorative arts. Construction of the palace began in 1802, designed by Italian architect Francisco Javier Fabri and José Costa e Silva who took over. Building was halted in 1807 when the royal family fled to Brazil and resumed again in 1813.

The rather heady extravaganza includes lavish tapestries designed by Francisco Goya, which were given as a gift to King João VI by the King of Spain in honour of his marriage in 1785 to Princess Carlota. Far from a marriage made in heaven, João was renowned for his troublesome piles and was by no means an Adonis, while ambitious Carlota was an imperious dwarf and attempted on many occasions to get the unpleasing and inept King committed. Still, for all their flaws, they produced nine heirs.

King João V 'the magnificent', hit the jackpot in the first half of the 18th century when diamonds were discovered in Brazil. So, with unprecedented wealth, and little restraint, he placed his downright excessive orders for superlative gold- and silver-work in Paris. His successor King José I (1750-77) had similar tastes, accumulating over 1,000 pieces from the Germain goldsmiths, most of which is to be found here.

By the reign of King Luís (1861-89), the monarchy really knew how to have a good time, hosting receptions, balls and concerts, all of which required a lavish setting bearing the hallmarks of acclaimed artists, designers and master craftsmen of the day. Chamber music concerts were held in the Music Room which contains precious oriental porcelain from the Ch'ien period. In the Despatch Room a Sèvres porcelain urn was a gift from Napoleon III in 1867.

The Blue Room was the everyday sitting room of King Luís and Queen Maria Pia and was designed by Possidonio da Silva in 1865. The desk by Paul Sormani decorated with 'Vernis Martin' is an exceptional piece of Louis XV style. The agate stone ceiling of the Winter Garden room was a gift from the Viceroy of Egypt.

Maintaining the 19th-century tradition for things oriental, the Chinese Room's centrepiece is a particulary quirky chandelier, made from Imari tea cups, bowls and lids. The climax of the tour is King Luís' echoing Throne Room, which corresponds to the size of the entire south wing. The ceiling was painted by Manuel Piolti, themed 'Heroic Virtue'. The walls are covered with embroidered blood-red silk, the two magnificently gilded thrones are lined with sumptous velvet, decorated with mischievous cherubs and flanked by priceless porcelain jars from the K'anghis Dynasty.

Ajuda's 18th-century **botanical gardens**, *Calçada da Ajuda, T 21 362 25 03*, are believed to be the first in Portugal, created to nurture plants yielded from the exotic lands. The area is covered with hedges, trees over 100 years old and aromatic plants.

Northern Lisbon and the Gulbenkian

*The broad avenues of the 'Estados Novos' (New States) which stretch beyond Parque Eduardo VII bear the imperious imprint of fascist Prime Minister Salazar (1936-70). Thrusting 1940s office blocks and monolithic apartment buildings don't exactly secure the area an entry onto most vistors' hit lists but nestling in between there are fine examples of elegant prize-winning architecture. The **Casa-Museu Dr Anastácio Gonçalves** is an acclaimed decorative arts museum worth visiting for its swirling art nouveau façade alone. Lisbon's number one attraction, the **Museu Calouste Gulbenkian**, lies in its own serene, 17-acre garden housing an outstanding collection of*

*Western and Eastern art. Further north is a clutch of niche museums, including the rather fusty **Museu de Cidade**. Unveiled for Euro 2004, Sporting Lisbon's new stadium straddles the busy transport nexus of Campo Grande and Benfica's over-hauled football shrine glimmers in its rather down-at-heel eponymous suburb. With an old-fashioned fun fair, zoo and toy museum within a 20-minute metro ride, the northern reaches of the city also offer plenty of child-friendly activities.*

▶▶ *See Sleeping p131, Eating and drinking p153, Kids p213, Sport p201*

Sights

★ Museu Calouste Gulbenkian
Av da Berna, 45-A, **T** 21 782 34 61. *Wed-Sun 1000-1800, Tue 1400-1800. €5, free Sun. Metro São Sebastião. Map 1, D6, p246*

As monumental in its scope as in its quality, the Gulbenkian covers the major periods of Western and Eastern art from 2,800 BC onwards. Armenian entrepreneur and art fanatic, Calouste Sarkis Gulbenkian (1869-1955), bequeathed to Portugal some 6,000 works. When Turkish Petroleum Ltd was distributed among four oil companies, Gulbenkian secured for himself the 5 per cent of the capital, earning him the sobriquet 'Mr Five Percent'. But his passion for the arts derived from the artistic and aesthetic beauty of each item rather than from its market value. His fervour, however, knew no bounds and each item had to be the best. If what he desired was not available on the open market he would simply approach the Rothchilds of the world and tenacious bartering would ensue.

Egyptian and classical antiquities This collection, although slender, spans all periods of the civilization from the Old Kingdom to the Roman period. Gulbenkian devoted great time and money to the aquisition of a bronze sculpture of the Torso of Pedubast, encrusted with copper and gold, from the reign of King Pedubast (818-791 BC), the Dynasty XXIII, Third Intermediate Kingdom. The

Saite period (664-525 BC) is represented by a series of striking, amazingly preserved bronze cats. Bastet, the goddess of fertility, was one of the multiple deities in Egypt's polytheist religion endowed with a cat's head.

The collection of **classical antiquities**, presents a series of ancient Greek coins (575-75 BC) and the 3rd-century Roman head of Alexander the Great, or the Abouquir Medallion. Discovered in 1906, debate raged for decades as to its authenticity.

Decorative arts The decorative arts collection is dominated by the French Regency, revealing Gulbenkian's fondness for the elegance characterized by the Louis XV and Louis XVI periods. Designs from the drawing board of France's finest cabinet makers include Jean-Henri Riesener's Louis XV-style cylinder desk, made in 1773 for the wife of the future Louis XVII.

Islamic art Gulbenkian's interest in Islamic art developed from formative years in spent in Turkey. There are more than 250 pieces from the period spanning the Mongol invasions of Gengis Khan to the end of the 18th century, including ceramics, costumes, Isfahan carpets from Persia (16th to the 17th-century Ottoman periods), Persian silks and lustrous Ottoman *azulejo* tile panels (16th century), mosque lamps from the Mamluk period (14th century), as well as textiles, lacquer doors and remarkable jade. It's an revealing insight into the fervent religious beliefs and unbridled luxury in which the upper classes lived. One of the highlights is the stunning mural relief from Assyria-Nimrud (884-859 BC), Mesopotamia.

Oriental art From the Far East, there is 18th-century porcelain from the Qing Dynasty, semi-precious stones from China and laquer work from Japan, reflecting the collector's preference for the fanciful decoration of the porcelain of the T'sing Dynasty. The crowd puller is the 'Coromandel screen' from 17th-century China. Also alluring is the Japanese writing box, laquered with relief decoration and ornte *inros* (tobaco pouches).

European art This collection spans the period from the 15th-20th century. The 15th- and 16th-century Flemish and Italian schools are represented by a selection that includes works by Roger van der Weyden, Carpaccio and Ghirlandaio. There are many works by 17th-century Flemish and Dutch masters Peter Paul Rubens, Franz Hals, Anton van Dyck and Rembrandt van Rijn.

One of Gulbenkian's paintings, Rubens' *Helena Fourment* (1577-1640), is one of the highlights of the entire collection, a ravishing portait of the artist's wife dressed in black satin, which constrasts with her silky rosy hue flesh. Gulbenkian acquired the painting from the Hermitage Museum, whipping it from right under the nose of legendary dealer Sir Joseph Duveen. The 18th century is also represented by an area devoted to the work of the Venetian painter Francesco Guardi (1712-93). The *Veduta*, considered one of Guardi's masterpieces, shows the Piazza San Marco decorated for the *Festa della Sensa*. In *Portrait of a Young Woman* (1485), the alluring model dressed in a Florentine red dress and a coral necklace radiating from her neck, captures the essence of the *quattrocento* Florence, the realism and naturalism which defined the last half of the 15th century.

Another area focuses on the works of English painters and includes a collection of portaits by Thomas Gainsborough (1727-88). Throughout the collection, in paintings and sculpture, women in all their glory whether in naked liberation, or closed modesty, lithe or curvaceous fascinated Gulbenkian. Gainsborough's full-length portrait of the youthful Elizabeth Garth, painted in celebration of her wedding to her cousin William Lowndes-Stone shows the Flemish influence upon 18th-century English portrait painting. But with dashing spontaneity and elegance this is considered to be one of Gainsborough's finest portaits, earning him the title, the 'ideal artist to portray the English woman'. There are also two Turners, windswept elemental masterpieces, including the turbulent, *Wreck of a Transport Ship* (1810).

Sculpture The collection focuses on French works from the 18th-19th century. From the 18th century there is the polemical masterpiece of Jean-Antoine Houdon, the marble statue of *Diana*, which belonged to Catherine of Russia. Running, quivering, naked, Houdon's work caused a sensation at the time and was regarded as excessive and inappropriate.

Not to be missed is the magnificent Jean D'Aire sculpture by Rodin. Cast in bronze in the late 19th century it formed part of the sculptural group which was a monument to the valiant Burghers of Calais; the six martyrs who surrended themselves as hostages to Edward III of England, so he would raise the siege of the city and save the starving population during the Hundred Years' War. Rodin immortalized the hostages as they prepare themselves for execution. Each figure embodies the different states of mind on facing martyrdom. The most valient of the group, holding the keys to the city, Jean d'Aire, has become the most famed of the six. August Rodin kept this piece in his possession until his death in 1917, when it was acquired by Gulbenkian.

Lalique Jewellery Gulbenkian was a great admirer and close friend of René Lalique and this glittering art nouveau collection is unrivalled anywhere in the world. As a child, Lalique felt a great affinity with nature and would observe the world around him in great detail. Green was one of his favourite colours and he frequently used birds of prey, associated with the darkness of night. A fine draughtsman, he produced the drawings for his jewels himself. Imbued with elegance and eroticism, the orchid was one of the flowers that symbolized the aesthetic movement of the late 19th century and featured in many of Lalique's creations.

The exuberant Jewel for the eagles and pine choker (1889-1901) was bought directly from Lalique in 1901 when Gulbenkian was just 12 years old. Made in cast and chased gold and enamelled in green, its centrepiece is an enormous square cabochon opal. The rectangular plaque is quite sinister, harbouring glaring demonic eagles enamelled in dark blue.

Perhaps the most stunning piece of all is the Female Face Pendant featuring poppies, one of the most emblematic flowers of art nouveau, associated with dream worlds. A languid female face, another recurrent image in Lalique's work, is surrounded by waves of silver hair, draped with a huge baroque pearl, and framed by a hood of four voluptuous poppies.

Jose de Azeredo Perdigão Centro de Arte Moderno

Gulbenkian Museum, Av da Berna, T 21 782 34 74, €3, €5 joint ticket with the Gulbenkian, free Sun. Wed-Sun 1000-1800, Tue 1400-1800, closed Mon. Metro São Sebastião. Map 1, D6, p246

Opened in 1983, this museum houses the best collection of 20th-century Portuguese modern art in the country, as well as an important collection of British art since the 1960s. Just to the left of the entrance is *Pintura* (1917), the abstract work of one of the gallery's most prominent artists Amadeu de Souza-Cardosa (1887-1919), Portugal's most influential figure in transcending conventional forms and introducing modern art schools already established in Europe. In 1906 he studied in Paris, immersing himself in the bohemian gatherings of the cubists; the influence of his friend Picasso is clear. Working through the major avant garde trends from abstractionism, cubism, futurism and expressionism, his exhuberant work was characterized by splashes of fanciful colour and inventive subject matter. Just short of his 31st birthday, Souza-Cardosa died in the great influenza epidemic that swept across Portugal.

On the first floor there are works by Almada Negreiros, the father of Portuguese modernism, including his self portrait which was displayed in Café A Brasileira, see p147, until the 1970s. On the lower ground floor, there are monochrome canvases by Helena de Almeida (1934). The 1960s are represented by an almost fetishistic obsession with the human body, apparent in the powerful portrayals of internationally acclaimed artist Paulo Rego, artist in residence at London's National Gallery during the 1990s. Also on the lower ground floor, the slender British contingent includes Bridget Riley's *Metamorphosis*, David Hockney's *Renaissance Head* and Harold Cohen's *Quadratic*.

★ Casa-Museu Dr. Anastácio Gonçalves

Avenida 5 de Outubro, 6-8, **T** 35 40 823/09 23. *Tue 1400-1800, Wed-Sun 1000-1800. €2. Metro Saldanha/Picoas. Map 1, D7, p247*

War veteran, renowned ophthalmologist and friend of Gulbenkian, Anastácio Gonçalves (1889-1965) devoted his life to a profound appreciation of the arts. During his life he amassed some 2,000 works, demonstrating a collector's zeal refreshingly driven by personal taste and aesthetic stimulation rather than commerce.

While the collection is phemonenal, the Valmor prize-winning building that houses it is a visual feast in itself. Casa Malhoa was built in 1904 by one of the most revered architects of the period, Manoel Joaquim Norte Júnior. In the shadows of the *Sheraton* monolith, it is a delightful neoclassical anachronism. The austerity of the neo-Romanesque windows is set off by *azulejo* friezes, ornate borders and exuberant motifs.

The exhibition begins with a mesmerizing collection of Chinese porcelain, which includes many blue and white porcelain pieces from the Zhengde and Jiajing periods of the Ming Dynasty (1506-1566), as well as lustrous Wucai (five colours) pieces from the transitional period (1620-1683) and enamelled pieces from the *famille verte* and *famille rose* of the Qing dynasty.

A large part of the collection is dedicated to 18th-century Portuguese furniture and provides an insight into its evolution from the austere 17th-century designs to a more flamboyant French style. The collection includes the works of some of France's most renowned cabinet makers, including JL Cossen and M Ohneburg.

Gonçalves was particulary enamoured of the naturalist paintings of the "Grupo de Leão" especially the work of António Silva Porto, the pioneer of Portuguese naturalism, the majority of whose works are displayed in Malhoa's original studio. Notable highlights are *A Ciefa* (*The Harvest*, 1884) and *Raparigas do Paço de Lumiar*. Another of Gonçalves's favoured landscape artists was João Vaz (1859-1931) and his ethereal *A Praia*, (*The Beach*, 1890) dominates the studio.

Palácio dos Marqueses de Fronteira

Largo São Domingos de Benfica, **T** 21 778 20 23. *Guided tours must be booked in advance: Jul-Sep 1030, 1100, 1130, 1200. Oct-May 1100, 1200. Map 1, D4, p246*

Built in 1640 as a hunting pavilion for João de Mascarenhas, the first Marquês de Fronteira, this charming palace is on the edge of the bucolic idyll of Monsanto forest. The interior is delightful with a profusion of lustrous *azulejos* and 18th-century rocaille stucco, suffused with the colonial exoticism of Indo- Portuguese furniture, paintings and tapestries. Even more crowd pleasing are the two beautiful romantic **gardens**, heavy with Pre-Raphaelite languour. Laid out in 1660, they are considered to be the finest example of the original Portuguese approach to gardening, despite being more representative of the 16th-century Italian Renaissance style.

Parque das Nações

*The Expo 98 site of Parque das Nações is a far cry from the medina streets of Alfama and the colonial triumphalism of Belém. This one-time industrial wasteland to the northeast of the city has been transformed into a modernist playground, united by the theme "The Oceans, a Heritage for the Future". Coinciding with the 500th anniversary of Vasco da Gama's 'discovery' of the sea route to India, Expo 98's exhibits were unashamedly intended to flaunt Portugal's maritime triumphs. Today, the park is one of the best places in the city for all-round family entertainment. Stretching for 2 km along the Tagus, cable cars glide above coastal walkways and exotic gardens to the highest lookout point in the city, the **Torre de Vasco da Gama**. The state-of-the-art **Oceanarium** is the largest in Europe and the **Interactive Science museum** reveals the park's educational dimension. Perhaps nowhere in the city is the dynamism of New World Lisbon more apparent than in the concordian elegance of **Oriente**, the new metro and railway station designed by Spanish master architect Santiago Calatrava.*

*The discount card, **Cartão do Parque**, is available from the kiosk in front of the Vasco da Gama shopping centre on Alameda dos Oceanos. It allows free entry to the Oceanarium, Torre Vasco da Gama, round trip on the cable car, 50% discount on the Knowledge Pavilion, 20% discount on bike hire, 15% discount on bowling and 15% discount on selected restaurants. Adults €14, under 12s €7. Bikes hire from Tejo Bike, next to the information kiosk, 1000-2000 summer, 1000-1800 winter, €4 per hr, €2 ½ hr and €1.50 for every addtional ½ hr, children €3 per hr, ½ hr €1.50, each addtional ½ hr €1.*

Sights

Around the park
Map 1, A11, p247

Calatrava's **Oriente metro station** is a cathedral to modernity, a three-aisle nave with steel-supported glass archways like gossamer wings and flooded harmoniously with blue sky. The subway terminal itself is a collage of tile murals, designed by some of Lisbon's best contemporary artists. The train station serves the eastern zones of Lisbon and TAP and Swiss Air passengers can even check in here.

Emerging from the station, a walkway leads to more slithers of steel and sheets of glass, the **Vasco da Gama Shopping Centre**. Passing though here brings you out at the centre of the park in front an information booth on Caminho da Água, selling maps, discount tickets and passes. Turning right brings you to the southern section of the park with its showcase Oceanarium and the Science Museum, see below. The first attention-grabber is the **Pavilhão de Portugal**, designed by Portugal's leading architect Álvaro Siza Vieira, the man behind Chiado's reincarnation. It's a remarkable sight, its roof undulating like a silver wave. The **Teatro Camões** at the southern fringes is a key venue for classical theatre productions and in front is the eye-catching **Reflexo do Ceú Navigante**, a shimmery sculpture of a compass by Japanese archictect, Sasumu Shingu.

★ Oriente
Brave New Lisbon. The iconic metro station designed by the Spanish architect Santiago Calatrava.

Turning left, directly in front of you is the giant mushroom shaped **Pavilhão Atlântico**, an excellent concert venue which has played host to Bob Dylan, Massive Attack and Robbie Williams. Skirting its left-hand side will bring you to the riverside walkway where cable cars pass along **Olivais dock**, above a line up of chain restaurants alongside the herbaceous **Garcia de Orta** gardens. Visible from any vantage point is the **Torre de Vasco da Gama**, see below, and adjacent is the **Sony Plaza**, another sports and concert arena.

Pavilhão do Conhecimento Ciência Viva

Alameda dos Oceanos, **T** 21 891 71 00. *Tue-Fri 1000-1800, Sat, Sun and holidays 1100-1900. €5, children 7-17 years €2.50, 3-6 years €2, 2 and under free, family ticket €11. Map 1, A11, p247*

The Interactive Science Museum was opened in 1999. Themed exhibitions include the Exploratorium, the concept of American physicist Frank Oppenheimer and premised on harnessing the human perception of nature. While stuffy science classrooms may come to mind, kids love the diverse range of interactive displays and simulations. Children can experiment with their own physical strength, attempting to launch a hydrogen rocket. To keep the under-six amused The Unfinished House is a kids'-only construction site with foam bricks and panels, pulleys and wheelbarrows. There is also a bookshop and cybercafé free of charge with entry ticket.

Oceanário

T 21 891 70 02 21. *Summer 1000-2000, winter 1000-1900. €9, children under 12 years, €4.50. Map 1, A11, p247*

Lisbon's wonderous Oceanarium draws weekend-liberated *Lisboetas* and kids on school trips by the coach load. The second largest in the world (Japan is the largest), it is the innovative design and mesmerizing odyssey of marauding maritime roamers, rather than its size which makes it one of Lisbon's best sights for all round family entertainment. Designed by Bostonian Peter Chermayelf with 30 cm-thick transparent concave acrylic, it gives you the feeling that you are entering the ocean.

The 'one ocean' theme embraces every coastal habitat and temperature zone. It's transfixing. Sinister requiem sharks and barracudas roam, manta rays rood and a not-so-pretty sergeant fish cruises alongside sand tigers, needle fish and the largest inhabitants, two massive bullsharks. Don't miss the furry sea otter All Stars Eusebio and Amália.

Descending to the lower level, you experience, close up, life on the ocean floor, with living coral reefs, heavenly sea dragons, Roman hermaphrodites and South Australian fish, including the Port Jackson sharks, which live apart but during breeding season will travel over 800 km to meet each other.

Torre Vasco da Gama and Ponte Vasco da Gama

Cais das Naus, **T** 21 891 80 00. *1000-2000. €2.49. Cable cars between the Vasco da Gama tower and the Olivais Marina Locks: Jun-Sep weekdays 1100-2000, weekends and holidays 1000-2100, Oct-May weekdays 1100-1900, weekends and holidays, 1000-2000. €3 one way, round trip €5, children €1.50, round trip €2.   Map 1, A11, p247*

Standing 140 m-high, the Vasco da Gama tower is the tallest building in Lisbon. You can ride up to the top, where there is an expensive restaurant and exhilarating panoramic views of the city and across the river. It's even more memorable at night, with the sea silver-streaked under a bright moon.

Ponte Vasco da Gama is a beautiful feat of engineering. The longest bridge in Europe spanning 17.2 km, it was inaugurated on 4 April 1998 to commemorate the 500th anniversary of the discoverer. The aim was to create a north-south traffic bypass and it was built to withstand an earthquake four times greater than the Great Earthquake of 1755. More than 300 families were relocated from slums and rehoused to enable its construction.

Listings

Museums and galleries

- **Casa do Fado e da Guitarra Portuguesa** The evolution of fado traced through audio-visual presentations, p68.
- **Casa-Museu da Fundação Medeiros e Almeida** Extraordinary decorative arts museum, p60.
- **Casa-Museu Dr. Anastácio Gonçalves** Former home of modernist Portuguese painter Jose Malhoa houses an eclectic collection of decorative arts, p95.
- **Casa-Museu Fernando Pessoa** Astrological charts, manuscripts, letters and portraits reveal the inner workings of the mind of Lisbon's most cryptic resident, p80.
- **Cinemateca** 19th-century camera equipment and movie paraphernalia in an art nouveau setting, p59.
- **Convento e Museu Arqueológico do Carmo** Late Neolithic artefacts, Visgothic funerary stones, medieval sculpture and pre-Columbian mummies, p54.
- **Design Museum** Homage to cool, packed with gadgets and furnishings galore, within a historical framework, p85.
- **Fundação Arpad Szenes-Vieira da Silva** Brooding expressionism from a 19th-century vanguard painter, p61.
- **Fundacão Ricardo Espiritú Santo Silva** One of the finest decorative art collections in the country, housed in the 17th-century Azurara Palace, p73.
- **Igreja-Museu de Santo António** Religious artefacts and iconography reveal the life of Saint Anthony, p72.
- **Igreja de São Vicente da Fora** The church's serene cloisters are adorned with stunning azulejos, while the former refectory houses the pantheon of the House of Bragança, p67.
- **Jose de Azeredo Perdigão Centro de Arte Moderno** Gulbenkian's 20th-century Portuguese art collection, spearheaded by the work of one Portugal's most influential modernist painters Amadeu de Souza-Cardosa, p94.

Museums and galleries

- **Museu Calouste Gulbenkian** The acclaimed art collection of "Mr Five Per Cent", oil baron and philanthropist, is without peer in Portugal, p90.
- **Museu do Chiado** The great 19th- and 20th-Portuguese Romantics, surrealists and modernists and a slender collection of French sculpture, p57.
- **Museu e Igreja de São Roque** Lavish religious artefacts, 16th- and 17th-century sacred art and *retablos*, p47.
- **Museu do Teatro Romano** The history of Lisbon's Roman Theatre, originally built by Emperor Augustos, p71.
- **Museu Nacional das Coches**, Praca Afonso de Alburquerque, T 21 361 08 50. €3, free Sun 1000-1400. The coach museum provides an insight into Portugal's lavish court life. Gilded coaches, sedan chairs and royal portraits.
- **Museu Nacional de Arte Antiga** Lisbon's Ancient Art Museum includes great works of 14th to 20th century decorative arts, sculpture and paintings, p81.
- **Museu Nacional do Azulejo** The Madre de Deus convent provides the serene backdrop for lustrous *azulejo* tile panels and exhibits relating to ancient production techniques, p76.
- **Olissipónia** Multimedia snapshot of the history of the Lisbon in the former Moorish palace of Castelo de São Jorge, p74.
- **Palácio Nacional de Ajuda** A lavish collection of decorative arts, including the most complete set of 18th-century tableware in the country, housed in the neoclassical 19th-century residence of the Portuguese royal family, p88.
- **Panteão Nacional de Santa Engrácia** Lisbon's national pantheon; the final resting place and cenotaph for Lisbon's legendary cultural, social and political figures, p66.
- **Sé** The cloister of Lisbon's fortress-like cathedral contains evocative Phoenecian, Roman and Moorish artefacts, p70.

Sintra 105 UNESCO World Heritage Site. An arcadia of velveteen hills nestled with Moorish palaces, eerie ruined castles, hobbit hermitages, and the greatest act of architectural blasphemy in Portugal – the Palácio da Pena.

Cascais and the Lisbon coast 112 The 'Portuguese Riviera'. Rugged Atlantic beaches, backed by the spruce former fishing village of Cascais, an ex-pat haven with a shiny marina and designer labels. A coastal stroll away lies Estoril, one-time enclave of playboys and exiled monarchs, oozing faded grandeur with palm-lined promenades flanked by peeling mansions.

Mafra and Ericeira 115 The baroque marvel of Palácio de Mafra, the most potent symbol of Portuguese imperial excess, taking 13 years and 52,000 men to construct. Close by, the amiable and buzzy seaside town of Ericeira with huge Atlantic rollers and great seafood.

Queluz 117 The elegant Palácio de Queluz is a paradigm of Portuguese rococo with lavish formal gardens.

Sintra

Poets have raved and pagans have revelled in the Elysian Fields of Sintra, one of the oldest places in Portugal, recaptured from the Moors in 1147. It's a truly ethereal landscape where castles rise from the mists of emerald mountain ranges. On sloping terraces, carpeted with lush pine forests, erupts a rhapsody of Bavarian kitsch in the form of the slapstick **Palácio da Pena**, the epitome of 19th-century decadence. In the valley, the cobblestone streets of quaint Sintra Vila, the old quarter, fan into Moorish courtyards, festooned with flowers and palms – all very chocolate box, but none-the-less alluring.

The tourist magnet is the sublime **Palácio Nacional**, steeped in Arabian myticism, Shakespearean dramas and the imprint of cavorting kings. Close by, in Estefania, the wonderful world of Warhol is on display, part of the **Berardo collection**. Around Sintra, the stunning **Quinta da Regaleira**, with mystical grottos, reels with tales of alchemy and masonic mythology. **Monserrate**, a blend of imperial exotica and Victoriana, is where England's richest brought rituals, romance and lashings of kitsch.

▸▸ *See Eating and drinking p154, Festivals p186, Sport p201, Kids p213*

See Eating and drinking p154, Festivals p186, Sport p201, Kids p213

There is a **tourist office** at the train station and in the centre of Sintra Vila on Praça da República. Further information, www.cm-sintra.pt Sintra is less than 30 km from Lisbon. **Trains** run from Rossio every 15 mins, journey time around 45 mins, stopping at Queluz after 20 min. €2.20 return trip. The **Stagecoach bus** (number 434) runs a circular service every 20 mins from Sintra train station through Sintra Vila and then up the mountain to the Palácio da Pena and Castelo dos Mouros. Flat flare is €3.80. It takes a good hour to walk up to the palace. Alternatively the day rover ticket, €6.50, can be used on the **Stagecoach** services which connect Sintra with Cascais (45 mins) and the beaches of Guincho.

◉ Sights

★ Palácio Nacional de Sintra

Largo Rainha D Amélia, **T** 219 23 00 85. *1000-1300 and 1400-1700. Closed Wed. Last admission is 30 mins before close.* €3.

Around Lisbon

The two gargantuan conical chimneys of the National Palace dominate Sintra's skyline. Classified a national monument, this 14th-century building is the finest medieval royal palace in Portugal, a palpable symbol of the power of the Avis Dynasty which reigned during Portugal's Golden Age (1385-1580). Layered with history and oozing Arabian mystique, the palace provided the backdrop for royal intrigue and courtly shenanigans before the cry of freedom for the republic in 1910.

A fantastical hotch potch of Moorish, Gothic and Manueline architectural styles, each tendency was grafted onto the original structure according to the whim of each successive monarch. The Magpie Room, Stag Room and Swan Room should form a hurried snap-shot visit and are best visited very early in the morning, or late afternoon, to avoid the masses.

Beginning on the ground floor, the **Sala das Pegas** (Magpie Room) features 140 magpies which strut across the octagonal panels of the ceiling. Unconventional lothario King João I (1357-1433), known as the 'kissing king', showed a similar lack of restraint with the ladies as he did with his architectural vision and royal equity, building whatever he fancied, however he fancied. The story goes that when his royal highness was caught cavorting with a lady-in-waiting, the courtly gossips didn't waste much time in alerting the cuckolded Queen Philippa of Lancaster. As his case for the defence, the wooing casanova had the magpies painted with scrolls bearing the words, 'Por bem' ('It's for the best'), in their beaks.

With the coffers brimming and the ego bolstered by colonial endeavour, Dom Manuel I (1469-1521) lavished one of the world's most splendid *mudéjar* tile collections on the **Sala das Armas**,

(Armour Room, also known as the *Sala das Brasões*). He also left his fanciful imprint on the exterior of the palace, embellishing the windows, doors and frames with late-Gothic Manueline flourishes, characteristic of the period.

The National Palace provided the setting for one of the monarchy's more Shakespearean subplots. It was here that Dom Afonso VI was imprisoned by his brother. In his youth Afonso was quite the wild child. When his mother, acting as regent, was banished to a convent by an insurgent courtier, Afonso was forced to marry the demure French fancy, Marie-Françoise. Embroiled in political intrigue, Afonso fled to England and his mortified bride also locked herself away in a convent. Afonso's younger brother Pedro was swift to stake his claim, thanks to a clutch of very persuasive nobles, and he moved into the royal palace, married his sister-in-law and had Afonso imprisoned until his death in 1683. Afonso's cell, with very well-trodden floors, can be visited.

★ **Palácio Nacional de Sintra**
The emblematic chimney cones of the mystical National Palace define Sintra's skyline and grace tourist brochures the world over.

Away from the crowds, the greatest appeal of the palace lies in its serene atmosphere. Inner patios reveal intimate alcoves where the aroma of orange and lemon trees mingles with the calming aura of trinkling water fountains.

The palace continues to be a venue for cultural events such as Sintra's classical music festival in June and ballet festival in July, see p183, as well as the setting for ceremonial receptions.

Castelo dos Mouros

Estrada da Pena, **T** 21 923 73 00. *0900-2000 summer, 0900-1900 winter. €3. Bus 434 from Sintra Vila, first stop.*

Snaking along the mountain ridge, blasted with Atlantic winds and engulfed by low cloud, the fortifications of the seventh-century Arab stronghold are a mystical place, with a palpable air of bloody conquest. Centuries of neglect have left only protruding slabs of crumbling stone as testimony to its formidable history. One of the oldest Moorish sites in Portugal, the Moors were defeated here by the advancing troops of Afonso Henríques in 1147. Legend has it that the Moors hid their treasures from the oncoming crusaders beneath the ramparts. On a clear summer's day, it's a wistful place to escape the crowds in the valley below and to take in the breathtaking views along the coast.

Palácio de Pena

T 21 910 53 40. *Summer 1000-1800, winter 1000-1700. Closed Mon, and Jan 1, Easter Sun, May 1 and Dec 25. €5 palace and gardens. The circular Sintra bus 434 from the centre of town drops you at the entrance to the palace park and the ticket and information office.*

Pena Palace sprawls improbably down the mountainous pinnacles overlooking Sintra. A truly outlandish concoction of Renaissance, baroque, Moorish, Gothic and Manueline styles, it was conceived by Dom Ferdinand II of Saxe-Coburg-Gotha, arguably the maddest

Bavarian of them all, and architect Baron Von Eshwegem, who was responsible for a roll call of brazen castles on his native turf.

A 15-minute stroll uphill through the palace gardens leads to a Bavarian riot of candy pink spires, purple ramparts and shimmering gilded onion domes, woven into a tapestry of cobblestone streets and serpentine stairwells, where gargoyles and lurching demons stare menacingly from Moorish gateways.

While the exterior might feel hallucinogenic, the interior is more likely to make you weep with its unrestrained opulence. The serenity of the Moorish-style tiled cloister is something of an anomaly, as is the original monastery chapel. The exquisite *retablo*, the work of French master Nicolau Chanterène (1528-32), is an acclaimed masterpiece of the Portuguese Renaissance.

But from the sublime to the ridiculous – the Meissen room is the most extravagant of all, dripping with priceless porcelain. The ballroom is where things get really crazy with neo-Gothic chandeliers in gilded bronze, stained-glass bay windows and four golden turbaned Turks holding blazing torches aloft. The palace is preserved as it was when Queen Amelia lived there at the beginning of 20th century and her chambers, with stuccoed vaulting and mosaic tiled walls, are quite suffocating. The queen's terrace provides much-needed relief with breathtaking views of the Sintra hills. The statue nestling among the craggy peaks in the distance is the mad architect himself.

The palace gardens provide a soothing antidote, a blissful retreat of shady arbours, Moorish fountains and shocking pink camellias, making an ideal picnic spot. Nestling in the outer reaches of the park is a small house that Ferdinand of Saxe-Coburg-Gotha had built for his trysts with his opera singer mistress.

! Primitive Iberians were so bewitched by Sintra's natural wonders that it became a place of cult worship. They christened it Sintra, Mountain of the Moon, after the Celtic Goddess.

Museu de Arte Moderna

Av Heliodoro Salagado, **T** 21 924 81 70, www.berardocollection.com
Wed-Sun and holidays 1000-1800, Tue 1400-1800. €3, free on Thu.
Turn right when exiting the railway station and it's a 5 to 10 min walk to
the pastel lemon mansion on the left.

The Berardo collection is the finest collection of modern art in
Portugal, a chronological tour through the most important artistic
movements from the Second World War to the present day.
Inaugurated in 1997, the stunning neoclassical former casino
provides an excellent backdrop. The vast private collection of José
Berardi boasts more than 500 works of European and American art,
sculptures, paintings and installations, and was brought together
by Francisco Capelo, the media mogul behind the fantastic Design
Museum in Belém, see p85. Alongside the work of Man Ray,
Pollock, Miró, Picasso and Vieira da Silva, sit iconic pop art images
from Andy Warhol and Roy Lichtenstein. There is an excellent café
and restaurant with great views of Sintra.

Palácio e Parque de Montserrate

Estrada de Monserrate, **T** 21 923 73 00. *Gardens open 0900-2000*
summer, 0900-1900 winter. Visits inside are not permitted. 4 km from
Sintra Vila centre, 50-min walk; maps available from the tourist office.

Usually escaping the attention of the tourist hordes, this splendid
estate, exuding 19th-century faded grandeur, is a rhapsody of
English romanticism and bohemian decadence. Set amidst romantic
gardens, with gigantic sequoias and arucarias, it was designed by
James T Knowles in 1858, the architect of the *Grosvenor Hotel* in
London. William Beckford, one of England's most notorious and
wealthy eccentrics lived here when he was exiled from England in
1787, aged 26, following a homosexual affair which scandalized
prudish England. The romantic traveller came in search a bucolic
dreamscape, where he could enjoy the finer things in life and plenty

of youthful eye candy, and find it he did. Francis Cooke bought the estate in the mid-19th century, before being made the Viscount of Monserrate by his royal neighbour. Cooke revamped the Gothic house, creating a Moorish-style palace with bulbous cupolas and plundered exotica. He also laid out the subtropical gardens which consisted of microcosms from regions as far flung as Mexico, Australia and India and a crumbling chapel. The story has it that Francis decided to accelerate the chapel's decay in order to add to its romantic allure. While visits are not permitted, due to renovation works, the palace is sufficiently bewitching from afar.

Around Lisbon

Quinta da Regaleira

Jan-Dec 1000-1730, Feb-May and Oct 1000-1830, Jun-Sep 1000-2000. €10. Self-guided tours with maps provided. Guided tours 1100, 1230, 1430, 1600. 10 mins walk from Sintra Vila.

This 20th-century palace and UNESCO World Heritage Site is one of the most mystical places in Portugal. A hotch potch of Gothic, Manueline and Renaissance style, the estate has been much derided for its architectural irreverence. It was built by Brazilian António Augusto Carvalho Monteiro (1848-1920), together with extrovert architect and scenographer Luigi Manini, a man not renowed for his restraint and understatement – he had worked on La Scala in Milan – and completed just before the 1910 Revolution. It's a magical setting, with fairy-tale turrets, pre-Raphaelite gardens and leafy grottos but its main interest lies in its supernatural revelations and its fusion of pagan and divine. In the gardens a spiral staircase leads down to an intiatory well.

! Lisbon has the *pastel de nata*, Sintra the famed *queijada de Sintra*, delicious bite-size cheesecakes made from *queijo fresco* (cottage cheese) and featured in Eça de Queiroz's masterpiece *As Maias*, see p233. The best place to sample *queijadas* in Sintra Vila is Casa de Piriquita, see p155.

Mosteiro de Santa Cruz dos Capuchos

Serra da Sintra, 9 km from Sintra Vila, **T** 21 923 73 00. *0900-2000 summer, 0900-1900 winter. Guided visits only. €3. No public transport; taxis are available from Praça da República in Sintra Vila, or it's an excellent hike; route maps available from the tourist office.*

Founded in 1560 by Dom Álvaro de Castro, the son of the Viceroy of India, Capuchos Convent lies in the remote mountain reaches of Sintra. An austere Fransciscan hermitage in every sense, it consists of a warren of cork-lined cells carved out of the rock face, its miniscule dimensions more fit for hobbits and dwarfs than human beings; and set against a stunning mountain backdrop, it feels more Middle Earth than western Europe.

Cascais and the Lisbon coast

*Once upon a time sedate **Cascais** was a humble fishing village before becoming a royal retreat in the 19th-century and an enclave for a crop of exiled monarchs – the Duke of Windsor for one – in the 20th century. Easy on the eye, it's a twee town, its traditional roots still gleaned along cobblestone streets lined with whitewashed houses and swaying to a southern Mediterranean rhythm. Satisfyingly, traditions still continue. Alongside the pistachio sea, where craggy rocks shelter colourful fishing boats moored in the shadows of sleek cruise liners, weather-beaten fishermen still hold* lotas, *auctioning off their daily catch. Today, Cascais smells of new money, drawing an international jet set possy of Prada-clad wannabees and a cluster of British expats. Despite the smattering of Anglophile attractions, the conspicuous golden arches and the odd chalk-boarded promise of tea like your mum makes, Cascais has more than its fair share of seaside charm.*

*Just down the road, or a pleasant meander along the coast, **Estoril**, immortalized in Ian Fleming's* Casino Royale, *was an enclave for spies and spooks, before drawing Testerosa playboys with fast cars and foxy*

chicks to its Grand Prix circuit, casino and Beverly Hills-style palm-lined
promenade, earning it the sobriquet 'Portuguese Riviera'.

▸▸ *Eating and drinking p155*

*Cascais **tourist office** is at Combatentes da Grande Guerra 25,*
*Cascais, **T** 21 486 82 04. Mon-Sat 0930-1900, Sun 1000-1730 winter,*
Mon-Sat 0900-2000, Sun 1000-1800 summer. There are efficient,
comfortable, air-conditioned trains approximately every 20 mins
*(0530-0230) from Cais do Sodré. €2.10. Information, **T** 21 888 40 25.*

 Sights

Cascais
Map 7, p256

Exiting the train station, crossing straight over the mini roundabout,
past *Macdonald's* on your right, will bring you out onto the town's
main cobblestone street, **Rua Frederico Arouca**, a very bijou affair
punctuated with prissy houses, sassy boutiques, generic restaurants,
patisseries, sarong sellers and more than a whiff of ex pat living.
Turning left is nightlife enclave **Largo Camões**, centred around the
brash *John Bull's* pub, replete with all the relevant brawn and
bravado and a cluster of open-air over-priced cafés and restaurants.

   Continuing in the direction of the sea, the town hall is just off
Largo 5 de Octubre, alongside the small cove of **Praia das
Pescadores** (Fishermen's beach), where colourful boats bob in the
harbour, the endearing legacy of Cascais' fishing village roots.
Climbing around the bay, past the fort, Avenida Dom Carlos leads to
the sumptuous 19th-century mansion of the Count of Castro
Guimarães, the **Palácio de Conde de Castro Guimarães**, *Tue-
Sun from 1000-1230, 1400-1700, €1.50*. The museum exhibits the
count's extensive collection of antiques from the 17th and 18th
centuries including porcelain, silverware, artwork and an immense
collection of more that 25,000 books. The most important being a

rare 16th-century illuminated manuscript of the *Chronicle of Afonso Henríques* by Duarte Galvão. There are also prehistoric finds from a network of underground caves, just outside of Cascais, the **Grutas de Alapraia**, discovered in the 19th century. The original features and decor of the house have been maintained, providing an intriguing insight into the life and times of a 19th-century count. The palace is set in the grounds of the **Parque da Gandarinha**, a lovely place to stroll with an array of 18th-century *azulejo* tile panels, attributed to Bartolomeu Antunes, peaceful eucalyptus-scented lanes, romantic rose gardens and pergolas draped with vines. There is Gaudi-esque play area for kids, a mini zoo (chinchillas and birds), picnic lawns, an *estufa* (hot house) and a café with an esplanade.

The best way to spend an afternoon in Cascais is to wander around its traditional backstreets of spruced whitewashed houses, splattered with bougainvillea, nudged up against rustic *tascas* and neighbourhood grocers, which, on a languid hot summer's day, feel more reminiscent of an Andalucian *pueblo blanco* (white village).

On the leafy Largo da Assunção stands the 16th-century **Igreja de Nossa Senhora da Assunção**, *T 21 484 74 80, daily from 0900-1300 and 1700-2000*, which features 17th-century paintings by Josefa de Obidos (1634-84), revered for her tender religious paintings and portraits and one of the few female painters of the period to have achieved international recognition; more of her work can be seen at the Museu de Arte Antiga, see p81.

Just in front of **Praia da Ribera**, close to the town hall, free cycles are provided by the town council. A **cycle lane** runs parallel to the Guincho road, a windswept 7.5 km trail where waves crash thunderously across the rock face, spraying pearly mists upon you like icing sugar. **Guincho**, with some of the best rollers in Europe attracts dreadlocked dudes the world over to its surfing championships. The dramatically entitled **Boca do Inferno** (Mouth of Hell), just outside Cascais is named after its lashing waves. Over time, the elemental rage has been so intense that a gaping hole has been sculpted in the rock face.

Estoril
Map 7, p256

A former spa town and fashionable seaside resort, Estoril had its
glamorous heyday in the 1930s. Graced with a Grand Prix track,
international casino and glitzy hotels, it lured the bold and the
beautiful to its immaculate boulevards and glorious regal mansions.
During the Second World War both Allied and Nazi spies pitched up
at the rococo elegance of the **Hotel Palácio**, creating a hotbed of
intelligence operations and sinister subpots. Ian Fleming set his first
Bond novel, *Casino Royale*, amid the tacky glamour of Estoril's casino.
On Her Majesty's Secret Service was also filmed here and more
recently it provided the backdrop for Richard Wilson's novel *A Small
Death in Lisbon*, see p233. Estoril also had its fair share of noble exiles:
Spanish King Alfonso, Umberto II of Italy, Juan de Bourbon of Spain,
Karl Hapsburg of the Austro-Hungarian Empire and Carol of Romania.

Estoril has few sights of interest but it's a pleasurable 20-minute
walk along the coast from Cascais. In summer, the beaches, lined
with friendly bars and fish restaurants, are mobbed with body
borders, surfers and scantily-clad *Lisboetas* and tourists, bringing
an infectious sense of modernity to Estoril's faded grandeur.

Mafra and Ericeira

*West of Lisbon, less than two hours by bus, the sublime baroque
convent-palace of Mafra is the symbol of Portugal's unbridled
opulence following the discovery of diamonds in Brazil. As the bank
balance became ever more healthy, so Dom João V and his famed
German architect Ludovice became evermore ambitious. Its original
humble vocation as a monastery for Franciscan monks was soon
usurped by thrifty João's desires for a palace to rival El Escorial close to
Madrid. Down-at-heel Mafra offers little else to detain, but just 10 km
lie the gusty surfing beaches of Ericeira, Lisbon's Newquay, a surfing
mecca with a charming but rapidly developing old town.*

*Mafra is 40 km northwest of Lisbon. Mafrense **buses** depart hourly from Campo Grande and Martim Moniz in Lisbon (1 hr 45 mins-2 hrs). €2.70. Ericeira is 50 km northwest of Lisbon, 10 km from Mafra. There are no direct rail services but buses leave Martim Moniz hourly (1 hr). €3.20. There are also hourly buses from Sintra (1 hr). Touisprai buses run from Ericeira to Ribeira das Ilhas to the north and Lizando to the south. The **tourist office** is on Largo de Santa Marta, T 261 863 122.*

Sights

Palácio Nacional de Mafra
Daily 1000-1700, closed Tue. €3.

Construction of this magnificent baroque convent-palace began in 1717 to fulfil Dom João V's vow that if his wife Queen Mariana gave him an heir he would build a convent. With the arrival of Princess Bárbara and with the coffers full, the king set out to honour God and to satisfy his own lavish ambitions and dreams of immortality. Other versions of the tale claim that the palace was built as penance for Dom João's sexual ardour.

More than 52,000 workmen drafted from all over the world were involved in its construction - quite something when you consider that a mere 20,000 were involved in the building of the Taj Mahal - and it was finally inaugurated in 1730. The interior is an eye-popping medley of baroque extravagance, dripping with marble and adorned with statues carved by the greatest Italian masters of the day. The rococo library, with a colossal collection of 36,000 books, includes a first edition of Portugal's national epic, Camões' *As Lusíadas*. Most of the sumptuous fittings were taken with the king when he fled from Napoleon to Brazil in 1807 but the remaining huge bells were the palace's most costly embellishement. Cast in Belgium in 1730 and renovated in 1993, they really were worth their weight in gold. Every Sunday at 1600 you can hear carillon concerts. The bells certainly tolled for one monarch, King Manuel II, who was the last Portuguese

monarch to sleep in the palace before he escaped to England shortly
before the declaration of the republic.

Ericeira
Map 7, p256

Ericeira, draped above the clifftops with narrow cobbled streets,
white-washed houses and kitsch Christmas decorations manages to
cling rather tentatively to its traditional village status. It was here in
1586 that one Mateus Álvares falsely declared himself to be King
Sebastião (the real King Sebastião was missing, presumed dead, on a
crusading mission in Ceuta) and went wholeheartedly into regal
character before he was arrested and sentenced to death.

Nowadays, Ericeira is more famed amongst Euro surfers for its
great rollers and with weekending *Lisboetas* for its supurb seafood,
and *mariqueiras*. There is a variety of beaches, small sheltered
coves and more expansive ribbons of creamy sands, lined with
shaggy peaked cliffs, breezey surfing enclaves, splattered with
iodized kelp and peopled by a high dude contingent.

Ribeira das Ilhas, lying between Ericiera and Ribamar (3 km
from Ericeira centre, near the village of Santo Isidoro) is fêted as
one of the best surfing spots in Europe and has hosted the World
Surfing championships since 1985.

Queluz

*The majestic palace of Queluz marks the half way point between Rossio
and Sintra. Arguably the most graceful example of the rococo style in
Portugal, behind the soothing candy pink façade the baroque interior
oozes French grandeur and Portuguese eclecticism, and is truly redolent
of 18th-century aristocratic court life. The formal Italian gardens are
worth a visit alone. The regal aura is palpable, and the palace remains
the setting for grand official functions. Apart from the palace, the
unbefitting and rather grotty town of Queluz has little appeal.*

***Trains** from Rossio to Queluz-Belas take 20 mins. €2.20 return. The Palácio de Queluz is signposted from the station, a 10 to 15 min stroll.*

Sights

Palácio de Queluz
1000-1300, closed Tue and during official functions.

Exuding French palatial pomp and circumstance and a lofty look-but-don't-touch factor, the palace of Queluz has appropriately been garlanded with the sobriquet 'Portugal's Versailles'. It was designed by architect Mateus Vicente de Oliveira to transform Dom Pedro III's 17th-century hunting lodge into a graceful rococo summer palace and was completed in 1747. The flamboyant interior is the epitome of 18th-century baroque with a profusion of tiles, Florentine paintings, ornate crystal chandeliers and Chippendale furniture. Look out for the stunning murals of Cervante's *Don Quixote* in the royal bedroom. Following the wedding of Dom Pedro III to Queen Dona Maria I in 1760, it was embellished further by French architect Jean-Baptiste Robillion.

More Italian in style, the gardens are quite out of keeping with the prevalent fad for all things French. From Holland came lime trees, chestnut trees, elms and boxwood. In all, some 233 statues were sculpted, painted and gilded in England, with Anglophile themes of classical mythology and allegories.

The royal kitchens have been converted into a restaurant *Cozinha Velha*, which serves traditional, rather mediocre, Portuguese food, although the wine list is suitable monumental.

! When William Beckford visited the palace in 1794, he witnessed the mental anguish of the queen, who went rather off the rails in 1788 when her 27-year-old son José contracted small pox and died – her religious conviction had prohibited vaccination.

From curvaceous art deco palaces to literary garrets and glitzy glass towers, Lisbon is well-stocked with accommodation for all budgets and tastes. It's advisable to book at least two weeks in advance throughout the year, but especially so during summer, the Popular Saints festivals in June and while any other key events are taking place, see p183. It's also a good idea to confirm your booking the day before you travel – given that many flights arrive late in the evening it is not unusual for bookings not to be kept, or a more expensive room allocated to you.

There are three accommodation categories, *pensões* and *residenciales* (guesthouses – graded one to three) and a variety of *hotéis* (hotels), many spruced up for Expo 98 and in preparation for Euro 2004. Popular with backpackers, the Baixa grid offers some of the cheapest beds, within walking distance of the old town sights and staggering distance of Bairro Alto's nightlife. Prices range from €10 for a moss-carpeted cell with no windows to €35-40 for a double room with en suite bathroom.

€ **Sleeping codes**

Price

LL	€300 and over	C	€75-99
L	€250-299	D	€50-74
AL	€200-249	E	€35-49
A	€150-199	F	€25-34
B	€100-149	G	€24 and under

Prices are for a double room in high season.

With many rooms overlooking raucous **Rossio** and **Praça da Figueira**, this area is not a good choice for the noise sensitive.

For a similar budget, *pensões* and *residenciales* in the northern reaches of the city, stretching **beyond Parque Eduardo VII** and east to **Saldanha** – 15 minutes by metro from Rossio – offer much better facilities including TV, air conditioning, heating and a more welcoming ambience. **Avenida da Liberdade** and its parallel streets have many functional three- and four-star hotels with spacious rooms, air conditioning, satellite Tvs and rather unintentionally retro decor.

The area skirting **Parque Eduardo VII** is one of Lisbon's most expensive postcodes and draws, for the most part, a suited and booted business clientele.

The most idiosyncratic places to stay are in **Alfama**, which has a cluster of charming guesthouses, arty *pensões* and a couple of sleeker four-star additions in 2003. Bohemian **Bairro Alto** is universally popular, with excellent value pastel-painted *pensões* at the heart of the nightime action. Neighbouring **Chiado** retains its literary character with hotels named *Borges* and the plush new *Regency Chiado*.

Out west in filthy-rich **Lapa**, a 15-minute ride on Tram 28, mystical converted convents and charming *Heritage* hotels nestle in leafy streets, while for unbridled luxury and good taste the *Lapa Palace Hotel* is set in lush tropical gardens and invites a serious wallet haemorrhage.

Baixa and Rossio

Sleeping

A **Hotel Metrópole**, Praça do Rossio, 30, **T** 21 346 91 64, www.almeidahotels.com *Above Café Nicola. Map 2, D8, p248* With unrivalled views over all that is Rossio, the Metrópole is a stately 1920s classic with characterful rooms of various sizes and design, many with original art nouveau and *azulejo* tile features and antique furniture. Service is charming and courtly. Great value.

B **Portugal**, Rua João das Regras, 4, **T** 21 887 75 81, www.hotelportugal.com *Map 3, C2, p250* This elegant hotel, in a prime position, has a welcoming, refined ambience. The classical features in the hallways and haughty living room – ornate high ceilings, chandeliers and a profusion of *azulejo* tiles – give way to functional modernity in the light and airy bedrooms, which have marble-clad bathrooms, TV, phone and air conditioning. Breakfast is served in the sunny dining room. A good, central, mid-range option.

D **Hotel International**, Rua da Betsega, **T** 21 324 09 90, www.hotel-internacional.com *Map 3, D1, p250* Overlooking Lisbon's main square, this old world hotel, while rather rough around the edges, has comfortable, if small, rooms, decent service and plenty of undeliberately 1960s retro touches. Some rooms have balconies with great views of the castle and the city. A disappointing breakfast is included (bread roll in a bag).

D **Pensão Residencial Gerês**, Calçada do Garcia, **T** 21 881 0497, www.pensaogeres.web.pt *Map 3, B1, p250* In the heart of downtown Lisbon, this cosy, family-run *pensão* has built up a reputation for having a warm atmosphere, plenty of character and being spic and span – the hallways are beautifully tiled throughout with *azulejos* and festooned with cheery nick nacks. Some of the slightly prissy rooms have great views over the Teatro Nacional and Rossio through large, shuttered windows.

D Residencial Florescente, Rua Portas de Santo Antão, 99, **T** 21 342 66 09, www.residencialflorescente.com   *Metro Restauradores. Map 2, A7, p248* Flanked by seafood restaurants, this charming *residencial*, with chintzy, tiled hallway and dining room, offers good value comfortable rooms to suit most budgets. Ask to see several rooms before you commit. However, note that the staff can be exceedingly gruff and reservations are not always kept.

E Residencial Duas Naçoes, Rua Vitória, 41, **T** 21 346 07 10, **F** 21 347 02 06. *Pedestrianized street which bisects Rua Augusta. Map 3, F1, p250* One of the more appealing options amid a cluster of downright sleazy places for travellers who would prefer to sacrifice creature comforts for location. Tired rooms are reasonably spacious although in serious need of upgrading, especially the bathrooms. A sociable dining area, where breakfast is served, injects it with a youthful traveller vibe, particulary in the summer.

F Pensão Beira Minho, Praça da Figueira, 6, 2°, **T** 21 346 18 46, **F** 21 346 90 29. *Map 3, C1, p250* Musty rooms are redeemed by stunning views from behind the equestrian statue of Dom João V. The price you pay for this is the noise, between midnight and 0100, of Praça Figueira being cleaned. Quieter cells (€10), without windows, are about as low as you can go for price and comfort in this prime location. The quirky staff are friendly, and Brazilian Delí can tip you off on where to samba and, if your Portuguese is up to it, entertain for hours on the origins of his bullet wounds and his mates back in Rio, apparently stars of *Cidade de Deus*.

F Pensão Portuense, Rua Portas de Santo Antão, 151, **T** 21 346 41 97. *Map 2, A7, p248* A modest *pensão* with a family feel and attentive service. Basic, but comfortable, rooms vary in size, from the decidedly pokey, to the liberatingly spacious (with separate lounge areas). All have surgically clean private bathrooms and power showers. An above-average continental breakfast.

Bairro Alto

C Casa São Mamede, Rua Escola Politécnica, 159, **T** 21 396 31 66, **F** 21 395 18 96. *Map 6, H2, p254* A beautiful apartment building, built shortly after the 1755 eathquake and converted into a hotel in the 1940s. With many original period features, it's a conservative option, close to Bairro Alto. Spacious, old-fashioned rooms have parquet floors, modern bathrooms, TVs and air conditioning. But a cluttering of antiques, gold drapes and flouncy pink satin sheets lend a rather fusty air and it lacks the privacy of some guesthouses.

D Pensão Residencial Camões, Travessa do Poco da Cidade, 38, 1°, **T** 21 346 75 10, **F** 21 346 40 48. *Map 2, E5, p 248* Peppermint-coloured rooms have telephones and friendly Mozambiquan owner Rogério has plans to put TVs in each room in time for Euro 2004. Rooms vary in size and price, and there are two huge attic apartments sleeping six with private bath for €100. Attic rooms have views over the red-tiled rooftops of Bairro Alto but street-facing rooms are noisy. Basic breakfast is included.

D Pensão Residencial Santa Catarina, Rua Dr Luís de Almeida e Albuquerque, 6, **T** 21 346 61 06, **F** 21 347 72 27. *Map 2, F3, p248* This temple to 1960s kitsch is 10 minutes' walk from the bars and restaurants of Bairro Alto on a tranquil and picturesque street. Furnished with retro irony; garish rooms are decked out with floral orange fabrics, wood panelling, chunky furniture and brown shag-pile carpets. Breakfast is served in the cavernous rock-walled cellar with stained-glass windows and hanging plastic fruits.

E Pensão Londres, Rua Dom Pedro V, 53. **T** 21 346 22 03, **F** 21 346 56 82, www.pensaolondres.com.pt *Map 2, B4, p248* This grand old building is close to hip Príncipe Real, flanked by classy restaurants, antique shops and boho bars. With soaring ceilings and ornate chandeliers, rooms exude faded grandeur, with the added allure of magnificent far-reaching views across Bairro Alto and the River Tagus. Room 304, romantic, breezy and flooded with light, is the one to book. A simple breakfast is included, served in the ever so regal dining room.

F Pensão Globo, Rua do Teixero, 37, **T** 21 346 22 79. *Map 2, B5, p248* Perfectly located on one of Bairro Alto's more tranquil leafy streets, *Pensão Globo* has built up a reputation for offering excellent good-value accommodation with the charm and cordiality of an English B&B. The 20 spotless and cosy rooms all have small en suite bathrooms and feel reasonably spacious despite the medieval proportions. Attic rooms have poetic vistas over the eaves of Bairro Alto. Proudly managed by charming and helpful Luís and Carmina, who can provide good information on excursions and tours.

Chiado

A Hotel Lisboa Regency Chiado, Rua Nova do Almada, 114, **T** 21 325 61 00, www.regency-hotels-resorts.com *Map 2, F8, p248* Occupying the upper levels of the *Armázens do Chiado* shopping mecca, the Regency boutique-style hotel was designed by Álvaro Siza Viera. The interior design – the work of Pedro Espírto Santo – is a fusion of classical Portuguese style with Oriental and African flourishes. The spacious, well-appointed rooms have soothing, minimalist decor. *Superior* rooms have magical views of the castle.

D Hotel Borges, Rua Garrett, 108, **T** 21 346 19 51, **F** 21 346 66 17. *Map 2, F7, p248* One of the oldest hotels in Lisbon, its grandeur is more than a little faded. Still, rooms are comfortable enough and the ambience retains a classical aura, making it popular with Americans and processions of Italian tour groups. Breakfast is included, but a *bica* and *pastel de nata* at the iconic *Café A Brasiliera* next door would be a better option.

Avenida da Liberdade and around

LL Ritz Four Seasons, Rua Rodrigo da Fonseca, 88, **T** 21 381 1400, www.fourseasons.com *Map 6, B1 (off), p254* Founded by Salazar in the 1940s, when there were no hotels luxurious enough to welcome foreign presidents, the brutal bombastic lines of this concrete monolith belie the 18th-century grandeur and style of its interior. The best rooms have balconies overlooking Parque Eduardo VII. With all the superlative services that you would expect and a highly rated, exclusive restaurant. Essentially geared to business travellers.

AL Le Meridien Park Atlantic, Rua Castilho, 149, **T** 21 381 87 00, **F** 21 381 87 00. *Map 6, B1 (off), p254* Behind the soaring glass façades, stylish contemporary rooms offer the highest standards and facilities replete with Philippe Starck designed washbasins. Many rooms have sweeping views across Lisbon and out over the River Tagus. The staff are very personable and efficient, the guests mainly living it up on chunky expense accounts.

AL Hotel Avenida Palace, Rua 1° de Dezembro, 130, **T** 21 321 81 00, www.hotel-avenida-palace.pt *Map 2, C7, p248* Designed by José Luís Monteiro in 1890, the classical French style of Lisbon's first luxury hotel was intended to establish the city's cosmopolitan credentials. Exuding belle époque grandeur, the huge lobby is a truly over the top Aladdin's Cave. Oppressive rooms are crammed with period furniture and Portuguese celebs skulk in the bars wearing designer shades giving it a rather pretentious vibe.

A Hotel Britânia, Rua Rodrigues Sampaio, 17, **T** 21 315 50 16, www.heritage.pt *Map 6, F6, p254* Designed in 1944 by renowned architect Cassiano Branco, this intimate *Heritage* hotel has fabulous art deco features including port hole windows and unbridled luxury with its glitzy lobby dripping in marble and crystal chandeliers. Tastefully restored and spacious rooms have all the frippary of classical furnishings and functionality of the desired mod cons including soundproofed windows, airconditioning and satellite TV.

A Hotel Lisboa Plaza, Travessa Salitre, **T** 21 321 82 18, www.heritage.pt *Map 6, G6, p254* This warm hotel avoids the sterile aloofness of many of the upper-range hotels. The service is excellent and the understated, luxurious atmosphere has a home- from-home feel, with a burning log fire in winter, well-stocked bookcases, fresh flowers and peopled with bespectacled intelligensia. The 96 marble-clad rooms are equipped with satellite TV, modems, minibar and double glazing. Excellent American-style buffet breakfast.

A Hotel Tivoli, Av da Liberdade, 185, **T** 21 319 89 40, www.tivolihotels.com *Metro Avenida Map 6, G6, p254* A renowned five-star hotel on Lisbon's main boulevard, just 10 minutes' walk from Rossio. Spacious rooms combine classical ambience with contemporary facilities. The outdoor heated swimming pool with poolside bar, set in an idyllic tropical garden provides a city oasis but one of the hotel's major claims is the terrace restaurant, where you can enjoy highly rated cuisine and stunning views over the city.

B Best Western Hotel Eduardo VII, Av Fontes Pereira de Melo, **T** 21 356 88 00, www.hoteleduardovii.pt *Map 6, A4, p254* A monolithic mass overlooking Parque Eduardo VII, the hotel's star attraction is the rooftop cocktail lounge-restaurant, with breathtaking views across the city and the Tagus, highly regarded for its Portuguese and Brazilian cuisine; residents receive a 20 per cent discount. Very good value for budget-conscious business travellers with four meeting/banquet rooms. Parking available.

B Hotel Veneza, Av da Liberdade, 189, **T** 21 352 26 18, www.3khoteis.com *Metro Avenida Map 6, F5, p254* Minimalists should retreat in haste from this ostentatious Lisbon landmark, a former palace built in 1886. The entrance hall is a striking example

Sleeping

of unrestrained pomp and circumstance with a coiling turn-of-the-century spiral staircase, modern pastel painted mural of Lisbon by Pedro Luis Gomez, classical archways and statues with colonial era exotisicm. Bedrooms have the necessary concessions to modernity.

D Don Sancho I, Av da Liberdade, 202, **T** 21 351 31 60, **F** 21 354 80 42. *Close to Tivoli Forum. Map 6, F6, p254* Welcoming, characterful guest house with art nouveau features, à la Manueline style, with stained-glass windows and *azulejo* tiles decorated with maritime imagery. Pleasing rooms have wooden floors and pristine modern bathrooms and double glazing which does its best to keep out the sound of roaring traffic on the Avenida. An above average cooked breakfast is served. With an international upbeat atmosphere, it appeals to young couples and families.

D Hotel Miraparque, Av Sidonio Pais, 12, **T** 21 352 42 86, **F** 21 357 89 20. *50 m from Metro Parque. Map 6, A4, p254* One of the cheapest hotels near Parque Eduardo VII. It's a classic case of ironic 1960s retro with lashings of PVC, floral swirls and staff with big collars and unruly side burns. Rooms have satellite TV, phone, hairdryer and air conditioning and there is a passable restaurant and a good fall-back bar, but the overall impression is rather lacklustre.

E Residencial Castilho, Rua Castilho, 57-4°, **T** 21 386 08 22, **F** 21 386 29 10. *Map 6, D2, p254* This friendly 1860s apartment building has plenty of character and is smoothly operated by charmer Manuel. Ornate, high ceilings, decorative cornicing, antique lighting and swirling ceiling fans give a classical feel to the public areas but the period charm fails to extend to the rooms, which although comfortable and clean are furnished with *MFI*-style specials.

E Residencial Londrinho, Rua Castilho 61-1°, **T** 21 386 36 24, **F** 21 386 06 25. *Map 6, C1, p254* This 19th-century apartment building has classical period features and a range of spotless rooms with phone, TV, air conditioning, decent size en suite bathrooms and high ceilings. Conservatively managed by three families, it has an old-fashioned guesthouse feel replete with fussy flowery decor and nick nacks. Breakfast is served in the prim living/dining room.

Alfama, Castelo and around

A **Hotel Olissipo**, Rua Costa do Castelo, 112-126, **T** 21 888 12 30, olissipo@netcabo.pt *Just below the walls of Castelo de São Jorge Map 3, C3, p250* Opened in May 2003, this swish four-star hotel is eager to please, offering 24 plush, tastefully furnished rooms and suites. The soothing rooms with TV, minibar and marble-clad bathrooms blend classical features with modernist touches. The main pull is the private terrace, complete with sun loungers and poetic views across Mouraria. The staff are charming and attentive.

A **Solar dos Mouros**, Rua Milagre de Santo António, 6, **T** 21 885 49 40, **F** 21 885 49 45. *Map 3, E4, p250* This designer showroom-cum-art gallery with tasteful minimalist furnishings, feels more SoHo, NY, than old world Lisbon. The artful rooms, flooded with light, have river views and are decorated with the abstract paintings of Luís Lamos, whose gallery is connected to the hotel by an enchanting garden. The building's medieval dimensions seem to have curtailed the designer's aspirations and hotel facilities – there is no dining room, breakfast is served in your room. The top attic room, reached by a precipitous spiral staircase, has its own spectacular terrace.

C **Sé Guest House**, Rua de São João da Praça, 97, **T** 21 886 44 00. *Map 3, G5, p251* This 19th-century family house has bags of character with walls decorated with family photos, African travel memorabilia, cinema posters and an iconic photo gallery. The four rooms with stripped wooden floors are homely and idiosyncratic, and have TV, minibar and room service. On the downside, the bathrooms are shared with the other guests so it's rather overpriced.

D Pensão São João da Praça, Rua de São João da Praça, 97- 2-2°, **T** 21 886 25 91, **F** 21 888 04 15. *On the next floor above the Sé Guest House, see above.* *Map 3, G5, p251* A good, budget choice with a variety of simple but bright, cheerful rooms with TV and fridge. An excellent value family room, sleeping four, has a separate lounge area, €63, including breakfast. Doubles with bath or shared bathroom. Be sure to request a room with Tagus panoramas.

E Pensão Ninho das Águias, Costa do Castelo, 74, **T** 21 885 40 70. *Just below the walls of Castelo de São Jorge.* *Map 3, D3, p250* This is one of the best *pensãos* in the city. It was originally a church, then a haven for political refugees, before its present incarnation as a guesthouse. Its spectacular setting has lured many a movie maker and artist in need of inspiration. A steep spiral staircase leads to the leafy terrace with unrivalled views and an eerie calmness. The interior is full of character, with original church features stained-glass windows, conspiratorial alcoves and a stuffed eagle. Comfortable rooms with high ceilings are spotless, some with private bathrooms (cheaper rooms share facilities). Proud owner Luís is utterly charming and devoted to the history of the place and the city in general.

São Bento, Estrela and Lapa

LL Hotel Lapa Palace, Rua do Pau de Bandeira, 4, **T** 21 394 94 94, www.lapa-palace.com *Map 5, F1 (off), p253* The height of luxury and good taste, the Lapa Palace is the place to blow your budget into orbit. A one time 19th-century noble palace, it opened as a hotel in 1992 and has become the first choice of A list celebrities, political movers and shakers, and royalty, from George Bush to Tina Turner. Each room is individually and tastefully styled, with gorgeous marble bathrooms and many with awesome views of the Tagus. Set in 10 acres of lush tropical gardens, with a heated swimming pool and fantastic sports facilities. The suitably pricey *Cipriani* restaurant serving northern Italian cuisine is one of Lisbon's finest restaurants.

A York House, Rua das Janelas Verdes, 32, **T** 21 396 25 44. *Close to Museu de Arte Antiga. 25-minute walk from Rossio, or Tram 28. Map 5, H2, p253* A one-time 17th-century convent, Convento dos Marianos, this is one of the most charming and inviting places to stay in Lisbon. Discreetly located behind a pastel-pink garden wall, lavishly decorated with fine antique furnishings, *azulejo* tiles and parquet floors. Big, period rooms are individually styled, some with romantic four-poster beds, and all the creature comforts and modern amenities you'd expect. The highlight is the Pre-Raphaelite courtyard garden.

A As Janelas Verdes, Rua das Janelas Verdes, 47, **T** 21 396 81 43, www.heritage.pt *Map 5, H2, p253* This Heritage hotel was once the 18th-century home of Portuguese novelist Eça de Queiroz, where he found inspitation for his greatest work, *Os Maias*. Extensively renovated, the quaint hotel retains a sedate literary ambience and charming period features. There is a help-yourself bar with stunning terrace views over the Tagus and a serene vine-covered courtyard where an American-style buffet breakfast is served in summer. Some of the smaller rooms can feel rather cramped though.

Northern Lisbon

A Sheraton Lisboa Hotel and Towers, Rua Latino Coelho, 1 **T** 21 312 00 00, www.sheraton.com/lisboa *Metro Picoas, 10 mins walk from Marquês de Pombal.* The archetypal chain hotel, the Sheraton, spanning 28 floors and the tallest building in the city before the Torre Vasco da Gama stole the mantle in 1998, is a Lisbon icon. While the exterior is an ugly mass of 1970s modernism, the hotel provides five-star services and a vast range of amenities including two restaurants, pool, solarium, gym, communication centre and a banquet and conference hall. Standard, moderate-sized rooms are well equipped, although lacking in charm and character. More expensive – €265 – *Tower* rooms have delirious views, parquet floors, internet access and a personal butler. The 26th floor has a bar with panoramic views and nightly live music.

D Pensão Residencial Canadá, Av Defensores de Chaves, 35, **T** 21 351 34 80, **F** 21 351 34 82. *Metro Saldanha.* Very handy if you are arriving by bus, this quirky *pensão*, which was recently renovated, is homely and meticulously managed. Large, airy rooms are decorated with Barbara Cartland-esque pink curtains and bedspreads and all have private peppermint-green tiled bathrooms. Rooms with verandas overlooking the bus station are inevitably noisier, try to get one of the more peaceful rear view options. Breakfast is included, served in the 1960s-style wood-pannelled dining room.

D Residencial Horizonte, Av António de Aguiar, 42, **T** 21 353 95 26, www.hotelhorizonte.com *Metro Saldanha.* Excellent value *Rresidencial* with reasonably spacious comfortable rooms with private bathroom, satellite TV, hairdryer, safe, air conditioning, soundproof windows and phone. Efficient, friendly service, and the bargain rate, €57, includes American-style buffet breakfast, which you can have in bed. Parking at €10 per day. Children under 12, sharing parents room, are free.

E Residencial Saldanha, Av da República, 17, 1°, **T** 21 354 64 29, www.residencialsaldanha.pt Metro Saldanha. This charming *residencial* is the best budget option in the city. The 12 spacious and comfortable rooms are spotless, and have cable TV, private bathrooms, air conditioning and radio. The ambience is welcoming and relaxing and manager Carlos is extremely friendly and helpful and has a cult following with many repeat and long- stay guests. Although it is slightly far out, 15 minutes' walk from Marquês de Pombal, the metro is right on your doorstep, as is *Café Versailles*, see p154. Possibly the best place in Lisbon for a morning coffee and pastry. Highly recommended.

Eating and drinking

With pastries named 'nun's belly' and 'angel's breast', 356 recipes for codfish, racing-green soups, searing African spices and porridgy hinterland specialties, eating out is deliciously bewildering. Chi chi Chiado offers Portuguese traditional cuisine at its finest, while the Baixa is pretty straight up – all golden arches, laminated menus and meal deals – with the exception of the seafood strip of Rua de Santos de Antão (also home to the best greasy spit-roasted chicken this side of Louisiana). Doca de Santo Amaro and Parque das Nações feature the bland chain gang eateries churning out overpriced dishes. Doca de Jardim de Tabaco has scooped all the culinary and clubbing kudos right now, while eating in well-to-do Lapa could mean rubbing shoulders with Prince and Catherine De Neuve, although the memory will cost you an arm and a leg. Alfama is prime tour group territory, where spacious restaurants produce mediocre dishes to a soundtrack of diluted fado. Bairro Alto cuts across the gastro divides – hip food, soul food, Portuguese staples and polycultural delicacies, all scattered abundantly through its quirky narrow streets.

€ **Eating codes**

€€€ €30 and over
€€ €20-29
€ €19 and under

Price per head for a two-course meal excluding drinks.

Portuguese dining rituals tend to follow the Mediterranean siesta body clock, although unlike in Spain, lunch times tend to be a more conscientious one- to 1½-hour affair, and go easy on the soporific stodge.

Breakfast is sweet and strong. Like all good *Lisboetas*, head for a fine art nouveau *pastelaria*, such as *Café A Brasileira*, see p147 or *Versailles*, see p154, and head straight for the *balcão* (the counter) for a turbo-charged *bica* (seriously strong expresso) pull out a crisp white *servietta* and select your cake of choice; the best intiatiation being a *pastel de nata*.

Dinner is eaten quite late, never before 2100 and more like 2200-2300, especially during the summer. In Bairro Alto, restaurants stay open until around 0200, in the outer districts, 2400-0100. Most restaurants close on either Sunday or Monday.

Delightfully, old world Portugal serves food at old world prices, with the some of the cheapest meals in western Europe. Most main fish and meat dishes in Bairro Alto are on average around €10-12. Generally speaking you should easily be able to eat a decent three-course meal with wine and appetizers for less than €20. If you are on a budget, take the *menu del dia* (usually three courses for around €10), nibbling on *pasteis de bacalhão* (cod cakes) and *pasteis de nata*, between meals.

Vegetarians don't have an easy time in Lisbon, with Italian being the predictable mainstay and a none-too-fertile crop of buffet-style canteens, where vegetables are treated rather mercilessly and the surroundings are grim. See language glossary p234 and menu reader p236.

Baixa and Rossio

Restaurants

€€€ **Gambrinus**, Rua Portas de Santo Antão, 23, **T** 21 342 14 66. *Daily 1200-0130*. *Map 2, B8, p248* One of Portugal's best seafood restaurants, Gambrinus, established more than 70 years ago, is something of a local institution. There is an extensive and varied menu of seasonal specialities, with tantalizing exotic flavours, served by knowledgeable and friendly staff, in the moody wood-panelled dining room. Specials served daily include *empadão de perdiz* on Mondays and *sopa rica de peixe* on Wednesdays.

€€€ **Solmar**, Rua Portas de Santo Antão, 108, **T** 21 342 33 71. *1200-1500, 1900-2300*. *Map 2, A7, p248* With soaring marble pillars, underwater mosaic tiles, ornate fountains and huge aquariums jammed with lobsters, Solmar is a shimmering 1950s classic. Famous among well-heeled *Lisboetas* for its abundant seafood and in particular its *açorda de mariscos*. In winter more heart-warming dishes such as wild boar and venison are also served. The adjacent *Solmar Café* is a popular post-theatre hang-out.

€€€ **Terreiro do Paço**, Lisboa Welcome Centre, Praça do Comércio, **T** 21 031 28 50. *Mon-Sat 1130-2300, Sun 1230-1500*. *Map 3, I1, p251* Featuring on *Condé Nast Traveller*'s list of the world's top 50 restaurants, Terreiro do Paço certainly hasn't rested on its laurels. Award-winning chef and creative zealot Júlia Vinagre creates thoroughly modern renditions of ancient Portuguese recipes and regional specialities including roast kid and veal. *Açorda* devotees will relish the *açorda de camarão*. The wine list is superb and the traditional, intimate setting, under colonnaded arcades, hard to beat.

€€ **Casa Alentejo**, Rua Portas de Santo Antão, 58 , **T** 21 346 92 31. *Daily 1200-1500, 1930-2400. Map 2, B8, p248* The 17th-century neo-Moorish Palácio Alverca is now home to the Alentejano cultural centre and restaurant and is worth a visit alone to admire the central courtyard, designed by Portuguese architect Silva Júnior in 1914 and richly decorated with *azulejo* tiles and paintings. Upstairs is where nostalgic *Alentejanos* partake of hearty *açorda* soups (a runny mixture of stale bread and garlic, topped with boiled egg). There is codfish *açordas*, delicious octopus rice, grilled seabass and 'bullock's entrecôte cooked the wine trader's way'. The stewed turbot with pasta is highly recommended.

€€ **Valentino**, Rua Jardim de Regedor, 15-30, **T** 21 346 17 27. *Daily 1200-2400. Map 2, B7, p248* Reliable, conveniently located Italian restaurant with outdoor seating and a cavernous, split level interior with intimate alcoves. Popular with *Lisboetas* enjoying lazy Sunday lunches, there is a child-friendly repertoire of decent thin base pizzas, oozing calzones and rich pastas. The portions are mammoth but meagre use of herbs and spices can render some dishes rather bland. Fine fish and meat dishes push the prices up to the expensive price category. Excellent tiramisu for desert.

€ **Bom Jardim**, Travessa de Santo Antão, 11 **T** 21 342 43 89. *Daily 1200-2300. Map 2, B7, p248* Known as the 'Rei del Frango', The *King of Chickens* has become a Lisbon legend, famous for its spit-roasted chicken. And its a bargain, dished up with fries, salad and jugs of rough house wine, for less than €10. Troubadours, theatrical waiters and persistent flocks of rose sellers add to the rustic charms.

Cafés

Café Martinho da Arcada, Praça do Comércio, 3, **T** 21 886 62 13. *Mon-Sat 0800-2300, closed Sun. Map 3, H2, p251* The oldest café in Lisbon, opened in 1782, is one of the essential stops on the trail of

★ **Vegetarian eats**

Best

- Os Tibetanos, p148
- Stasha, p144
- Império dos Sentidos, p142
- Gulbenkian Museu de Arte Moderno, p154
- Casanova, p151

Lisbon's most famous son Fernando Pessoa, who spent many hours here, writing poems on menus which are now displayed in the restaurant. In 1991 the café began hosting *tertúlias* drawing venerable figures such as Jorge Sampaio, Jorge Amado, Siza Vieira and Amália Rodrigues. The expensive restaurant serves grilled fish, duck and *bacalhão do Martinho* but to revel in the literary garret-style ambience, simply order a *bica*, a *pastel de nata* and muse under the colonnades on dignified Praça do Comércio.

Café Nicola, Praça do Rossio, 24, *Mon-Fri 0800-2300, Sat 1000-1300*. *Map 2, D8, p248* Opened in 1929, Nicola initiated Lisbon's long tradition of the café as a place of literary and political meeting point, and wowed Lisbon's denizens with its stunning design of wood and steel, the work of award-winning architect Norte Júnior. Following a 1935 redesign in art deco style, characteristic of 1930s taste, only the sculpture of one its original literary patrons Manuel Mia Barbosa do Bocage, remained. Sadly, nowadays, little of the literary charms remain, with grumpy staff, cakes only so so, and more tourists than Lisbon literati. Still, the pricy seats under canary yellow canopies on Rossio, are hard to beat for a *bica* with a view.

Confeitaria Nacional, Praça da Figuiera. *Mon-Fri 0800-2030, Sat 0800-1400*. *Map 3, D1, p250* When it opened in 1829, this sugary haven wowed Lisbon society with its elegant salon. With its bright mirrored interior, small shiny marble counters and adjacent tea room, it's still a wonderful place for a sugar boost, with no end of glazed pastries, shiny brioche and all manner of gooey treats.

Pastelaria Suiça, Praça Dom Pedro IV, Rossio, 100, **T** 21 321 40 90. *0700-2130. Map 3, C1, p250* Largely occupied by tourists, this legendary café serves up thickly glazed pastries and hot croissants and, for a late-night snack, door-stopper *toradas* (thick slices of toast) oozing with butter accompanied by a hot chocolate. Staff rarely break a smile though, and the pre-pay system and modernist interior have removed much of its historic charm.

Bairro Alto

Restaurants

€€€ **Comida de Santo**, Calçada Engenheiro Miguel Pais, **T** 21 396 33 39. *Daily 1230-1530, 1930-0100. Map 2, A1 (off), p248* For inspired Brazilian cooking and an effervescent atmosphere, this unassuming restaurant decorated with cheerful Brazilian paintings, is worth a splurge. The *Vatapá*, €14.50 and *Picadinha à Mineira*, make for a reliable initiation. The highly potent caipirinhas are the best in town. Worth reserving at the weekend.

€€€ **Consenso**, Rua das Academia de Ciências, 1-1A, **T** 21 343 13 13. *Closed lunchtimes Sat, Sun and holidays. Map 2, B1, p248* Classy restaurant in the cellar of the former house of the Marquês de Pombal, combining a classical atmosphere with inventive international cuisine. There are four themed dining areas to choose from; fire, earth, water and air. Thoroughly indulgent gastronomy including grilled monkfish served with a rich cream sauce and duck with sticky chocolate sauce.

€€€ **Conventual**, Praça das Flores, 45, **T** 21 390 91 96. *Mon and Sat 1930-2300, Tue-Sun 1230-2330*. *Map 2, D2, p248* Favoured by prime ministers and pop stars, Conventual is one of Lisbon's gastronomic highlights. Inspired dishes are served in a dining room decorated with religious artefacts (testifing to its previous incarnation as a convent). Memorable dishes include partridge flambéed with brandy and served with a chestnut sauce.

€€€ **Pap d'Açorda**, Rua Atalaia, 57, **T** 21 346 48 11. *Tue-Sat 1230-2330, two servings for dinner 2000-2030, 2200-2230*. *Map 2, E4, p248* This former bakery is now one of the most fashionable eateries in the city. Behind the plush velvet curtains, the young, arty types stand cheek-by-jowl at the sleek long bar, waiting to be seated in the lush winter garden dining room, glittering with centrepiece crystal chandeliers. Its eponymous *açorda* is served with shellfish in a clay pot. The wine list is monumental. Book early.

€€ **Águas do Bengo**, Rua do Teixeira, 1, **T** 21 347 75 16. *Tue-Sat 2000-2400*. *Map 2, C5, p248* Tucked down one of Bairro Alto's leafier and more tranquil streets, this atmospheric African restaurant-bar is owned by famed Angolan musician Waldemar Bastos. Piquant Angolan cuisine, including steamed fish and vegetables, is served to hip-swaying African music. Waldemar often gives impromptu performances when in town.

€€ **Alfaia**, Travessa da Queimada, 22, **T** 21 346 12 32. *1200-1530, 1900-0300*. *Map 2, D5, p248* A welcome Bairro Alto newcomer which combines a refined international style and presentation with superb traditional Portuguese dishes and attentive service. Main course dishes, average price €9, include wonderfully fresh *dorado*, tasty *bacalhão a minhote*, cod with onions, chicken wrapped in bacon and octopus skewers. Delicious home-made ice cream and tiramisu. Very popular, especially at the weekend. Booking advised.

€€ Bizarro, Rua da Atalaia,133, **T** 21 347 18 99. *Daily 1700-0100. Map 2, D4, p248* With its kaleidoscopic exterior strewn with fairy lights, Bizarro is true to its name. The interior continues the grotto theme, with walls painted with *varinhas* (fishwives), trams and traditional Lisbon scenes. Fish and meat dishes cooked on a charcoal grill, to the sound of fado, is the speciality.

€€ Bota Alta, Travessa da Queimada, 35, **T** 21 342 79 59. *Daily 1200-1500, 1900-0200. Map 2, D4, p248* Opening out onto the street, in the heart of the Bairro Alto nexus, this eccentric wood-panelled tavern is a classic. Decorated with gnarled boots, gingham tablecloths and intriguing art, a faultless repertoire of Portuguese classics provides the mainstay of the menu. Favourites include steaks in red wine, cod with port and sausages.

€€ Casa Nostra, Travessa do Poço da Cidade, 60, **T** 21 342 59 31. *1200-1500, 1900-2300, closed Sun and Sat lunch. Map 2, E5, p248* Casa Nostra is a far cry from the red-and-white check tablecloths and frenzied Italian waiter cliché. The almost soporific mint and white decor, discreet service, and well-executed, if rather predictable, Italian cuisine has sparked a cult following. The success has spawned an even cooler off-spring down at the docks, *Casanova*, see p151. The house special is a very rich spinach and ricotta roulade. The desserts are worth leaving room for.

€€ Charcutaria Francesa, Rua Dom Pedro I, 52-54. *Daily 1200-1500, 1900-0200, Sat and Sun 2000-0200. Map 2, A3, p248* Close to Príncipe Real, delicious fresh fish and meat dishes are cooked with Parisian panache in this small, arty restaurant close to Príncipe Real. Choose from sole fillets with garlic sauce, swordfish with banana and monkfish with saffron rice. A large selection of Portuguese and international wines. A very civilized Saturday brunch at 1030 is the perfect hangover cure.

€€ **Cravo e Canela**, Rua da Barroca, 70, **T** 21 343 18 58. *Daily 1700-0200, closed Tue. Map 2, E5, p248* Contemporary designer bar- restaurant with stylish decor. Reasonably priced international dishes ranging from traditional grilled fish to Asian specialities. Mouth-watering duck with champagne and pepper is recommended. The groovy bar area fills up after midnight, playing mellow jazz to laid-back, young media types.

€€ **Império dos Sentidos**, Rua Atalaia, 35-37. **T** 21 343 18 22, imperio.dos.sentidos@clix.pt *1900-2400, closed Mon. Map 2, F4, p248* This very popular, stylish restaurant serves a Mediterranean menu of fish, pasta, crêpes and meat dishes. There are plenty of vegetarian options including tagliatelli with spinach and cream. The intimate candle-lit tables, ambient music and minimalist decor is offset by a bizarre collection of rather disturbing paintings. Reservations are advised at the weekend, or have a drink and people-watch at the small bar while you wait. Gay friendly.

€€ **Inox**, Rua da Barroca, 129-A, **T** 91 957 44 98. *1900-0200, closed Sun. Map 2, F4, p248* Medieval lanterns flaming outside, chunky wooden tables draped in check tablecloths and black and white photos, give old-world charm to the contemporary jazzy ambience of this boho newcomer. Dishes are a totally tropical take on Portuguese traditionalism with succulent Brazilian kebabs, steaks with damasc and pepper sauce, chicken with yoghurt sauce, and fish fillets served with tangy mango salad.

€€ **O Cantinho das Gavéas**, Rua das Gavéas, 82-84, **T** 21 342 64 60. *Map 2, E5, p248* An inviting tavern that has made the leap from rustic *tasca* to restaurant yet still retains a traditional ambience. Wonderful unadulterated fresh fish is served to the fanfare of a steady stream of lively regulars. Very popular at lunchtime with Bairro Alto's suited media types and jammed in the evening. A recommended first initiation to the delights of *açorda de gambas*.

€ € **Restaurante Maio 1**, Rua Atalaia, 8, **T** 21 342 68 40. *Sat 1200-1500, Mon-Fri 1200-2230. Map 2, F4, p248* Queues day and night outside this old-style tavern testify to its enduring popularity. It's a firm favourite choice with locals as well as tourists. The food is predictable traditional Portuguese, the decor rather worn and the service often brusque. The Alentejo region is particularly well-represented on the varied menu of fish and meat staples. Worth trying is the *carne do porco Alentejano* (pork with clams).

€ **Ali Há Papas**, Rua da Italaia, 95, **T** 21 347 41 43. *Tue-Sat 2000-2400. Map 2, E4, p248* A charming Moroccan restaurant with all the pre-requisite Arabia themed nick nacks, including Moorish tiles, hanging lanterns, trotting camels, burning incense and hand-painted walls. Tagine chicken and cous cous dishes are served, as well as traditional Moroccan sweet desserts including *seffa* and mint tea *infusiones*. A far superior choice to its Moroccan competition several doors down, *Pedro das Arábias*.

€ **Casa Faz Frio**, Rua Dom Pedro V, 96, **T** 21 346 1860. *0900-2400. Map 2, A3, p248* Quirky rustic tavern with 18th-century marble floors and original *azulejo* tiles, proudly managed by charming José Dandelaras Sequeira who had been dishing up homely Portuguese staples for the last 45 years. For discreet dining you can hire one of wood-panelled cubicles where revolutionaries once plotted the overthrow of Salazar. Copious portions of traditional Portuguese dishes, including, oven-baked duck rice, seafood stew, or even paella, (€20 for two people). Excellent value, inviting atmosphere.

€ **Cantinho de Bem Estar**, Rua do Norte, 24. T 21 342 79 59. *2130-0100, closed Mon. Map 2, F5, p248* Queues of locals and tourists line up eagerly outside this homely tavern. Always brimming with lively banter, it has bags of quirky charm, with lacy curtains, religious bric a brac, azulejo tiles and statuary niches. Simple, robust, four-course set meals are €9.00.

€ **Restaurante Cataplana**, Rua de Diário de Notícias, 27, **T** 21 342 29 93. *1200-1500, 1900-0200.* *Map 2, E5, p248* From 2000 each night, locals and tourists are jammed into this snug living room-cum-restaurant, tucking into abundant portions of octopus rice and *açorda de marisco*. The decor perhaps vies for the prize of the highest kitsch factor in Lisbon – statues of Saint Anthony watch over the TV and fado paintings, aquariums and bird cages compete for wall space. The slightly fazed, but ever congenial, staff seem to forget they are running a restaurant. Check the blackboard outside for live music, which often features *fado vadio*.

€ **Stasha**, Rua das Gáveas, 29-33, **T** 21 343 11 31. *Mon-Sat 1200-1500, 1900-2300.* *Map 2, F5, p248* The young and beautiful Bairro Alto bohos flock to *Stasha*, where the eclectic menu includes imaginative Mediterranean and Brazilian dishes. Despite the high hip factor, the Moorish-Portuguese setting is relaxing and decorated with modern art and mosaic *calçada* tiled floors. Great daily specials include, *vatapá* (a Brazilian spicy fish curry) and mango chicken served with rocket salad and fresh coriander. One of the best value lunches in the city, at around €4.50. Charming, beautiful staff.

€ **Tripa-Forra**, Travessa das Mercés, 16, **T** 21 343 31 51. *Mon-Sat 1200-1500, 1900-0200, closed Sun.* *Map 2, E4, p248* Opened in May 2003, this simple Bairro Alto eatery serves some of the cheapest fish dishes in the area with friendly and obliging staff keen to make an impression. Unapologetically simple, Portuguese dishes are served ranging from beef with mushrooms to grilled salmon and cod with onions.

Cafés

Cultura de Chá, Rua das Salgadeiras, 38, **T** 21 343 02 72. *Daily 1000-2130. Map 2, F5, p248* A tea lovers' heaven with a two-page menu of black, green and herbal varieties from gunpowder tea to *Chá Li-Cungo* (Mozambique) and *Pai Mu Tan* (white Chinese tea) served in one of the most tranquil spots in Bairro Alto. The Mexican-style decor is fun, if rather incongruous, with brightly painted wooden chairs and tables, artisan crafts, ceramics and huge gilded mirrors. Advertised as a gallery, the work of local artists is displayed on the walls. There is a wide selection of bountiful salads, warm scones served with delicious jams, cheesecakes and croissants. Service can be rather brusque.

Padaria São Roque, Rua Dom Pedro V, 57. *Daily 0700-1900. Map 2, B4, p248* With a huge ornate ceiling, towering pillars and marble counter decorated with *azulejo* tiles, this is an operatic setting for a humble bakery doing a brisk trade in fresh bread, pastries and coffee to chattering locals seated on incongruous white plastic chairs, in the glow of a flashing neon sign.

Pão de Canela, Praça das Flores. *Mon-Sat 0800-2000, Sun 1000-2000. Map 2, B1 (off), p248* Smart, friendly café with outdoor seating on one Lisbon's most romantic squares, with an almost Montmartre feel. Popular with arty types lingering over books, sipping coffee and devouring mouth-watering pastries. Good spot to meditate. There is also a kid's playground in arm's reach.

Chiado

€€€ **Belcanto**, Largo de São Carlos, 10, **T** 21 342 06 07, belcanto@netcabo.pt *1200-1500, 1900-2300. Map 2, G7, p249* A Chiado institution, Belcanto draws an aspiring yuppie crowd to its hallowed wood-panelled dining room, which oozes old world mystique and serves traditional Portuguese cuisine. The desserts are divine, the wine list superb and the staff utterly charming.

€€€ **Tavares Rico**, Rua da Misericórdia, 35, **T** 21 342 11 12. *Closed Sun.* *Map 2, F6, p248* Dating back to 1784, this is the oldest restaurant in Lisbon and attracts visiting dignitaries and aspirational artistes. The Edwardian-style decor is palatial and the food first class with a well-conceived menu of veal, cod dishes and shellfish. More humble meals are served in the café upstairs.

€€ **Atira-te ao Rio**, Cais do Ginjal, 69-70, Cacilhas, **T** 21 275 13 80. *1600-2400, closed Mon.* It's worth taking the ferry at sunset to 'Throw yourself in the river', a Spanish-owned restaurant which dishes up superb Brazilian food, including wonderful *picanha* and *feijoada*. With stunning panoramas across the Tagus, the setting is hard to beat.

€€ **Brasserie de L'Entrecôte**, Rua do Alecrim, 117, **T** 21 347 36 16. *Mon-Thu 1230-1500, Fri-Sun 1230-1600, 2000-2400.* *Map 2, G6, p249* Highly rated classic French cuisine served in a traditional wood-panelled dining room, with impeccable service and presentation. A favourite haunt of Chiado's upper crust, the two-course daily menu (€13.50) includes, not suprisingly, first-class entrecôte drenched in a cream sauce.

€€ **Cervejaria Trindade**, Rua Nova da Trindade 20, **T** 21 342 35 06. *Mon-Sat 2000-2400.* *Map 2, E6, p248* As renowned for its museum piece *azulejos* as for its traditional cuisine this vaulted 19th-century beer hall-restaurant with a lively atmosphere is a reliable option for a light evening snack, a generous portioned meal or even just a few beers. Stick to meat and *açorda* and it's good value, but opt for grilled seafood dishes and the bill will soar. There is also a peaceful garden in summer.

€ € **Café no Chiado**, Largo do Pinheiro 10-12, **T** 21 346 05 01. *1100-0200. Map 2, G6, p249* Beers and *bicas* are served by young, friendly staff to an eternally clocking-off, media crowd. The cool minimalist interior is a favourite with Chiado's ladies who lunch. There is a small, competently executed menu, featuring rich and creamy Portuguese specials, *Bacalhau a nata* (€8), shredded cod with potatoes and cream, a selection of beef dishes and a range of wholesome salads, €6-7.50. Save room for the sublime desserts.

€ **Oriente**, Rua Ivans 28, Chiado, **T** 21 343 15 30. *Daily 1200-2300. Map 2, F7, p248* A vegetarian and macrobiotic restaurant, *Oriente* is a misnomer, serving an eclectic all-you-can-eat buffet, ranging from spinach lasagne to vegetarian *feijōada*, cous cous, roasted peppers and a variety of salads. The atmosphere is more upbeat and the cooking far superior to most of Lisbon's generally uninspiring health orientated eateries. Delicious non-dairy desserts include blackcurrent cheesecake and chocolate cake.

Cafés

Café A Brasileira, Rua Garrett. Daily *0800-0200. Map 2, F6, p248* The first and last place for a *bica* and a *pastel de nata*. With opulent guilded display cases, a wooden 19th-century clock and floor to ceiling mirrors, this much-loved coffee house is an institution, the stomping ground of Lisbon's late great literati, Fernando Pessoa among them. By night, *Café A Brasiliera* is a popular gay meeting point, first stop on the Bairro Alto bar hop.

Panificação do Chiado, Calçada do Sacramento, 26-32, **T** 21 342 40 44, www.panificacaodochiado.pt *Mon-Sat 0700-2000. Map 2, E8, p248* With aromatic vapour still rising from the bread, this is one of the loveliest and least touristic breakfast spots in Chiado. There are delicious pastries, scones and smooth golden brioches served on doilies. With just three tables it can be difficult to get a seat.

Pastelaria Bénard, Rua Garrett, 104-106. *Daily 0800-2400. Map 2, F7, p248* Romantic Pastelaria Bénard, opened in 1912, remains a historic landmark among Chiado's residents. The mouth-watering croissants, prepared to a secret recipe, entice passing commuters with their buttery aroma. There is outdoor seating on Rua Garrett and a moody old world interior. Bénard's place in history was secured when it featured in the film *Fábula em Veneza* which stared Vitorino de Almeida.

Avenida da Liberdade and around

€€€ **Casa da Comida**, Travessa Amoreiras, 1, **T** 21 388 53 76. *Mon-Fri 1300-1500, 2000-2300, Sat 2000-2300. Map 6, D1, p254* Set in an 18th-century garden with an outdoor patio, this is one of Lisbon's most acclaimed, and expensive, restaurants. With an artful philosophy towards the glory of food and the pleasure of eating, award-winning chefs conjure delicious renditions of Portuguese traditional dishes including pheasant cooked in red wine, kid with fine herbs and to finish off apple and ricotta pudding. If money is burning a hole in your pocket, this is one of the finest ways to spend an evening in Lisbon.

€ **Caruso**, Rua Artilharia Um, Páteo Bagatella, Loja O, **T** 21 383 04 55. *Daily 1130-1530, 1930-2300. 10 minutes' climb from Rato Metro and Praça das Amoreiras.* Cheerful Italian serves a decent line-up of inexpensive and abundant pasta and pizza dishes on its breezy outdoor patio, under shady canopies.

€ **Os Tibetanos**, Rua Salitre, 117, **T** 21 314 20 38. *Mon-Sat 1200-1500, 1930-2300. Map 6, G4, p254* On the ground floor of the Buddhist centre, this is one of few pure vegetarian options. Eastern equanimity prevails, with pan piped music, zen decor and a warm welcome. However, the food is rather hit and miss. The juices are heavenly, soups satisfying and the salads bountiful but some main course dishes – pastas, risottos and crêpes – can be rather bland. Busy at lunchtime with suits getting in touch with their inner self.

Alfama, Castelo and around

Restaurants

€€€ **Bico do Sapato**, Avenida Infante Dom Henrique, Armázan B, **T** 21 881 03 20. *Mon 1700-0100, Tue-Sat 1200-0100, Sushi bar 1900-0100. Map 4, F5, p252* Unquestionably the hippest restaurant in Lisbon with a stunning setting alongside the Tagus, beautiful people and masterful reworkings of old school Portuguese classic cuisine. Owners John Malkovich, restaurant guru Fernando Fernandes, of *Pap d'Açorda* fame and *Lux* owner Manuel Reis, have transformed this one-time warehouse into the most talked about place in Lisbon, forever frothed over by the international arbiters of style. There is a sushi bar and café-bar but the truly gorgeous line up of models, poseurs and kudos-boosting glitterati flock to the über-cool international restaurant.

€€€ **Faz Figura**, Rua do Paraíso, 15B, **T** 21 886 89 81. *Mon-Sat 2000-0100. Map 4, F4, p252* A gourmet landmark, whose sumptuous 1920s lounge-style reincarnation has managed to retain the traditional, formal atmosphere and cultivated a loyal clientele. There are stunning views across the Tagus. The menu is a refined selection of Portuguese classics from baked cod with Serra cheese and roast goat. For dessert try the Alentejo speciality *sericaia*.

€€ **Santo António de Alfama**, Beco de São Miguel, 7, **T** 21 888 13 28, santoantonio@excite.com *2000-0100. Closed Tue. Map 4, H1, p252* Owners Fernando Heitor and pianist João Paulo Soares have managed to combine an old world Alfama ambience with contemporary service and style and an imaginative international menu. The salty potato-skin appetizers are a sensation. Some of the more adventurous main courses often don't live up to expectation but stick to traditional Portuguese fish and meat options and excellent pasta dishes, and you can't go wrong.

€€ **Malmequer Bemmequer**, Rua de Sao Miguel, 23-25, **T** 21 887 65 35. *Daily 1200-1500, 2000-2300, closed Mon. Map 4, H1, p252* Despite its position, well on the tourist track, this family run, unpretentious restaurant serves superb fresh fish on the charcoal grill, at suprisingly reasonable prices. Try the grilled sea bream, drizzled with olive oil and rubbed with coarse sea salt, stacked against a mound of salad and wedged with herby potatos. Charming Moorish decor and lyrical fado music. Booking advised.

€€ **Mercado de Santa Clara**, Campo de Santa Clara, Alfama, **T** 21 887 39 86. *Tue-Sun 1200-1430, 1930-2230. Map 4, E2, p252* Located at the heart of Feira da Ladra flea market, traditional Portuguese fare is cooked to perfection by acclaimed gourmet Carlos Braz Lopes. There are delicious tomato *açordas*, as well as more inventive twists on *bacalhão* staples. The real draw, however, is the spectacular panoramic views across the Tagus.

€ **Cantinho do Aziz**, Rua de San Lourenço, 3-5, Mouraria, **T** 21 887 64 72. *1200-2330. Map 3, C2, p250* A living room, kitchen and dining room rolled into one, serving African dishes in pyrex dishes on formica table tops. Football matches blasting from the TV, competing with smashing pans in the kitchen doesn't make for the most relaxing backdrop but for cheap and cheerful spicey curries, and an authentic Mouraria vibe, this is a hit.

€ **Cartuxinha de Belinha e Adelino**, Rua das Farinhas, 7, **T** 21 88 50 154. *Daily 1200-0200. Map 3, C3, p248* Tucked away in the earthy Mouraria district, this modest, hospitable, Mozamiquan family restaurant serves inexpensive spicy African chicken, curries and fried plantains, in a neat *azulejo* tiled dining room.

€ **Casanova**, Cais da Pedra a Bico do Sapato, Loja 7, Armazem B, Santa Apolonia, **T** 21 887 75 32. *Tue 1900-0200, Wed-Sun 1230-0200, closed Mon.* *Map 4, F5, p252* One of Lisbon's hippest new eateries. Inside, local whizz kids and hip middle-youth with designer kids in tow, engage in lively banter at communal wooden tables, while relaxing summertime lunches are to be had on the breezy garden patio with superb views. The super-thin wood-oven pizza bases and calzones, oozing spinach and mozzarella live up to the hype, and the *crostini*, stacked with mozzarella and sweet cherry tomatoes, is reason enough for visiting.

€ **Haweli Tandoori**, Travessa do Monte, 14, Graça, **T** 21 886 77 13. *Daily 1200-1500, 1900-2230.* *Map 3, A6 (off), p250* Tucked away down a small pedestrian street in Graça, this popular Indian restaurant does a good line in inexpensive Goan and Kashmiri dishes. Despite the gauche decor and snaking queues at the weekends, a calming Eastern ambience generally prevails.

São Bento, Estrela and Lapa

Restaurants

€€€ **Sua Excelência**, Rua do Conde, 34, **T** 21 390 36 14. *Mon-Fri 1300-1530 and 2000-2330, Sat and Sun 2000-2330.* In the embassy quarter of Lapa and run by Angolan chef Francisco Queiroz de Andrade, this snug Lapa town house dining room, has an intimate atmosphere and an impeccably prepared menu – translated by the charming staff – ranging from spicy African dishes to some of the most imaginative Portuguese cuisine in the city.

€ **Restaurante Bahia de Todos os Santos**, Poço dos Negros, **T** 21 390 26 29. *Daily 1200-1500, 2000-2400. Map 5, E6, p253* In the earthy São Bento district, this Luso-Brazilian-Italian hybrid serves an inspired range of dishes to suit most tastes. The feisty *caipirinhas* provide a kick start to the evening.

Cafés

Simples Pecados, Rua de Santa Amaro, 6A, **T** 21 396 29 69. *Daily 0800- 1830. Map 5, B4, p253* The '*Sweet Dreams*' café and art gallery is a smoky, local's hang-out which makes for a good breakfast stop en route to Estrela and Lapa. Sunny blue and yellow decor and an eclectic 'gallery' ranges from abstract modernist works to traditional Portuguese *azulejo* tiles.

Belém and the western waterfront

Restaurants

€ € € **Alcântara Café**, Rua Maria Luísa Holstein, 15, **T** 21 362 12 26. *Daily 2000-0100, bar open until 0300. Map 1, G4, p246* A renovated 600-year-old warehouse that has become the haunt of Lisbon's style police since it opened in the 1980s. The decor is a dazzling art deco fusion of brushed steel and sumptuous red velvet. The delicious, inspiring cuisine doesn't come cheap, with abundant Portuguese classics, reinvented with international panache. The sole with oyster sauce and prawns with lemon cream sauce have become a Lisbon gourmet's rite of passage. Undeniably cool.

Cafés

Antiga Pastelaria de Belém, Rua de Belém, 90. *Daily 0800-2330. Map 1, G12, p247* An average of 10,000 salivating locals and tourists come to worship each day at the shrine of most famous bakery in Portugal. No one will dispute that the best *pastéis de nata* are lovingly prepared here, in strict adherence to a centuries' old recipe. The spark of culinary genius originated with the monks from neighbouring Mosteiro dos Jerónimos, who developed a secret recipe that not even one seriously rich Japanese business can get his hands on. The cavernous interior is a warren of 17th-century *azulejo* tiled walls, which erupts with orgiastic rapture as tourists are initiated into the cult of the über-tart. The record for the most sold in one day is a staggering 55,000. Unquestionably the best way to spend €0.70 in Lisbon.

Zonadoca, Doca de Santo Amaro, Armazén, 7A, **T** 21 397 20 10. *Map 1, H4, p246* Just under Ponte 25 de Abril, this restaurant-café with great views makes for a refreshing stop off on the riverside stroll from Belém. There are wholesome salads, heavenly ice creams and waffles and crêpes drenched in chocolate sauce and peaks of cream.

Northern Lisbon and the Gulbenkian

Restaurants

€€ **Cervejaria Portugália**, Avenida Almirante Reis, 117, **T** 21 885 10 24. *1000-0130, closed Tue.* A Lisbon institution, this archetypal beer hall is famous for its good value steaks and shellfish. If you don't fancy a full meal you can nibble on *petiscos* at the bar and soak up the classical family atmosphere. Try the *bife á Portugália*, a colossal steak, topped with a fried egg, served with a rich cream sauce. Reservations advised.

€ **Galeto**, Avenida da República, 14, Saldanha, **T** 21 354 44 44. *Closed Wed.* For a slice of ironic 1960s retro and a great post-clubbing breakfast setting, this 24-hour restaurant is hard to beat. The decor is classic, with dark wood-panelling, formica tabletops and PVC chairs. Overpriced fish and meat dishes are served but stick to the snack bar menu and you can't go wrong. Try a *tosta de quejo y perú* (turkey and cheese toasty) or hamburgers served on warm brioche.

€ **Gulbenkian Museu de Arte Moderna**, Avenida de Berna, 45-A, **T** 21 782 3000. *Tue-Sun 1000-1745*. A local's lunchtime favourite with the best quality self-service buffet in the city. Choose four items for €4.10, or six for €5.50, from a huge line up of broccoli, slices of quiche, Greek salad, tuna pasta, fettucine with coriander, and risottos, as well as fresh fruit and cream cakes galore for dessert. Super speedy staff keep the long queues moving quickly. Excellent choice for vegetarians.

Cafés

Versailles, Avenida da República,15-A, **T** 21 354 63 40. *Daily 0700-2200*. It's worth the trip north to this wonderful turn-of-the-century café, a dizzying baroque confection, oozing aristocratic grace and taste. Batallions of dapper waistcoated waiters take it all very seriously, serving *Saldanha's* silly moneyed and suited and booted. Displayed in an endless shimmering glass case are the most tantalising sweet and savoury confections in the city.

Sintra

€€€ **Café Paris**, Largo Rainha D'Amélia, Sintra Vila, **T** 21 923 2 3 75. *Café 0800-2400, restaurant 1200-2300*. Smack bang in front of the Palácio Nacional it's not surprising that this café-restaurant is a tourist trap. Still, the outdoor seats provide great views of the palace.

€€ **Tulas**, Rua Gil Vicente, No.4-6, Sintra Vila, **T** 21 923 23 78. Rustic family restaurant where the morning catch is transformed into one of the house specialities - *bacalhão de natas* (cod with cream). There's no fish served on Mondays, but locals still come out in force in for succulent *cabrito* (goat) and *pato* (duck).

€ **Casa da Avó**, Rua Visconde de Montserrate, 46, Sintra Vila, **T** 21 923 12 80. *Daily 1230-2300, closed Thu.* Amidst a cluster of very overpriced restaurants this is one of the cheapest in town. The hearty, no frills recipes use only the freshest local ingredients. It does a roaring trade at the weekends with sizeable *menu del dias* which are popular with visiting *Lisboetas*.

Café

Casa da Piriquita, Rua das Padarias, 1. *Daily 0800-2000*. This hospitable café with a warm atmosphere is especially inviting during the winter. It's the best place to head for Sintra's local delicacy - the heavenly *queijada* (cheesecake). Also serves delicious home-made quiche and *travesseiros* (almond pastries).

Cascais and the Lisbon coast

€€€ **O Pescador**, Rua das Flores, **T** 214 832 054. *Mon-Sat 1230-1500, 1930-2300*. Delicious fresh fish and inspired international twists. Excellent service.

€ **Adega do Gonçalves**, Rua Afonso Sanchez, 54, **T**214 830 287. *Daily 1200-2400*. Mammoth platters of tasty Portuguese staples served in a rustic wine cellar. Happy mix of tourists and locals.

€ **Esplanada Santa Marta**, Praia Santa Marta. *Mon-Sat 0700-1400, Sun 0700-2200. 15 mins walk from Cascais*. Nestling in a craggy cove overlooking the Atlantic, with a laid-back vibe and welcoming owners, this is a great place to stop off on a walk/cycle ride to Guincho. Sizzling stacks of sardines are served *no carvão* (charcoal grilled).

Mafra

There is a paucity of decent restaurants in Mafra. Far and away the best option is to nibble on pastries and *pão caseira* (home-made bread) at one of the many excellent cafés on Largo da República right opposite the palace, and then head to Ericeira for excellent seafood by the sea.

€ **Solar del Rei**, Rua Detrás dos Quintais, 18, **T** 261 81 47 77. *Daily 1200-2400*. Just around the corner from the palace this is the best choice in town with a broad good-value menu serving copious portions of unadorned fish and meat dishes and a buzzy vibe at lunchtime when it can get crammed with locals.

Ericeira

€€ **Mar a Vista**, Rua de Santo Antonio, 16, **T** 261 86 29 28. *1230-2300, closed Thu*. An excellent range of seafood and fish dishes and a good place to try the local speciality *açorda de mariscos*. It's worth booking ahead to secure one of the tables which has breezy sea views.

€ **Patrio dos Marialvas**, Rua Dr. Eduardo Burnay, 29, **T** 261 86 25 49. *1100-2400, closed Mon*. Serving a broad range of traditional fish and seafood dishes this popular family-run restaurant has a warm atmosphere and the added draw of al fresco seating. At the weekend it can soon fill up with a regular local crowd and visting *Lisboetas*.

In a city where the national song is a mournful longing for glories past, howled by tearful black shawled divas, you would think Lisbon's cutting-edge credentials and Bacchanalian status would be pretty lacking. But the city has well and truly cast off its melancholy malaise and lightened up. It seems that the Euro-zone clubbing capital may well have shifted a few hundred kilometres out west. It all began in the 1990s when the doyen of Lisbon's clubbing scene Manuel Reis opened *Frágil* in Bairro Alto, a utilitarian space where cool music and stylish scensters remapped every hip young *Lisboeta's* rite of passage. Rampantly, the action has been moving down to the river. In Alcântara Mar a string of decrepit warehouses have been reincarnated as classy clubs like *Kremlin* and *Kapital*, where fêted guest DJs play gunfire techno. Further west, Doca de Jardim de Tabaco is the epicentre of cool. In the 1980s this string of bleak warehouses looked more like an offspring of Sellafield, now a tide of the blonde, bold and beautiful sip cocktails on flashy terraces to a quality soundtrack of funky house, electronica, latin, and touchy-feely disco.

In an increasingly pretentious scene, Bairro Alto remains the city's great leveller and the best place to kick start an evening. Along the main drag, Rua da Atalaia, and its spidery offshoots, down-to-earth *tascas*, sleek gay joints, 1920s-style jazz bars, loungy clubs and funky discos come to life after 2200. The coffee shops of Chiado and *ginginha* bars of the Baixa provide a customary meeting point.

Lisbon's home-grown beers are *Sagres* or, for the more street savvy, *Super Bock*. An *imperial* is a draught 20 cl, a *caneca*, a half litre, costing around €1.50. Rough wine by the glass will set you back upwards of €1.50, while searing cocktails, particulary the sugary cool *caipirinhas* and *caipiroscas* usually €3. In the dockside über clubs and Bairro Alto's more fashionable bars, prices will double.

It would just be rude to show up at a club in Lisbon before around 2000 and hard-core revellers rarely leave before dawn. Admission and cover charge is usually at the whim of the bouncers who can be merciless in their fascist cherry pick of the pretty and the powerful. During the week, admission is often free, while at the weekend clubs like *Kremlin* and *Kapital* can charge anything from €15-30. *Consumo minimo* often applies, where you are stamped to ensure you drink enough.

Baixa and Rossio

Bars

A Ginginha, Largo de São Domingos, 8. *0800-2400. Map 2, B8, p248* It has become something of a ritual to imbibe *uma ginhinha*, a syrupy cherry brandy liquor, in a cloudy Duralex glass, at one of the rather insalubrious hole-in-the-wall bars across the city. From morning until night a motley crew of *Lisboetas* spill out onto the square from this sticky joint. A glass delivers the requisite sample kick, for less than a euro, and you can buy bottles to take home. Unless you aspire to catatonia, eating the cherry is best avoided.

Bairro Alto

Bars

Artis, Rua de Diário de Notícias, 95-97, **T** 21 342 47 95. *2100-0400. Map 2, D5, p248* This mellow dimly lit jazz bar is something of a Bairro Alto institution for jazz devotees. With chunky wooden furnishings, classic old movie posters and a smoky 1920s-style conspiratorial ambience, it is perfect for a close encounter with Lisbon's sultry side.

Café Buenos Aires, Calçada (Escadinhas) do Duque, 31B, **T** 93 661 36 72. *Tue-Fri 1800 2300, Sat-Sun 1500-2300, closed Mon. Map 2, D7, p248* On the steps that lead down from Igreja de São Roque to Rossio, this charming, friendly wood-panelled bar, with swirling wooden fans and impassioned Tango music, feels more La Boca than Bairro Alto. Snacks, pasta dishes and salads are served but it is worth a visit alone for its industrial-strength *caipirinhas* at €3.00

Café Targus, Rua de Diário de Notícias, 40, **T** 21 34 298 61. *Mon-Sat 2000-0400, food served until midnight. Map 2, E5, p248* The rather seedy looking exterior belies the zen harmony of this sushi bar, decorated with modernist paintings by up-and-coming artists. The glitter ball reveals Targus' post-midnight alter ego, playing mostly chilled out jazz and funk to a boho crowd. The sushi is not bad either.

Cafédiario, Rua de Diário de Notícias, 3, **T** 21 343 24 34. *2000-0400. Closed Sun. Map 2, F5, p248* Cafédiario's gregarious Chilean owner has created an up tempo and welcoming bar, so popular that it spills out onto the pavement at the weekends. The *mojitos* and *caipirinhas* are downright dangerous and the music, ranging from Cuban salsa to Brazilian samba reggae, infects the most rigid of northern European hips.

Capela, Rua Atalaia, 45, **T** 21 347 00 72. *Mon-Sat 2000-0400*. *Map 2, E4, p248* At the weekend, Lisbon's self-proclaimed arbiters of style are rammed into this former Gothic chapel. The music is an excellent repertoire of electronica and funky house. But at the more 'cutting edge' of Lisbon's scene, *Capela* can have a rather pretentious vibe. If you are in need of spiritual deliverence, the drink of choice should be the 'Holy Sacrament'.

Chafariz do Vinho, Rua da Mãe de Água, Príncipe Real, **T** 21 342 20 79. *1800-0200, closed Mon*. *Map 2, A3, p248* Not renowned for its refined bar culture, Lisbon's only wine bar is a classy place to develop a finer appreciation of Portuguese (and foreign) wines and port. Housed in the cavernous interior of Lisbon's old 11th-century reservoir, the setting is wonderfully atmospheric. There is an excellent selection of *petiscos* and more substantial dishes.

Clube da Esquina, Rua Barroca, 30, **T** 21 342 71 49. *Mon-Sat 2000-0200*. *Map 2, E5, p248* A favourite among Lisbon's sexier masses, this ersatz Bairro Alto watering hole is *the* place to see and be seen. The split-level interior is a cool fusion of modern and retro. Black-clad staff strut and sashay beneath the interior steel frames and the stark, low-level lighting is offset by intimate alcoves and swirling ceiling fans. The excellent roll call of talented DJs doing a fine line in hip hop, electronica and chilled out house.

House of Vodka, Rua da Escola Politécnica, 27, Príncipe Real, **T** 21 325 98 80. *Map 2, A1 (off), p248* One of Lisbon's hottest bars, with futuristic decor and different music nightly provided by up-and- coming DJs. There are over 250 different kinds of vodka, and excellent, but expensive, food served until 2300.

La Bodiguita del Lado, Travessa da Queimada, 17, *1800-0200 daily*. *Map 2, D5, p248* This combustable Cuban bar, decked out with all manner of Cuban nick nacks and scrawled inscriptions on the walls, is a homage to the original *Bodiguita del Medio,* in Havana, Hemingway's 50s haunt. Pumping salsa is courtesy of DJ Junior, allegedly from Habana Vieja, Cuba, and the staff certainly know how to have a good time. Great fun, but you probably won't remember.

Lisbona Bar, Rua da Italaia, 196, **T** 21 347 80 13, www.lisbonabar.com *1900-0200. Map 2, B4, p248* At the rather seedy end of this funky street, turf of hash peddlers and hawkers, *Lisbona* has a more authentic vibe. The rough-hewn decor, with black and white tiles festooned with football scarves and improvised scrawls, an eclectic musical score and gregarious crowd, is a pleasing antidote to Lisbon's more self-consious venues.

Luso Bar, Travessa da Queimada, 10. *1900-0200. Map 2, D5, p248* Carved out of the 18th-century Palácio São Roque, this smart bar, annexed to the 1930s *Café Luso* fado house, successfully fuses the characterful features of the palace with contemporary glass and steel decor. Candles, laid-back music and slinky bartenders create a more sophisticated vibe than most of Luso's Bairro Alto peers and attracts Lisbon's more gilded youth and pre-fado tour groups.

Majong, Rua da Atalaia, 3, **T** 21 342 10 39. *2130-0400. Map 2, F4, p248* A magnet for Lisbon's more penurious bohos, this minimalist former Chinese restaurant is a popular launch pad for a Bairro Alto bar hop. It is decorated with cinema posters and plays danceable world music. An in-crowd cliquey vibe can prevail before the more late-night stupor sets in, thanks to the highly intoxicating *bebidas.*

Pavilhão Chinês, Rua Dom Pedro V, 89, **T**21 342 47 29. *1800- 0200, Sun 2100-0200. Map 2, B4, p248* Behind chunky pillar box red doors, this is one of the most ludicrous watering holes in the city. An eye-popping medley of kitsch and classic paraphernalia, from Marilyn Monroe dolls to caricatures by Rafael Bordeiro Pinherio, are jammed into glass classes and suspended from the high ornate ceilings. Imbued with the decadence of an opium den, dapper waiters serve a wide range of pricey cocktails at the dazzling bars.

Portas Largas, Rua da Italaia, 105, **T** 21 346 63 79. *1900-0330. Map 2, D4, p248* The Bairro Alto nightlife scene pivots around the huge wooden doors of this perenially convivial drinking den. True to its *tasca* roots, the original decor and ambience remains with marble-top tables, silver streamers and wailing fado. While ostensibly gay, it attracts a mixed crowd from, the stylish to the grizzled, who spill out onto the street drinking sangria from plastic cups and icy *caipirinhas*.

Solar do Vinho do Porto, Rua de São Pedro de Alcântara, 45, **T** 351 347 57 07. *Mon-Sat 1430-2400. Map 2, C5, p248* In an old palace built by the architect João Federico Ludovice the Port Wine Institute was established in 1947 with the aim of boosting port consumption following the Second World War. Now orientated towards the tourist euro, port devotees can select from a menu of over 200 varieties, with prices ranging from €1-22.50 a glass. The light-starved interior is rather fusty and oppressive, the service invariably brusque and the cheaper options usually not available.

Tertúlia, Rua de Diário de Notícias, 60, **T** 21 346 27 04, tertuliabar@hotmail.com *Map 2, E5, p248* Behind the plush red curtain, unpretentious Tertúlia has a understated early 20th-century literary aura. With newspapers and magazines, art

! The story goes that in 1703, a reciprocal treaty between England and Portugal gave Portugal first rights over English wool, while England would be given priority over Portugal's finest wines from the Douro Valley. Finding the wine rather sharp for the novice English palate, two Liverpudlian seafarers added brandy to the wine and thus created port.

exhibitions and mellow jazz, it is popular with an older crowd of aspiring Pessoas, artisans, solo travellers and musicians.

WIP, Rua da Bica Duarte Belo 47-49, Bica, **T** 21 346 14 86. *1300-0200 Mon-Sat. Map 2, F4, p248* Halfway down the Elevador da Bica gradient, über-cool WIP (Work in Progress) moved to this site from across the street, where exposed brick and industrial pillars provided the backdrop for a hairdresser, streetwear shop and bar all-in-one. WIP bar is now a entity in its own right with a *movida* edge. Lisbon's avant garde self-consciously sip cocktails while DJs play a superb mix of house, breakbeat, soul, drum'n'bass and reggae. WIP also organizes carnival-esque street parties along the Elevador da Bica.

Clubs

Frágil, Rua da Atalaia 128, **T** 21 346 95 78. *2330-0400 (don't even think of showing up before 0100) Thu-Sat. Free but restricted admission. Map 2, D4, p248* Doyen of the Lisbon *movida*, Manuel Reis opened Frágil in 1983 and it soon became a legend. For years, its reincarnations kept it at the cusp of the city's clubbing scene. However, when Reis joined up with friend John Malkovich, to open *Lux*, see p166, the club was left in the hands of former customers and has since fallen out of favour with the clubbing elite. Still, at the weekend, the tiny space, with just one bar, is rammed with an ostensibly gay, but essentially mixed, upbeat crowd. After 0100 till late, the small dancefloor erupts to house, techno and electronica.

Incógnito, Rua Poiais São Bento 37, **T** 21 390 87 55. *Tue-Sat 2400-0400. Map 2, F1, p248* Despite the rather forbidding exterior, this is an intimate, welcoming dance venue in the stylish Príncipe Real. A cosmopolitan crowd of gays and straights, groove to everything from rap to indie and retro pop on the basement dance floor, while the quieter loft bar, connected by a chrome stairwell, is popular with local Príncipe Real sophisticates.

Chiado

Bars

Amo-te Chiado, Rua Nova de Almada, 105, **T** 21 092 70
10. *2000-0400. Map 2, F8, p248* This bubble-gum bar in the hip
designer fashion emporium *Vyrus* attracts a young swaggering
crowd. The feel-good music, from pop to ambient house, does
little to defrost the self-consciously frigid vibe.

British Bar, Rua Bernadino Costa, 52, Cais do Sodré. *0730-2400,
Fri and Sat 0730-0200. Map 2, I6, p249* In the 1930s, this slice of
Anglophilia was the haunt of stevedores and sailors, site of contraband
and conspiracy. Nowadays, this butch bar still has more than a whiff of
riverside decadence. Retro wood panelling is the backdrop for a louche
ensemble of grizzled regulars, chugging pints of Guinness.

Hennessy's Irish Pub, Rua do Cais do Sodré, 32, **T** 21 343 10
64. *1200-0200, Fri-Sat 1200-0300. Map 2, J5, p249* All that is the
Irish theme pub, with a genuinely affable ambience, squidgy sofas,
dark wood panelling, live music from 2300, impromtu dancing and
flowing Guinness. Very popular with English language teachers,
expats and travellers.

Café Rosso, Rua Ivens, 53-61, Chiado. *1000-0200, closed Sun. Map
2, F7, p248* Tucked down a small passageway off Rua Garrett, the
outside courtyard of this café-bar is a relaxing spot for an afternoon
beer, away from the shopping crowds. In the evening, the minimalist
interior is jammed with a chatty crowd of arty types, musing and
boozing the evening into full swing. Snacks are also served.

Heróis, Calçada do Sacramento, 14, Chiado, **T** 21 342 00
76. *1000-0200, Sun 1700-0200. Map 2, F7, p248* Cool, minimalist

bar with modernist space pod seats and more comfy bean bags. Its hip factor is on the rise, with up and coming DJs playing a mixed bag of breakbeat, funky house and electronica to a youthful crowd of gay and straights. Great sandwiches and salads are also served.

Alfama, Castelo and around

Bars

Chapitô, Costa do Castelo, 1, **T** 21 887 82 25. *1900-0200, Sat-Sun 1200-0200. Map 3, E4, p250* Founded by Portugal's first female clown, Tété, Chapitô is a performing-arts school, bar, restaurant and circus. After 2000, there are regular free shows from pantos to wrestling to tap dancing. The esplanade bar has breathtaking views over all Lisbon and is a great spot at sunset, while a decent array of international cuisine is served in the restaurant.

Clubs

Lux, Avenida Infante Dom Henrique, Armazém A, **T** 21 882 08 90. *1800-0600 Tue-Sat, Sun 1600-2000. Map 4, E6, p252* Excruciatingly cool *Lux* is the epitome of Lisbon style. The brainchild of guru Manuel Reis, it's a dazzling concoction of retro cool. The first floor is decked out with funky 1960s furniture and a democratic rock and pop soundtrack provides a relaxed vibe. Downstairs, from 0300 the midriff-flashing fashion posse dance to an excellent musical repertoire ranging from house delivered by top-class DJ Rui Vargas to deep gunfire techno, jungle and breakbeat from Dinis and Nuno Forte. Best of all is the breezy cocktail terrace with beautiful views.

Belém and the western waterfront

Bars

BBC - Belém Bar Café, Av Brasília, Pavilhão Poente, **T** 21 362 42 32. *Mon-Wed 1200-0300, Thu-Sat 1200-0400.* *Map 1, H4, p246* One of the most hyped, stylish and expensive bar-restaurants of the moment. Resident DJs Nuno Barroso and Miguel Cavaco host the "Do you remember me" party on the first Thursday of each month. There are spirited live music performances each night from samba to bossa nova to mellow jazz.

Op Art, Doca de Santo Amaro, **T** 21 395 67 86. *Tue-Thu 2230-0100, Fri-Sat 2230-0600, closed Mon.* *Map 1, H4, p246* This tiny optical art glass cube is unquestionably the best nightspot option of the identikit warehouse conversions at Santo Amaro. The stunning location, alongside the Tagus, with a terrace scattered with bean bags and sassy clubbers, is the best place for post-clubbing sunrise euphoria. In the early evening the minimalist interior functions as a trendy restaurant, before the tables are cleared away for DJs playing electronica, hip hop and early morning chilled out house.

Clubs

Alcântara Mar, Rua da Cozinha Económica, 11 **T** 21 364 5250. *Wed-Sun 2300-0400* *Map 1, G4, p246* One of the first and trendiest clubs in the region, this converted manor house has great ambience, a young party crowd and diverse musical offerings. House and techno music abound. Regular local band appearances.

Docks Club, Rua de Cintura do Porta de Lisboa, Doca de Alcântara, **T** 21 395 08 56. *Mon-Sat 2300-0600.* *Map 1, H5, p246* With kitsch colonial decor, leopard prints and a fun-loving cast of mature well-heeled regulars, this converted riverside warehouse plays a danceable mix from 1980s pop and rock to Cuban salsa. Tuesday is Ladies' night and Thursday is Latin night.

Kapital, Avenida 24 de Julho, 68, **T** 351 395 59 63. *Sun, Mon 2200-0430, Tue-Sat 2230-0600. Map 5, H11, p253* Before *Lux* stole the mantle, Kapital was the epicentre of the clubbing scene and just getting in has become something of a rite of passage to hip young *Lisboetas*. A Stalin-esque door policy weeds out the undesirable caste from the beautiful, rich and powerful. If you can face the prospect of social humiliation and have money to burn on crazy drinks prices and cover, its stylish interior, fantastic terrace, eye-candy clientele and excellent music from garage to techno and house (and Portuguese rock), makes it worth a try.

Kremlin, 5 Escadinhas da Praia, Santos, 1200, **T** 351 395 71 01. *Tue-Thu 1200-0600, Fri, Sat 1230-0900, best between 0300 and 0800. Map 5, H3, p253* Kremlin was one of the great forebearers of the Lisbon clubbing scene. During its 1980s hey day it was one of the most talked about clubs in Europe, with exhilarating techno, an underground vibe and cutting-edge clientele. The cavernous dance floor is still rammed at the weekend with fashionable, rich, young *Lisboetas*. The ever-changing decor pivots around a bizarre oriental theme with Buddahs flanked by collossal pillars and elephants perched on pedestals.

Salsa Latina, Gare Marítima de Alcântara, **T** 21 395 05 55. *Tue-Thu 2000-0400, Fri/Sat 2000-0600. Map 1, G4, p246* This hugely popular dance club and restaurant is the best place in the city for salsa and merengue, tango and mambo. There are live bands on Friday and Saturday when the white marble dance floor heaves with a sweaty crowd of Latin aficionados, from mature besuited gents to Lisbon's hipper youth. It's worth a visit just to enjoy a Cuba Libre on the bar terrace, with stunning views of the Tagus.

A 'sparking laboratory' is how many commentators have described Lisbon's contemporary arts scene. From experimental funky café theatres to rococo opera houses and the indigenous musical traditions of fado, Lisbon fuses its fine classical legacy with a new 21st-century dynamism. Portugal's former colonies have bequeathed to the city an exhilarating soundtrack embracing everything from African *mornas* to Brazilian samba reggae.

The passion and dedication of the Gulbenkian remains without peer. The foundation boasts an outstanding repertoire, nurturing a breed of talented home-grown composers.

With the rise of the modern multiplex, cinema audiences have been swelling – albeit on a diet of Hollywood pulp rather than on excellent local *auteurs*. A clutch of independent art house movies can still be found with excellent programmes.

The fortnightly tourist office booklet *Follow me Lisbon* has arts and cultural listings. The municipal government publishes the monthly *Agenda Cultural* (www.hpv.pt/lisboa /agenda/outras.html), which has detailed listings (an English summary in summer) as well as reviews of exhibitions, concerts and theatre performances. Event tickets can be purchased at the Agência de Bilhetes para Espectáculos Públicos (ABEP), on the southeast corner of Praça dos Restauradores or at Fnac in the Almázens do Chiado shopping centre. The *Diário de Notícias* newspaper has film listings and also features reviews on Fridays of the latest releases.

Cinema

Lisbon's art nouveau cinemas have sadly been eclipsed by international multiplexes serving popcorn-munching audiences and now forming a traditional Sunday day out for Lisbon families. Located in the northern reaches of the city, the behemoths show all the latest blockbusters, but often feature a slender selection of independent movies. Films are usually shown in their original versions, with Portuguese subtitles. Tickets cost around €5, €3.50 concessions. Reduced rates on Monday.

It is surprising that a country with such a strong *auteur* tradition – in 2003 prolific director Manoel de Oliveira was the world's oldest working director, still churning out films to critics' delight at 94 years' old – displays a far greater appreciation for American commercial fodder. However, home-grown, critically acclaimed, independent movies can still be seen in the Lisbon art house theatres.

Independent cinemas

Cinemateca Portuguesa, Rua Barata Salgueiro, 39, **T** 21 359 62 26. *Map 6, F4, p254* Lisbon's national film theatre, with a library (ID required) and museum, is highly recommended for film buffs. The excellent monthly programmes, with two daily showings, feature the history of international and Portuguese cinema from the silent era to classic themed Hollywood retrospectives and the work of some of Europe's most revered avant garde directors from Ingmar Bergman to Manoel de Oliveira.

Quarteto, Flores Lima, 16, Northern Lisbon, **T** 21 797 13 78. This atmospheric art house cinema with a reverential cult following is a forum for independent films.

Mainstream cinemas

Amoreiras, Av Eng Duarte Pacheco, **T** 21 387 87 52. *Metro Rato. Map 1, E6, p246* Loved and loathed in equal measure this modernist shopping centre houses an 11-screen cinema showing Hollywood blockbusters. On Sundays, it is hugely popular with teenage audiences and young families.

Monumental Saldanha, Av Fontes Pereira de Melo, **T** 21 314 22 23. *Map 1, D7, p247* With eight screens showing a mix of independent films and select Hollywood releases, fantastic sound quality and an appreciative art house ambience, this is one of the best cinema venues.

São Jorge, Av da Liberdade, 175, **T** 21 31 034 00. *Map 6, H6, p254* The last bastion of movie palace traditionalism with five screens and a classic 1950s ambience.

Vasco da Gama, Centro Vasco da Gama, Parque das Nações, **T** 21 893 06 01. *Map 1, A11, p147* On the upper level of the Expo 98 shopping centre, with 10 screens and excellent sound quality.

Fado

Finding an authentic fado venue in Lisbon is a bit like trying to find the Holy Grail. Repackaged for tourists, fado has become the antithesis of its primordial essence. Generally speaking, tour groups are packed into *casas do fado* to consume overpriced food and diluted fado while being flogged second rate CDs during intervals. Still, it is possible to hear authentic fado in Lisbon, to

★ Portuguese Music CDs

Best

- *Fado Curvo*, Mariza (Times Square Records, 2003)
- *Putumayo presents an Afro-Portuguese Odyssey*, Various Artists (Putumayo, 2002)
- *Red Hot and Lisbon Onda Sonora*, Various Artists (Bar None, 1999)
- *The Story of Fado*, Various Artists (Capitol Hemisphere, 1997)
- *Os Dias da Madredeus*, Madredeus (Capitol/Metro Blue, 1987/1997)

stumble across raucous amateur *fado vadio* performances, where the *fadista* arrives uninvited to a closet-sized *tasca* jammed with locals tucking into home-cooked *bacalhão* and rustic wine. Here, there's no formal programme, only an orgy of emotional catharsis. Down earthy backstreets late at night, you are just as likely to hear a haunting soliloquy which in a nanosecond can confer the wild emotional resonance that a pricey two-hour performance will often fail to fulfil.

In *casas do fado* admission prices are generally based on *consumo minimo*, which can range from €12 to €35 for a three-course meal. Prices are not reflective of the quality of the meal and can vary according to which artists are performing. It's always advised to check when you make a reservation which *fadistas* are scheduled to perform.

A Severa, Rua das Gáveas, 51, Bairro Alto, **T** 21 342 83 14. *Sat, Sun and holidays, 2000-0330, Mon-Fri 1200-0330. Consumo minimo €18. Map 2, E5, p248* The home of Maria Severa, one of Lisbon's most famous *fadistas* (see p66 and 75). Now a traditional tourist fado house, serving average Portuguese dishes including the house special, *Cabrito assado à Severa*.

A Tasco do Chico, Rua de Diário de Notícias, 3, Bairro Alto, **T** 96 50 59 670. *Mon and Wed, fado vadio, every day from 2000-0330. Admission €5. Map 2, F5, p248* "Ssshhhh....silencio por favor..." is the cue for often delirious fado at this rustic den of iniquity, strewn with football scarves, stained with wine and peeling walls that have seen it all. The spontaneous outpourings are hugely popular among locals, with queues usually snaking outside. The owner sings, as do the audience, when they feel the need to unload some angst.

Adega do Ribatejo, Rua de Diário de Notícias, 23, Bairro Alto, **T** 21 346 83 43. *Mon-Sat 1200-2400. Admission €8. Map 2, F5, p248* A great, unpretentious fado house with a fun atmosphere. Alongside the local fadistas, there are impromptu performances from the waitresses, chefs and the owners. This is one of the most reasonably priced venues.

O Faia, Rua Barroca, 56, Bairro Alto, **T** 21 342 67 42. *Mon-Sat 2000-0200. Average meal €35. Map 2, E5, p248* Despite its largely tourist clientele, O Faia has a reputation for being one of the best venues in the city for authentic fado performed by greats including Lenita Gentil, Maria Valejo, Maria do Rosário and António Rocha.

Parreirinha de Alfama, Beco do Espírito Santo 1, Alfama, **T** 21 886 82 09. *2000-0300. Consumo minimo €15-20. Map 3, E7, p250* Owned by the legendary *fadista* Argentina Santos, this is one of the most seductive fado venues in the city. Some of the best *fadistas* in Portugal perform here.

Taverna do Embuçada, Beco dos Cortumes, 10, Alfama, **T** 21 886 50 88. *Mon-Sat 2100-0200. Consumo minimo €20-25. Map 3, F7, p250* Co-owned by renowned *fadista* Teresa Siqueira, this suave Alfama fado house has been a launch pad for Lisbon's talent-rich pool of fado singers since its 1960s heyday. Cidalia Moreira performs here exclusively following a 30-year career in the theatre.

Singing the blues

Fado is poetry set to music. It is to Portugal what tango is to Argentina and what flamenco is to Spain. Understand fado and the Portuguese soul is laid bare. The name fado comes from the Latin *fadum*, meaning fate and embraces the idea of *saudade*, an almost untranslatable term which relates to Portugal's melancholy yearning for the glories of the past.

Lisbon and Coimbra, in Northern Portugal are the cradle of modern fado, but its historical origins remain a mystery. An earlier style *fado de marinheiro* is believed to have originated in sailors' drinking dens at the end of the 18th century. Many sailors were from Cape Verde and they would sing these mournful raptures as a form of catharsis as they left behind their lovers to depart on dangerous journeys. More evidence suggests fado is linked to Arab fatalism and that it has it roots in Andalucia. The minor key, perfectly suited to lyrical expression, was popular in the musical traditions of the Moors. In the 19th-century fado transcended social barriers as the cultural elite appropriated its emotional intensity revelling in the exotic decadence of pain and suffering that came to characterize late romanticism. Maria Severa was one of the first *fadistas*. She ran a brothel and her impassioned affair during the 1930s with Count Vimioso scandalized society. Fado's greatest 20th-century diva was Amália Rodriguez, see p45, who took fado into new realms, breaking with conventions and introducing more personalized themes of love, life, loss and politics. Fascinated with the music of the Maghreb, her lyricism provides further evidence of fado's Moorish roots. For many years during the 20th century fado became synonymous with the dictatorship as Salazar used its nationalist themes as a means of responding to liberal counter propaganda.

▶ Mariza

Mariza is the new darling of fado. With an extraordinary voice of shattering emotion, universal lyrics of love and loss, and a striking physique with diaphanous dresses and platinum blonde crimped hair, she has become a rising star on both sides of the Atlantic. Mariza was born in Mozambique but spent her childhood in the Mouraria neighbourhood of Lisbon. Mariza began to sing fado at the age of five, but during her teens she dabbled in funk, soul and jazz before rediscovering fado in her early twenties. Her big break came in 1999 when she sang on national television in tribute to the late Amália Rodriguez, with whom she has been compared both for her charismatic presence as for her astounding voice. In less than a year she walked away with the European prize at the year's Radio 3 World Music awards, converted thousands at the Womad festivals and appeared in sell-out concerts in London's Barbican Centre. In 2001, her debut CD *Fado em Mim* received great critical acclaim, comprising largely of heartwrenching melodies and love homages to Lisbon.

With her second album, *Fado Curvo*, produced by Carlos Maria Trindade (of Portugal's most internationally renowned group *Madredeus*) Mariza's live vocals are backed by a small acoustic band and with an emphasis on spontaneity rather than technical perfection.

Timpanas, Rua Gilberto Rola, 24, Alcântara, **T** 21 390 66 55. *2000-0200, show starts at 2130. Consumo minimo €18-25. Map 1, H4, p246* It's worth getting off the beaten track to experience some of the most soulful fado performances in the city, where local singers perform with elemental passion to enraptured *Lisboetas*. Unpretentious vibe and delicious food.

Music

Unknown to most, Portugal has an excellent classical music legacy which has always inspired a passionate following. Tragically, much of Lisbon's classical repertoire was lost when Portugal's historical archives went up in smoke when the Torre do Tombo was destroyed by the earthquake of 1755. The long-suffering contemporary music scene, blighted by a lack of funds, has more recently been injected by the passion and cash of the Gulbenkian Foundation.

The rhythms of Angola, Mozambique, Cape Verde and Brazil have greatly influenced contemporary Portuguese music. Over time everything from African lundums and mornas to Brazilian samba and Musica Popular Brasileira have been layered upon and integrated into Portugal's own rich musical heritage. One of Portugal's most internationally well-known contemporary bands is Madredeus, whose blend of Gothic chants, folk themes and Argentine tango are delivered by the searing vocals of lead singer Maria Teresa Salgueiro.

Classical music, opera and dance

Fundação e Museu Calouste Gulbenkian, Av da Berna, 45, **T** 21 782 3000, www.musicagulbenkian.pt *Tickets, €10-25. Map 1, D6, p246* The flagbearer of Lisbon's cultural scene, the Gulbenkian foundation has a world-class orchestra, choir and ballet. The *Grande Auditório*, with state-of-the-art acoustics, hosts a stellar repertoire of classical concerts and occasional ballet performances, directed by Lawrence Foster, the Music Director and Principal Conductor of the Gulbenkian Orchestra. Under the direction of Iracity Cardoso, Ballet Gulbenkian has become one of Europe's most reverred contemporary dance companies. Critics worldwide have frothed over its 'sensational', 'exhilarating' and 'remarkable' performances. Free concerts are also held in the amphitheatre.

Culturegest, Caixa Geral Depósitos, Rua Arco do Cego, **T** 21 790 51 55. *Map 1, C7, p247* The cultural wing of the *Caixa Geral* bank hosts an erratic but exciting repertoire of avant garde theatre, music, dance productions and exhibitions from up-and-coming Lisbon artists.

Teatro Nacional de São Carlos, Rua Serpa Pinto, 9, **T** 21 325 30 00. *Map 2, G6/7, p249* Inaugurated in 1793 and dripping with gold trimmings and dazzling chandeliers, this national theatre is emblematic of Lisbon's high culture. It's worth buying a ticket to see the wonderful rococo interior, modelled on La Scala. The opera season runs from September to June (ballet and classical concerts also performed). There are regular performances by the Orquestra Sinfónica Portuguesa, the state-run orchestra.

Jazz

Catacumbas, Travessa Água da Flor, Bairro Alto, **T** 21 346 39 69. *Just around the corner from the Hotel San Donato.* *Map 2, D5, p248* The newly graduated talent from the Hot School play here on Thursday nights. There are plenty of Fame-style improvisations around the piano and a welcoming, colourful, young crowd.

Hot Clube Jazz, Av da Liberdade, Praça da Alegria, 39, **T** 21 346 73 69. *2200-0200. Map 6, H6, p254* This basement has hosted some of the world's greatest jazz names from Pat Metheny to Don Pullen. Stacked to the rafters with red Marlboro-smoking jazz devotees, its medieval dimensions can soon become alarmingly claustrophobic. There are concerts on Fridays and Saturdays and rousing jam sessions on Tuesdays and Wednesdays.

Speakeasy, Cais de Oficina, Rocha Conde de Obidos, Armázen 115, **T** 21 396 42 57. *Tue-Sat 2300-0400. Map 1, H5, p246* Very cool, funked-up bar with a 1920s speakeasy vibe. Popular with avant garde 30-something musos. There is a varied programme from Monday night jam sessions to experimental music on Tuesdays and Wednesdays and funky house on Saturdays.

Latin and African

A Lontra, Rua da São Bento, 157, **T** 21 396 10 83. *Tue-Sun 2200-0500. Map 5, E6, p253* One of the oldest dance clubs in Lisbon, this low-key disco, club and bar plays an eclectic range of African music with a seductive vibe. Often live performances at the weekend.

B.leza, Largo do Conde Barão, 50, **T** 21 396 37 35. *2200-0500, closed Sun. Map 5, F6, p253 The* venue for live Cape Verdean music. Housed in a remakable 16th-century Renaissance palace, run by Alcides Nascimento, this old time music hall exudes faded grandeur. Excellent Creole music from sultry *mornas* and *coladêras* to hip swaying *funaná*, infects the very sociable dancefloor. This legendary club has played host to Creole greats like Paulino Vieira and Danv Silva and Alcides himself often takes to the stage.

Enclave, Rua do Sol ao Rato 71A, Rato, 1250, **T** 21 388 87 38. *2200-0400, closed Sun. Map 1, F6, p246* Founded by Cape Verdean legendary Bana, Enclave is an unpretentious and welcoming venue, hugely popular due to the pulling power of musicians such as Tito Paris. For the full African experience, there is also an atmospheric restaurant serving fish and chicken *moamba* as well as delicious almond soup and Mozambique prawns.

Chafarica, Calçada de São Vincente, 81, Alfama, **T** 21 886 74 49. *Mon-Thu 2200-0300, Fri-Sat 2200-0400, closed Sun. Map 3, C7, p250*

> **!**
> Portuguese classical perfomers to watch out for include starry pianist Arturo Pizarro, blazing a trail on the international stage and 28-year old, Pedro Carneiro, one of the few Portuguese percussion players to gain international recognition as a soloist.

This welcoming, snug bar, with burgeoning *Brazileira* spirit, is a great place for live music from 2300. During the week, the ambience is more restrained with acoustic renditions of legends Gilberto Gil and Caetano Velosa. At the weekend the atmosphere is more upbeat, with frenzied consumption of mind-blowing *caipirinhas*.

Pé Sujo, Largo de São Martinho 6, Alfama, **T** 21 886 56 29. *2200-0300, closed Mon. Map 3, F5, p250* There is always a feverish up-close-and-personal vibe at the 'Dirty Foot', a jam- packed Brazilian bar boucing with live samba and carnival fervour. It's raw, it's hot and certainly not for the inhibited.

Ritz Club, Rua da Glória, 57, Praça da Alegria, **T** 21 342 51 40. *2000-0400, closed Sun/Mon. Map 6, H6, p254* Despite a recent sprucing, an air of vaudevillian decadence still clings to this one-time cabaret club, which hosts live Cape Verdean music on Fridays and Saturdays. A restaurant serves piquant African dishes and a variety of exotic bars and galleries have titillating views of the raunchy dance floor action.

Pop, Rock and World

Coliseu dos Recreios, Rua Portas de Santo Antão, 96, **T** 21 324 05 80. *0800-1900. Map 2, A7, p248* A Lisbon cultural landmark, the coliseum runs the gamut of contemporary music concerts. *Massive Attack* performed here to a sell-out audience in May 2003.

Sony Plaza, Parque das Nações, **T** 21 891 98 98. *0900-2000. Map 1, A11, p247* This imposing mushroom-shaped amphitheatre, built for Expo 98, is a great concert venue, with a hi-tech Jumbotron video screen and 8,000 seat capacity.

Centro Cultural de Belém, Praça Império, **T** 21 361 24 44. *1000-1830. Map 1, G11, p247* This stellar cultural centre's main auditorium, the largest in Lisbon, and small studio theatre, are used for opera, theatre and concerts. Free concerts are also held by the café every afternoon at 1900. Built in 1988, the modern, minimalist design lacks the intimacy of other venues.

Pavilhão Atlántico, Parque das Nações, **T** 21 891 84 09. *0900-2000. Map 1, A11, p247* Imposing, world-class stadium built for Expo 98 that has become a celebrated venue for some of Lisbon's seminal rock and pop perfomances.

Theatre

Superficially at least the performing arts in Lisbon are booming. There is an excellent range of theatre venues from the classical splendour of the Teatro São Carlos to troupes of kids enacting credible experimental theatre from shanty town suburbs to the grounds of inner city mental hospitals.

Only Portuguese classics – notably the productions of 15th-century dramatist Gil Vicente – escaped the brutal censorship of the Salazar regime. Portugal's answer to Shakespeare, Vicente is the country's most important playwright and his work is still widely performed. When the dictatorship was swept away in 1974 new companies began to spring up across the city including A Barraca – a nod to Lorca's travelling troupe, see below. When economic stagnation set in during the 1980s making productions for commercial gain alone was no longer a consideration, theatre entered the realm of pure experimentation. For more information on the performing arts in Lisbon, see gac7.tripod.com/gac/id7 (Portuguese).

A Barracca, Teatro Cinearte, Largo de Santos, 2, **T** 21 396 53 60, barraca@clix.pt *Map 5, G5, p253* Established in 1976, this dynamic group won the UNESCO International Prize for Promotion of the Arts in 1992 for their play *O Pronto de Maria Parda* by Gil Vicente.

With an eclectic and vibrant programme it remains true to its founding philosophy of 'art for all'.

O Bando, Vale de Bariss, Caixa Postal, 4117, **T** 21 233 68 50/9, www.obando.pt   The epitome of experimental contemporary Portuguese theatre. Founded in 1974 by veteran Portuguese director João Brites, the group upped sticks in 2000 and moved to the village of Palmela, some 50 km southeast of Lisbon. From a futuristic high tech scaffold clasped to the rugged hillside the group performs an experimental and traditional programme to a hinterland audience.

Teatro da Cornucopia, Rua Tenente Raul Cascais, 1A, 1250, **T** 21 396 15 15, www.teatrocornucopia.com *Map 6, H1, p254* Established in 1973 by Jorge Melo as a nomadic pre-revolutionary theatre group, funded from the Gulbenkian Foundation, performances span everything from Gil Vicente to Shakespeare and an increasingly more radical repertoire including Gertrude Stein and Edward Bond.

Teatro Nacional Dona Maria II, Rossio, **T** 21 325 08 00, www.clubdiapason.org *Map 2, C8, p248* Lisbon's most venerable theatre was built in 1843. Despite surviving the 1968 earthquake, the building was detroyed by fire and following a 14-year restoration project, it reopened in 1978. Criticism has raged for years over its rehashed and rather staid classical programme.

Teatro da Trindade, Largo da Trindade, 7, **T** 21 342 0000. *Tickets €6-12*. *Map 2, E6, p248* Built in the middle of the 19th century, the cosmopolitan Teatro de Trindade was at the apex of Lisbon's cultural scene. Eça de Queiroz made several references to the theatre in his novels. The lavish exterior was designed in 1967 by Maria José Salavisa, one of Lisbon's leading artists. This is one of the best venues in the city for experimental theatre productions.

The stereotype of the mild mannered, reserved and overly nostalgic *Lisboeta* is well and truly obliterated during the Festos dos Santos Populares in June. The celebration of Saints Anthony, John and Peter is the vibrant climax of the festival calender. On June 12, streets are festooned with paper chains, alleyways come alive with the sound of fado, the national fishing quota of sardines is consumed in one night and basil pots bearing love notes are exchanged. The Portuguese are intensely superstitious and there's a saint for seemingly every eventuality: marital strife, tax evasion or brooding spinsterhood. During May, many *Lisboetas* crawl on their hands and knees to the pilgrimage site of Fátima, where the Virgin Mary is said to have appeared to three shepherd children in 1917. Moorish palaces, ruined convents and serene monasteries in Lisbon, Cascais and the Sintra hills provide the stirring setting for world-renowned concerts and music festivals. While throughout the year, Lisbon's arbiters of liberal thought and style step up for festivals of film, fashion and gay pride.

February

Carnival (Feb 1-4 2004) Lisbon's Carnival celebrations have a distinctly Brazilian feel. Streets are jammed with people of all ages flamboyantly dressed and dancing to samba. Celebrations peak with the *Entrudo* on the final day, with colourful parades of floats and street artists. As well as the traditional celebrations and medieval atmosphere of Alfama and Baixa, a good place to head for more a more modern perspective is Parque das Nações. Drinks are free flowing and there are plenty of stalls selling regional delicacies. Events are free and festivities continue into the early hours.

March

Half marathon (Mar 28-30 in 2004 but dates vary, so consult www.maratonaclubeportugal.com) There are two half marathons in Lisbon, one in March and another in September, each beginning from opposite ends of the city. The March race starts on the south side of Ponte 25 de Abril, following the course of the River Tagus and finishing point in Belém at the Mosteiro dos Jerónimos.

May

Bullfighting season (May-Sep) The Campo Pequeno bullring is one of the largest in the world. In the north of the city, it's worth a visit to view its anachronistic Moorish architecture. The calendar of *corridas* and bullfighting events run until September. Renovation work has been ongoing for considerable time and the bullring is optimistically scheduled to reopen in summer 2004.

Pilgrimage to Fátima (May 12-13) On 13 May 1917 the Virgin Mary allegedly appeared before three shepherd children in the countryside close to Fátima. Today, this small town is Portugal's most potent symbol of Catholic devotion. Each year, more than four million pilgrims converge on the town.

Estoril Open Tennis (Dates vary)   The Estadio Nacional in Cruz Quebrada hosts this ATP/WTA international clay court event.

June

Gay Pride (last week in Jun)   A week of events organized by ILGA, see Gay and lesbian p209, above including debates, films, presentations, parties and transvestite shows held at various venues across the city. Celebrations culminate in the annual National Pride March which begins at Praça do Marquês do Pombal and climaxes with the Arrail Pride Party. See portugalpride.org for further details, or contact ILGA.

Festos dos Santos Populares (12-13 Jun 2004)   Lisbon's most buoyant festivities are the Feast Days of the popular saints. The Saints' days are: for Anthony (Jun 12-13), John (Jun 23-24) and Peter (Jun 28-29). On the night of the Jun 12, the whole city goes wild. Streets are decorated with paper chains and strewn with tinsel and fairy lights. Fado music pumps into every nook and cranny, sardines are consumed by the tonne and friends and lovers exchange basil pots with carnations bearing love notes. On Jun 12 there are also parades up the Avenida da Liberdade. The old town bairros of Alfama and Mouraria are particularly frenzied, with celebrations continuing until dawn. On St Peter's Day a boat procession sails along the Tagus.

July

Sintra Music Festival (early-mid Jul)   World-renowned classical music festival which features concerts and recitals by both Portuguese and international performers. Events take place at various sites in Sintra including the Palácio Nacional. Information and tickets, **T** 21 923 51 76, 21 923 11 57, www.cm-sintra.pt

Baixa Anima Street Festival (every weekend Jul-Sep) Lisbon's summer season kicks off with colourful festivities including musical performances, dancing, theatre productions and circus extravaganzas. Events centre on Rua Augusta.

Estoril Music Festival (Jul-Aug) First held in 1975, the Estoril Music Festival greets the summer with five weeks of great music. Just 15 km west of Lisbon, it's accessible even if you are visiting for a quick break.

August

Sintra Ballet Festival (throughout Aug) Also known as *Noites de Bailado*. Performances take place at various outdoors venues including the gardens of the *Hotel Palácio de Seteais*. Information and tickets, **T** 21 923 57 16, www.cm-sintra.pt

September

Gay and lesbian film festival (13-28) Excellent film festival showing all manner of films relating to gay and lesbian issues. For further information contact Associacao Cultural Festival de Cinema, Gay e Lesbico de Lisboa, Beco dos Contrabandistas, 29-2, Dito, 1350-083 Lisbon, **T** 21 395 54 47, www.lisboafilmfest.org

Half marathon See under March above.

October

Moda Lisboa (23-26) Portugal's top designers flaunt their wares on the catwalk to would-be fashionistas. The international glamour posse are drawn to the city by a series of swanky, high profile parties and after-show events.

December

Noite Magica (31) Lisbon celebrates New Year's Eve in style with grand parties in hotels and exuberant celebrations on the streets. Events centre upon Torre de Belém, which features a musical extravaganza, fireworks and a 'mega disco'. Events start at 2200, so to get a good view head down to Avenida de Brasilia early in the evening to get a good spot. There is a firework display at midnight followed by a huge party.

While Lisbon certainly isn't a shopping Shangri La to rival Paris, New York or Milan, it is one of the cheapest capitals in Western Europe when it comes to retail therapy.

The Baixa is the traditional shopping district, dotted with art nouveau storefronts, selling everything from ornate gloves to herbal remedies, hole-in-the-wall cobblers, cheap leather emporiums and delis stacked with pungent cheeses and lined with bottles of vintage port. In Chiado, hip youth brands rub shoulders with exclusive designer labels, antiquarian bookstores and cutting-edge interior design objects. Portugal's fashion kudos is most apparent in Bairro Alto with a crop of irreverent young designers flying flamboyantly on the coat-tails of Ana Salazar, the doyenne of Portuguese fashion. In funky boutiques, sharply tailored suits and figure-hugging leather hang from meat hooks where hungover bohos drink tea and DJs spin funky house and breakbeat. The Avenida da Liberdade maintains its status as the elite preserve of the silly-moneyed and the further north you climb, the higher the prices.

Generally speaking, traditional opening hours are Monday to Friday 0900-1300, 1500-1900 and Saturday 0900-1300. However, hours vary in Bairro Alto's hipper boutiques, where they usually open in the early afternoon and often don't close until midnight.

The best buys, and most predictable souvenirs, are port wine and *azulejo* tiles, which can vary from exquisite 16th-century antiques which will cost you an arm and a leg to more affordable reproductions. It's worth visiting the factories listed in the text to compare quality and price. They will also arrange shipping.

Books

Fnac, Armazáns do Chiado, Rua do Carmo, Chiado, **T** 21 322 18 00, www.fnac.pt *1000-2200. Map 2, F8, p248* Spread over three floors, this international French giant is beginning to dwarf Lisbon's old-fashioned book stores. But it is undeniably a convenient one-stop-shop.

Ler Devagar, Rua de São Boaventura, 115-119, Bairro Alto, **T** 21 324 1000, www.lerdevagar.com *Map 2, B3, p248* Welcoming and relaxed book shop-café and cultural centre with a large stock of English and French language books from novels to psychology to art and architecture. There is a music section with jazz, Portuguese rock, fado and Cape Verdean *mornas*. The auditorium hosts literary and artistic seminars and exhibitions.

Livraria Bertrand, Rua Garrett, 73-75, Chiado, **T** 21 342 19 41. *Mon-Fri 0900-2000, Sat 0900-2200, Sun 1400-1800. Map 2, F6, p248* Lisbon's oldest and most historic book store, founded in 1732, was once a hotbed of literary and political intrigue, appropriately located a stone's throw from *Café A Brasileira*. An erudite tardis with a large selection of books on Lisbon, English translations of Portuguese classics and contemporary popular fiction.

Livraria Británica, Rua de São Marçal 83, Bairro Alto, **T** 21 342 84 72. *Mon-Sat 0900-1900.* *Map 2, B1, p248* English language book shop close to Praça das Flores, with a large range of teaching materials, classical literature and popular fiction paperbacks. Very knowledgeable staff will order books that they do not have in stock.

Livraria Castro e Silva, Rua do Norte, 40-42, Bairro Alto, **T** 21 346 73 80. *Mon-Sat 0900-1900.* *Map 2, E5, p248* For over half a century this dusty, atmospheric book store at the foot of Bairro Alto has been keeping bookworms and collectors stimulated.

Livraria Eterno Retorno, Rua São Boaventura, 42, Bairro Alto, **T** 21 346 00 32, http://eternoretorno.no.sapo.pt *Mon-Thu 1800-2400, Sat-Sun 2100-2400.* *Map 2, C4, p248* Founded by Lisbon philosophy professor Nuno Nabais, this is a lively meeting place for aspiring Portuguese Nietzsches hosting book launch discussion groups to presentations of surrealist poets, art exhibitions and debates.

SeMedos Café Cultura, Rua da Rosa, 99, Bairro Alto, **T** 21 343 30 55, cemmedos@iol.pt *Tue-Thu 1400-2400, Fri-Sat 1400-0200.* *Map 2, D4, p248* Aspiring writers, actors and artists meet to muse over *bicas*, beer and wine. A calender of events is posted on the door. It's more than a tad pretentious, but interesting if your Portuguese is up to it.

Fashion and shoes

Agência, Rua do Norte, 117, Bairro Alto, **T** 21 346 1271. *1400-2300, closed Sun.* *Map 2, D5, p248* One of the first funky boutiques in Bairro Alto, *Agência* has been instrumental in Lisbon's fashion mutation from conservative to cutting edge. Something of a Bairro Alto landmark, the 1970s-style shop draws Lisbon's sexy masses with its slashed, ripped, cropped and tassled ranges of denim and lycra.

Ana Salazar, Rua do Carmo, 87, Chiado, **T** 21 347 22 89, www.anaslazar.pt *Map 2, E8, p248* The doyenne of Portugal's fashion scene, Ana Salazar began her career in the 1970s with innovative designs that catapulted Portuguese fashion onto the international stage. In the 1980s, she opened two stores in Lisbon, on Avenida de Roma and Rua do Carmo. In the 1990s, she expanded the collection to include perfume, interior design and accessories. She continues to be revered as the pioneer of Portuguese fashion.

Bad Bones, Rua do Norte, 85, Bairro Alto, **T** 21 346 08 88, www.bad.bones.com *Mon-Sat 1100-2000. Map 2, E5, p248* Behind the Frankenstein dummy, you can get pierced anywhere and anyhow, or select a tattoo from artfully gilded framed designs on the walls. Next door, behind a gyrating Elvis dummy, Bad Bones has expanded its punk attitude to fashion. Amidst the rock and roll kitsch: from Elvis to Marilyn Manson, you can peruse mags on the leopard skin sofas and check out rock chick labels including *Flufferstuff*, *Dixiefried* and *Hellsbelles*.

El Dorado, Rua do Norte, 23, Bairro Alto, **T** 21 343 12 39. *1400-2000, closed Sun. Map 2, E5, p248* Vintage classics from scratchy vinyl spinning on old gramophones, to a centrepiece Vespa scooter and Jackie O-style classic bags. There are new and second-hand psychedelic frocks, A-line skirts and high-rise platforms, as well as 21st-century clubbing gear.

Factolab, Av Infante Dom Henrique, Armazem B, Loja 9, Cais da Pedra a Santa Apolónia, **T** 21 882 28 98, www.factohair.com *Map 4, F5, p252* On the coolest strip in town is this sleek minimalist space pod dropped onto dockside Lisbon. Here you can funk up your feet with great collections of designer trainers and get a sculptured barnet in the hair salon, whilst revelling in the stunning views of the River Tagus.

Fake Lisbon, Rua do Norte, 113, Bairro Alto, **T** 21 346 12 70. *1400-2400, closed Sun.* *Map 2, D5, p248* Owned by Bairro Alto godfathers of fashion Carlos Barroso and Anselmo Ortega, Fake Lisbon is another one-stop-venue for shopping, funky house, hip hop music and people watching. The offspring of *Agência* and *Vyrus*, fusing the same lines of funky clubware with street savvy attitude, this boutique was opened to create a space dedicated to the *Skinfunk* brand. There are also plenty of hip accessories.

Fátima Lopes, Rua da Atalaia, 36, Bairro Alto, **T** 21 324 05 40. *Tue-Sat 1300-2300.* *Map 2, F4, p248* For the bold and the beautiful, achingly cool Fátima is one of Lisbon's cutting-edge designers. Skin-tight leather and lycra ensembles hang from metal rails in a steely chic warehouse-style boutique. Affordable end-of-season lines are often on sale, with discounts of up to 50%.

José Antonio Tenente, Travessa do Carmo, 8, Chiado, **T** 21 342 25 60. *Mon-Sat 1000-1900.* *Map 2, E7, p248* Former intern of Ana Salazar, Tenente opened his own Lisbon store in 1990, with a classically romantic collection of men's and women's fashions. Selected to participate in the Young Designer's Show in London, he has become one of the most hyped figures of Portuguese fashion.

La, Rua da Atalaia, 96, Bairro Alto, **T** 21 346 18 15. *Mon-Thu 1400-2000, Fri/Sat 1400-2200.* *Map 2, E4, p248* "For women who know what they want" is how Lena Aires characterizes her collection, an ethos embodied by this most thrusting designer. Feminine but edgy, the affordable range runs from kaleidoscopic prints, prissy polka dots and bold stripes, through to leather hot pants and coquettish sparkly dresses.

Otra face de la Lua, Rua do Norte, 86, Bairro Alto, **T** 21 347 15 70. *1500-2400, closed Sun.* *Map 2, D5, p248* Phenomenally cool, but surprisingly unpretentious, this fashion store stocks retro shirts, lurex blouses, Juicy Fruit bags, neon shirts and kitschy cool gadgets. The langorous café seems forever imbued with a just-got-out-of-bed vibe, with locals drinking tea over mags and nodding to funky house.

Sneakers Delight, Rua do Norte, 30, Bairro Alto, **T** 21 347 99 76, www.sneakersdelight.com *Mon-Thu 1400-2200, Fri/Sat 1500-2200, closed Sun. Map 2, E5, p248* Great selection of trainers including *Diesel* and *Adidas* brands. There is a DJ after 1900, to allow for more sample strutting.

Virus, Rua Nova de Almada, 105, Chiado. *Map 2, F8, p248* Clubby, urban fashion store which features very affordable designs from Portuguese up-and-coming fashion designers including 24-year-old Nuno Tiago whose bold designs are inspired by New York iconic disco *Studio 24*. Rails of more familiar labels, ranging from denims from *Gsus*, killer heels from *Forarina* and trainers from *Diesel*.

Food and drink

A Carioca, Rua da Misericórdia, 9, Bairro Alto, **T** 21 342 03 77. *Mon-Sat 0900-1900. Map 2, E6, p248* Since opening in 1937 with a swirling art nouveau façade, this charming coffee importer has provided the daily caffeine injections to strung out *Alfacinhas*. Tea and coffee from the former colonies dominates the range with blends from Cape Verde and East Timor. Also sells all manner of tea and coffee lover's paraphernalia.

Casa Macário, Rua Augusta, 272-276, Baixa, **T** 21 320 90 00. *Mon-Sat 0900-1900. Map 3, E1, p250* Founded in 1913, this traditional art nouveau fronted deli stocks a range of whisky, tea, coffee, cigars and chocolates and an excellent selection of dusty bottles of port including a 1948 vintage costing €928.

Chá Casa Pereira, Rua Garrett, 38, Chiado, **T** 21 342 66 94. *Mon-Sat 0900-1900*. *Map 2, F7, p248* Founded in 1930, by José Francisco Pereira, this family business is now run by the Pereira's widow. An indulgent array of vintage ports, home-made chocolates, syrupy *ginginhas*, herbal teas and heavenly aromatic coffee from East Timor, Brazil, Colombia, São Tomé blended and ground to your liking. There is another branch, *Casa Pereira da Conceição*, on Rua Augusta. Maintaining decades of traditionalism, the store has archived records of the type of coffee selected by individual clients and it is customary for many *Lisboetas* to select the brand enjoyed by their ancestors.

Manuel Tavares, Rua da Betsega, 1A, Baixa, **T** 21 342 42 09. *Mon-Sat 0900-1900*. *Map 3, D1, p250* Dating from 1860, Manuel Tavares is one of the oldest shops in the Baixa and the most renowned deli in Lisbon. The cavernous cellar is stocked floor to ceiling with fine wines and vintage ports including blends and vintages that are hard to come by anywhere elsewhere. Upstairs, there is a pungent array of cheeses and meats from the hinterland and exquisite home-made chocolates. The English-speaking staff are incredibly efficient and are always keen to aid with selection.

Napoleão, Rua dos Fanqueiros, 70, Baixa, **T** 21 886 11 08. *Mon-Sat 0900-1900*. *Map 3, D2, p250* Enormous port emporium near the junction with Rua de Comércio, with battalions of port experts on hand to guide you through its magnificent range.

Tábuas Charcuterie, Rua Barros Queirós, 45-51, Baixa, **T** 051 22 05 58. *Mon-Sat 0900-1900*. *Map 3, B1, p250* Wondeful deli, just off Largo São Domingos, with dangling hams, German sausages, smelly cheeses, fresh herbs and spices and bounties of tropical fruit and vegetables including *mandioca*. Attached is a snug *tasca* with *balcão* seating serving fresh *dourado*, *Alentejano* meat, and the house speciality *frango brosteado* (roast chicken). *Mon-Fri 0830-1930, Sat 0830-1930*.

Markets

Feira da Ladra, Campo de Santa Clara. *Tue and Sat 0700-1830. Map 4, E3, p252* Lisbon's famous flea market, at the foot of the Pantheon, flogs all manner of cheap clothes, CDs, contraband and twee handicrafts, see p67.

La Ribera, Av 24 de Julio, Cais do Sodré. *0500-1400, closed Sun. Map 2, J5, p249* Lisbon's answer to *La Boquería*, without the decorative touches, this bustling food market kicks off at 0600 selling meat, fresh fish and fruit and vegetables. The more tourist-orientated, and correspondingly pricey, ports, cheeses, olive oils, wines and flowers are sold upstairs.

Mercado Campo de Ourique, Rua Coelho da Rocha. *0630-1430, Mon-Sat. Map 1, F5, p246* On the plusher side of the tracks, this market sells fresh fruit and vegetables, flowers, sheaves of salted cod and meat of every derivation. No fish on Monday, when the boats have been moored.

Praça de Espanha, Praça de Espanha. *Mon-Sat 0900-1800. Map 1, G4, p246* With items ranging from knock-off watches and car stereos, to mobile phones and gold medallions, this frenetic market plonked on a roundabout, surrounded by heavy traffic has earned the overly poetic sobriquet *Centro Comercial do Céu Aberto* (the shopping mall of the open sky).

Music/CDs and records

V-Records, Rua de Diário de Notícias, 69, Bairro Alto, **T** 91 788 39 72, www.vrecords-dy.com *Mon-Sat 1200-2300 Map 2, E5, p248* Run by José Eduardo, also known locally as DJ Quiz, whose talents can be experienced first hand at the *House of Vodka*, see p161. The massive collection of vinyl is predominantly techno, electronica and trance but also features a good range of drum 'n' bass and soul classics.

Valetim de Carvalho, Rua do Carmo, 28, Chiado, **T** 21 324 15 70. *Map 2, F8, p248* Portugal's answer to *HMV*, this modern music mecca stocks an extensive collection of everything from fado to folk, Mozart to Marilyn Manson and Shakira to Shaggy. There is also a collection of music-themed books and books in English.

Shopping centres

Amoreiras, Rua Carlos Alberto da Mota Pinto/Av Eng. Duarte Pacheco, **T** 21 381 02 00. *Daily 1000-2400 Map 1, E6, p246* Loved and loathed in equal measure, this controversial monolith thrusting onto Lisbon's skyline was designed by Tomás Taveira. A sickly cinnamon-scented shrine to consumerism, it's downright unpleasant, especially on Sundays when it plays host to young families and *Lisboeta* youth with nothing better to do. Along with the 250 shops, there is a massive supermarket, a food court and a 10-screen cinema.

Centro Comercial Vasco da Gama, Parque das Nações, **T** 21 893 0601. *1000-2400 Map 1, A11, p246* This charismatic steel-groined structure, streaming with water, is the finest shopping mall experience in the city. All the major Portuguese brands are represented and thematically grouped to aid orientation. There is a 10-screen cinema and a clutch of restaurants and coffee shops, some with outdoor seating on the terrace with views of the Tagus. Usually packed with school trips doing Expo. Check out the funky loos.

Colombo, Av Colégio Militar, **T** 21 711 36 00, www.colombo.pt *Daily 1000-2400. Map 1, B6, p246* The largest shopping centre on the Iberian Peninsula with marble-tiled gallery walkways and a glass-domed ceiling. There are over 420 stores, including a large

Marks & Spencer, *Fnac*, designer labels and speciality shops including excellent value leather goods. There is also a 10-screen cinema, health club, bowling alleys and plenty of child-friendly activities.

El Corte Inglés, Av António Augusto de Aguiar, 31, **T** 21 371 17 00, www.elcorteingles.pt *Mon-Sat 1000-2200, closed Sun. Map 2, D6, p246* The large department store with Portuguese designers and international labels, household goods, supermarkets, restaurants and a 14-screen cinema.

Tiles

Sant' Anna, Rua do Alecrim, 95, Chiado, **T** 21 342 25 37, Santanna.tiles@oninet.pt *0900-2000. Map 2, H5, p249* Established in 1741, the Sant'Anna factory, very much aimed at the tourist market, produces contemporary *azulejo* tiles based on antique designs. Adopting the same century-old procedures, each tile is painted and glazed entirely by hand. Single tiles cost between €6.75 and €10.50, exquisite tile panels from €95. Shipping can be arranged. The factory is on Calçada da Boa-Hora 96, **T** 21 363 82 92.

Solar, Rua Dom Pedro V, 68-70, Bairro Alto, **T** 21 346 55 22. *Ring the bell for entry. Map 2, B4, p248* Wonderful display of antique *azulejos* from 15th-20th century, many taken from mansions, palaces and churches of European and Islamic origin. *Solar*'s vast stock includes 15th-century Ottoman tile murals (€15,000), 16th-century north German green glazed stone tiles and marvellous 1930s art deco tiles at a more affordable €30.

Viúva Lamego, Largo de Intendente, 25, Martim Moniz, **T** 21 885 24 02, www.viuvalamego.com *Mon-Fri 0900-1300, 1400-1730, Sat 1000-1400. Map 6, F12, p255* Internationally renowned *fábrica*, founded in 1849, with branches in Europe and the USA. Diverse collections from 16th-century antiques to Pombaline tiles and more contemporary designs. Tiles used in the public space art projects are manufactured here, as well as those which decorate the new airport in Macau and metro renovation projects on the Champs-Elysées.

Ratton, Rua Academia das Ciências, 2, São Bento, **T** 21 346 09 48. *Mon-Fri 0900-1300, 1500-1930. Map 2, D2, p248* Contemporary hand-painted tiles, designed by famed Portuguese artists including Paula Rego, Graça Morais, Julio Pomar, Jorge Martins. Correspondingly high prices but worth a visit to admire truly lustrous collector's items.

Sport in Lisbon is dominated by football, the one major sport where Portugal has enjoyed international recognition. The mere mention of legendary footballer Eusebio is enough to send the masses into messianic rapture and if you pass any backstreet *tasca* on a match day you will see eyes glued to snowy TVs featuring home-grown arch rivals Sporting or Benfica.

Portugal is one of the top European destinations for golf breaks and there are championship courses framed by spectacular scenery in the Sintra mountains. A gallop on a Lusitano horse, the equine equivalent of an Aston Martin, is another perfect way to appreciate Sintra's mystical forests or Cascais' rugged coastline.

With wind-lashed beaches and awesome rollers the surfer dude contingent is high in Lisbon, especially when nearby Guincho hosts its international surfing championship. For tamer water sports, there's also bodyboarding and windsurfing at the string of coastal resorts.

Bullfighting

In Portugal, unlike its Iberian neighbour, the bull isn't killed in the ring; a decree prohibiting the final slaughter was ordained by the Marquês de Pombal – a man not renowned for his compassionate approach to life – when the son of a duke was gored to death during a bullfight. Still, the torturous preamble, accompanied by all the familiar pomp and regalia and the bull's final culling outside the arena is bloody enough. Bullfights (*touradas*) last about two hours. You can organize tickets through agencies in Lisbon, who will charge about 10% commission. There is an *Agência de Bilhetes* kiosk on Praça dos Restauradores, **T** 21 346 11 89. Tickets generally cost between €11 and €130 (seats in the sun are the cheapest).

Praça de Touros, Av de República, **T** 21 293 24 42. *Map 1, C7, p247* This neo-Moorish extravaganza provides centre stage for bullfights in Lisbon. The ring has been closed for some time but is optimistically estimated to reopen by the beginning of 2004.

Alternatively, try **Monumental de Cascais**, Cascais, **T** 21 483 31 03, or for less tourist-orientated spectacles, head to **Santarém**, about a 50-minute car ride from Lisbon.

Football

Between 12 Jun and 4 Jul 2004 Portugal will host its greatest ever sporting event – **Euro 2004**. In preparation for the glaring media spotlight, Sporting's new 54,000-seater stadium was built at a cost of US$86 million but the final will be held at the 65,000- seater Estadio de Luz, Benfica's hallowed turf, which has been given a state-of-the-art overhaul.

The Portuguese Football League is often berated for being dominated by Benfica (www.slbenfica.pt), FC Porto and Sporting

Lisbon (www.sporting.pt). In 2001, Boavista broke the stultifying stranglehold of the big three by winning the Portuguese *liga*. The national team is another story entirely and has Portugal has earned the sobriquet 'the Brazil of European Football' for its innovative and exciting football, spearheaded by a roll call of greats like Luis Figo, Rui Costa and Nuno Gomez. While Figo and Co may be reaching the end of their careers, new talent is promising to shine through with Portugal's youth team dominating world football.

Following an early exit from the World Cup 2002 in Korea and after finishing in third place in the Euro competitions three times, Portugal, under coach Luiz Felipe Scolari, will attempt to win its first international crown. For further information check out the official website: euro2004.com, for fixtures, team information, news articles and press archives.

Golf

With some of the finest golf courses in Europe – including 19 courses in the Lisbon area – and an excellent climate, Lisbon is a great place to come to swing your irons. A round of golf will cost around €45 per person. For course details and event information, www.portugalgolf.com

Lisbon Sports Club, Casal de Carregueira, Belas, Queluz, **T** 21 432 14 74. The challenging Carregueira (par 69), is crossed by the River Jamor. The eighth hole (par 3), is considered by many to be faster than Augusta. €45 weekdays, €52 weekends.

Penha Longa, Estrada da Lagoa Azul, Linhó Azul, **T** 21 924 00 14. *Continue on the EN 9 in direction of Estoril-Sintra, turning left to Lagoa Azul.* A hilly championship course with spectacular scenery. Penha Longa was designed by famous golf architect Robert Trent Jones Jr on the site of the first convent of the order of Saint Jerome 1355.

There is a birdie chance on the 18th hole (par 5), depending on the wind. €81.70 weekday, €104.30 weekend/holidays.

Club de Golf do Estoril, Av da República, Estoril, **T** 21 923 24 61. The first nine holes of this course were built in 1929 by Fausto de Figueiredo, the gambling concessionaire at the Estoril Casino. The 18-hole course followed in 1945, designed by the great Mackenzie Ross, one of the world's most renowned golf architects. The 16th hole is considered by many to be one of the best holes in Portugal. €51 weekdays, €65 weekends.

Quinta de Beloura, Estrada de Albarraque, **T** 21 910 63 50. *Head towards Estoril-Sintra direction, on the EN9, turning off at Alcabideche. The course is 100m along on the left.* The most recent addition, this 60-hectare course straddles the Estoril Coast, between Cascais and Sintra, and was designed by the American architect Rocky Roquemore. €39 weekdays; €25 after 1600, €58 weekends.

Horse riding

There are excellent riding opportunities in the Lisbon area: quality forward-going horses and stunning scenery. A day out trekking through the verdant valleys of misty Sintra, galloping along the coastal plains, or across rolling countryside scented with pinewood and eucalyptus forests, is a wonderful experience.

Centro Hípico da Costa do Estoril, Chameca de Cascais, **T** 21 487 20 64. *Tue-Sun 1000-1300, 1400-1900, closed Mon.* Excellent classes for beginners and upwards, including expert dressage tuition on stunning Lusitanos and leisurely treks along the coastal plains of Cascais and across the Sintra ranges. Prices from €15 per hour.

Centro Hípico da Quinta da Marinha, Quinta da Marinha, 25, Cascais, **T** 21 486 92 82. *Tue-Sun 0900-1300, 1500-1900, closed*

Mon. With more than 350 horses, this wonderful equestrian centre provides lessons for all ages and levels, beginning at around €18 per hour. Treks to Sintra and Guincho can also be arranged.

Palácio de Seteais, Rua Borbosa de Bocage, 8, **T** 21 923 42 77, www.tivolihotels.com   Set in heavenly landscapes, this wonderful 18th-century palace is the apogee of unbridled luxury. A two or three-hour riding trek is the perfect way to get off the beaten track and discover Capuchos and Montserrate. Upwards of €20 per hour.

Tennis

Cascais Country Club, Rua dos Tordos, Lote B, Quinta da Bicuda, **T** 21 486 93 01. *0800-2100.* Four synthetic grass courts and two hard courts.

Clube de Ténis do Estoril, Av Conde de Barcelona, São João do Estoril, **T** 21 466 27 70. *0900-2200.* The Estoril tennis/social club has 14 floodlit hard courts and 4 slow courts.

Water sports

The fine white sand, sheltered coves and large breaks of **Guincho beach** make it ideal for surfing. Surfing championships are held in August. Waves generally range from 1-3 m but beware the under-current. Even more popular is **Ericeira beach**, north of Lisbon, see p117, or **Costa Caparica**. With constant winds in the region of Force 3 to 5, windsurfing is popular at Carcavelos and Cascais.

Clube Naval de Cascais, Esplanada Príncipe Dom Luís Felipe, **T** 21 483 01 25. *Closed Tue.* Runs the gamut of nautical sports including sailing, motor boats for rent, water skiing and harpooning.

Still in rehab from the straitjacket of the Salazar dictatorship, Lisbon might not immediately spring to mind as a gay-friendly, liberal-thinking kind of place. However, gay tourism is definitely on the up. Pretty, pink and intimate, it's the perfect backdrop for a buoyant gay and lesbian community nurtured by a clutch of pro-active organizations, upbeat nightlife, an inspired film festival and an annual gay pride event, see p186.

Príncipe Real is the centre of the gay scene, with correspondingly high property prices and stylish bars and restaurants. Parque Príncipe Real is one of the most popular, and safest, cruising areas in the city. The spirit of tolerance extends to Bairro Alto with streets lined with colourful mixed bars, gay-friendly restaurants and the kind of touchy-feely clubs that put Lisbon on every clubber's agenda during the 1990s (see also Bars and clubs).

Over recent years, facilities have improved with the opening of more salubrious saunas and the country's only exclusively gay hotel in Bairro Alto.

Associations

Centro Comunitário Gay e Lesbico de Lisboa, ILGA-Portugal, Rua São Lázaro, 88, **T** 21 887 38 18, www.ilga-portugal.com *Mon-Sat 1700-2130.*

Opus Gay, Rua Ilha Terceira, 34, 2°, **T** 21 315 13 96, www.opusgay association.com *Mon-Fri 1000-1300, 1600-2000.*

Bars

Água no Bico, Rua São Marçal, 170, Príncipe Real, **T** 21 347 28 30. *2100-0200, closed Sun. Map 2, B1, p248* Renowned throughout Portugal, this intimate bar is a well-established favourite. Despite the rather tacky, worn decor and older regulars, handy internet access makes it a popular traveller hangout.

Baliza, Rua da Bica Duarte Belo, Bairro Alto, **T** 21 347 87 19. *1300-0200, Sat 1600- 0200, closed Sun. Map 2, F4, p248* A humble canteen bar on the Elevador da Bica hill with steely decor and cool music. By day, it's a laid-back coffee stop off serving decent pastries.

Bar 106, Rua São Marçal, 106, Príncipe real, **T** 21 342 73 73. *Map 4, B1, p248* This tiny bar draws a regular crowd of gay and straight *Lisboetas* meeting up early evening. The setting is rather spartan, but once you are in (ring the bell), it's unpretentious and chatty.

Bric-a-Bar, Rua Cecilio de Sousa, 82, Príncipe real, **T** 21 342 89 71. *2100-0400. Map 2, A1, p248* Spacious bar/disco in the gay centre of Príncipe Real, with a dance floor that gets packed late on and a choice of moody bars ranging from the cliquey to the cruisey.

Heróis, Calçada do Sacramento, 14, Chiado, **T** 21 342 00 76. *1000-0200, Sun 1700-0200. Map 2, F8, p248* Just off Rua Garrett, this rather frigid bar attracts a young wannabee crowd with its aspiring modernist decor, guest djs and decent cocktails. Downstairs, the café serves an inventive range of sandwiches and salads.

Keops, Rua da Rosa, 157, Bairro Alto, **T** 21 342 87 73. *2200-0400, closed Sun. Map 2, C4, p248* With a Brazilian vibe and quirky Egyptian decor, this conspicuous Bairro Alto bar, undergoing something of a renaissance, is less democratic than most of its peers.

Portas Largas, Rua da Italaia, 154, Bairro Alto, **T** 21 346 63 79. *Map 2, D4, p248* This institution – with silver streamers, faded *tasca* decor and howling fado – is ostensibly gay but at some point every reveller in the city seems to end up drinking rough sangria at the foot of its huge wooden doors before piling into *Frágil* opposite.

Sétimo Céu, Travessa da Espera, 54, Bairro Alto, **T** 21 346 64 7. *Daily 1400-0200. Map 2, E5, p248* With minimalist decor, an upbeat Latin ambience and primmed and posey clientele, the 'Seventh Heaven' bar is the archityp al Lisbon gay bar. The crowd is mixed, and the owners are Brazilian, ensuring a fine line in potent cocktails. During the afternoon, it's less cliquey with lap top tapping and post-gym juicing.

Clubs

Finalmente, Rua Palmeira, 38, Bairro Alto, **T** 21 347 9923. *2200-0600. Transvestite show at 0200 (winter), 0300 (summer). Map 2, C1, p248* Appropriately named, most of Bairro Alto's never-say-die vampires end up here in the small hours. The decor is worn and the clientele gnarled but its jam-packed disco and outrageous drag shows make it one of the most happening places in the city.

Frágil, Rua da Italaia, 126, Bairro Alto, **T** 21 346 95 78, www.fragil.com *2300- 0400, closed Mon and Tue. Map 2, E4, p248*

The predominantly gay club that put Lisbon on every clubber's agenda, see p164.

Memorial, Rua Gustavo de Matos Sequeiro, 42, Príncipe Real, **T** 21 396 88 91. *Tue-Sun 1100-0400. Map 2, A1, p248* This is allegedly a lesbian-only club, although around a third of the clientele seem to be males on the pull. Entertainment includes drag shows, as well as camped up comedy perfomances.

Paradise Garage, Rua João Oliveira Miguéns, 38, **T** 21 324 34 00, www.paradisegarage.com *2300-0400. Map 1, G4, p246* A mixed club which is a popular gay hangout, especially on Thursday nights, when guests from *Heaven* in London have been known to appear. At the weekend there's an after-hours club, *Dub Delight*.

Trumps, Rua Imprensa Nacional, 104 B, Bairro Alto, **T** 21 397 10 59, www.trumps.pt *2300-0600, closed Mon. Map 2, A1 (off), p248* Rather erratic opening hours, mostly male crowd cruising upstairs in the intimate alcoves but also popular with lesbians. Floorspace challenged at the weekend on the dancefloor with people bouncing about to upbeat house on the dancefloor. Also has drag shows.

Gay-friendly hotels

Hotel Anjo Azul, Rua Luz Soriano, 75, Bairro Alto, **T** 21 347 80 69. *Map 2, E4, p248* The only exclusively gay hotel in Lisbon. Sleek and well-run with friendly informative staff. Double rooms with private bath from €50.

Pensão Globo, Rua do Teixeira, 37, Bairro Alto, **T** 21 346 22 79. See p125.

Pensão Londres, Rua Dom Pedro V, 53, Bairro Alto, **T** 21 346 22 03. See p124.

Saunas

In the early 90s, Lisbon's gay saunas gained a reputation for being rather seedy, unsafe and usually showing heterosexual porn films. In recent years they have been massively improved with facilities including cinemas, massage, Turkish baths and condoms usually provided. Saunas recommended by Opus are:

Spartacusum, Largo Trindade Coelho, 2, Chiado. *1500-1900. Map 2, D6, p248*

Viriato, Rua do Telhal, 4-B, Sete Rios. *Mon-Thu 1300-0200, Fri, Sat 1300-0500, Sun 1300-2400. Map 6, G8, p255*

Cruising

Parque Eduardo VII *Map 6, A/B2, p254*
Campo Grande Metro Station *Map A, B5, p246*
Oriente Metro Station (Public bathrooms) *Map 1, A11, p247*
Belém (Ferry terminal Trafaria) *Map 1, H2, p246*
Parque das Nações (Jardim Garcia da Orta) *Map 1, A11, p247*

Websites

www.portugalgay.pt
www.supersite.sapo.pt
www.terravista.pt/ilhadomel/1339
www.members.xoom.com/homem/index.html
www.members.xoom.com/altsport
www.lesbiacas.homepage.com
wwww.new.gay-portugal.eu.org
www.andromedical.com

With shrunken houses, castles that look like chess pieces and helter skelter tram rides, just wandering around the city can be a fantastical experience for imaginative kids or the most angst-ridden of teenagers. Restaurants, bars, cafés and shops all provide good facilities for children, who can prove a handy accessory when it comes to making friends with *Lisboetas*.

Across the city there are plenty of liberating green spaces, ideal for picnics and energy busting activities. Within easy reach of the city, the beaches of the Cascais and Estoril offer bucket and spade fun and a water sport adrenalin fix for hyperactive teens. For more focused pursuits and all-round family entertainment, head for state-of-the-art Parque das Nações, the water world theme park with a world-class aquarium and all manner of interactive wizardry.

There are excellent discounts for the under 12s at many museums and kids under four travel for free on the *Carris* transport network.

Attractions and museums

Belém *Map 1, G/H 10-12, p247 See p82* Epic Belém is a maritime adventure playground with plenty of activities to indulge a child's imagination. There are few children and teenagers who fail to be excited by the whimsical castles, sprawling parks, riverside activities and candy-coloured houses. The **Museu da Marinha**, see p84, has an excellent children's section with replica models and all manner of seafaring wizardry. For budding Patrick Moores, the **Planetário Calouste Gulbenkian** (Gulbenkian planetarium), Praça do Império, **T** 21 362 00 02, holds astronomy sessions including child-orientated programmes (*Sat 1530 and 1700, Sun 1100 (children), 1530 and 1700*). Style-conscious teens will enjoy the funky 1970s cheese grater chairs and marshmallow sofas at the kaleidoscopic **Design Museum**, see p85, and kids of all ages will be stirred by the Manueline whimsy of the Belém monastery and the Disneyland ice cream turrets of the **Torre de Belém**. Belém's sprawling parks provide plenty of release for hyperactive kids and are a great setting for al fresco picnics. Alongside the River Tagus, there are opportunities for rollerblading and cycling.

Parque das Nações *Map 1, A11, p247 See p96* Known as 'The Invented City', the Expo 98 site, with its breezy riverside walkways, cable car rides, themed gardens, cycle paths and child-friendly attractions, is the best place to head for varied all-round family entertainment, even when the weather is inclement. The fêted **Oceanário**, see p99, is guaranteed to keep kids exhilarated with its amazing underwater odyssey, populated by puffins, manta rays, requiem sharks, florescent corals and the All-Star seals Amália and Eusébio. For studious teenagers *Explore* terminals provide access to specific information about each species – including such marine trivia as the fact that Port Jackson sharks will travel over 800 km to meet each other during

Kids

215

breeding season – as well as technological and environmental information. The **Pavilhão do Conhecimento Ciência Viva** (Interactive Science Museum), see p99, is an inspired approach to increasing children's awareness of their environment.

For the under 12s, the **Music Garden**, **Skate Park** and **Pyramide do Gil Playground** are novel energy busters, while the **Parque do Gil**, next to Sony Plaza, €2, has a bouncy castle, plastic ball pools, tunnels and mazes.

Feira Popular, Av da República, (Entrecampos), **T** 21 793 44 35. *Mar-Oct 1900-0130 Mon-Fri, 1500-0130 Sat, Sun and Public holidays. Map 1, C6, p246* There is plenty of vaudeville fun at Lisbon's popular fairground, close to Campo Grande. As well as candyfloss, carousels and dodgems for younger kids, there is a stomach-churning rollercoaster. For good, all-round family fun, there are performances of Portuguese folk music and dance shows, plus the chance to sample some of Portugal's festive gastro treats, *faturas* (doughnuts fried in sizzling fat) and *no cavão* (sardines on the barbecue grill). A new Feira Popular akin to the Tivoli Gardens in Copenhagen is due to open in 2004.

Columbo Playground, Av Colégio Militar, **T** 21 711 36 00, www.colombo.pt *Daily 1000-2400. Map 1, B3, p246* On the upper floor of the Colombo Shopping centre, this high-tech arcade provides a thoroughly modern counterpart to the Feira Popular, with a bowling pavilion, virtual reality video games, a pirate ship and a go cart track.

Museu das Crianças, Rua Visconde de Monserrate, Sintra, **T** 21 910 60 16. *Tue-Sun 1000-1800, closed Mon, free.* Located in Sintra's old Fireman HQ, the quirky Children's Museum is home to more that 20,000 toys – ancient and modern – which provide an interesting insight into the social customs of each era. Amassed over 50 years by João Arbués Moreira, the eclectic collection ranges from Barbie dolls to model planes and toy soldiers. The oldest exhibit is a 3,000-year-old terracotta doll. There is also a Lego room, and an interactive computer section for older children.

Museu do Marioneta, Convento das Bernadas, Rua da Esperança, 146, **T** 21 394 28 10. *Wed-Sun 1000-1300, 1400-1800. €1.50. All display information in Portuguese. Map 5, G4, p253* A lovingly conceived collection of over 1,000 puppets, ranging from glove puppets from Italy to string-wire and stick controlled puppets from Burma and New Zealand. There are also theatrical exhibits which relate the history of the Portuguese puppetry traditions, including a display of the French theatre of Guignol. As the glass cases prohibit playful interaction, for more guaranteed child stimulation, it's worth calling ahead to check the programme of puppet shows which are frequently held.

Parks and beaches

Parque Eduardo VII, see p62 and the **Jardim da Estrela**, see p78, are the best of Lisbon's inner city parks with play areas for children, as the smaller parks tend to be populated by elderly men and hash peddlers. Be cautious, as there have been recent reports that the equipment is not well-maintained in many playgrounds and sandpits can harbour some distinctly un-child-friendly specimens. The **Botanical gardens**, see p48, are a great place for adventure, with dense jungly vegetation and exotic plant species. Outside the city, the beaches and parks of **Cascais**, see p113, provide a great release for restless tots and the fairy-tale palaces and Tolkein scenery of **Sintra**, see p105, will grab the attention of older children. Here, sporty teenagers can also play **tennis**, **waterski** or **surf**. **Horse riding** in the hills around Sintra is a great family day out.

Check out...

WWW...

100 travel guides, 100s of destinations,
5 continents
and 1 Footprint...

www.footprintbooks.com

Directory

Airline offices

Where addresses are not listed, the airline's main offices are at the airport. **British Airways**, Av da Liberdade, 32, 2°, **T** 808 200 125. **Air France**, Av 5 de Octubro, 206, 3°, **T** 808 202 800. **Iberia**, Rua Barata Salgueiro, 28, 6°, **T** 808 261 261. **KLM**, **T** 808 222 747. **Lufthansa**, **T** 214 245 155. **Portugália**, Av Almirante Gago Coutinho, 88, **T** 218 498 020. **Tap Air Portugal**, **T** 808 205 700.

Airport information

Aeroporto de Lisboa, **T** 21 841 3700, www.ana-aeroportos.pt

Banks and ATMs

Twenty-four hour *Multibanco* cash points are ubiquitous. Maximum daily withdrawal is €200 per day. Most banks accept international cards including Visa, Cirrus and Eurocheque. Credit card cash advances are not offered. Banks open from 0830-1500 Mon-Fri. Changing travellers' cheques will carry large commission charges.

Car hire

Autocerro, Rua Salgado Zenha, Quinta da Francelha de Baixo, Bloco 1-1°, **T** 21 940 05 55. **Avis**, Edifício Campo Grande, 390-2°, **T** 21 754 78 00. **Hertz**, Av Severiano Falção, 7-7A, **T** 21 942 63 00.

Consulates and embassies

Australia, Av da Liberdade, 200, 2°, **T** 21 310 15 00. **UK**, Rua São Bernardo 33, 1249-082, **T** 21 392 41 60, www.britishembassy.co.uk **US**, Av das Forças Armadas, Apartado 4258, **T** 21 727 33 00.

Credit card lines

Amex, **T** 06-72900347. **Diners**, **T** 800-8864064. **Mastercard**, **T** 800-870866. **Visa**, **T** 800-877232.

Cultural institutions

The British Council, Rua Luís Fernandes, 1-3, **T** 21 321 45 00.

Instituto Franco Portugais, Av Luis Bivar 91, **T** 21 54 43 89.
Alliance Française de Lisbonne, Rua Braamcamp 13-1º, **T** 21 315 88 06.

Dentists
Contact the main hospital (see below).

Disabled
Hilly, potholed and congested steets and limited facilities, make Lisbon a difficult city for disabled travellers. Before you go get in touch with the **Secretariado Nacional para a Reabilitação e Integração das Pessoas com Deficiência**, Av Conde Valbom, 63-1069-178, **T** 21 792 95 00, snripd@snripd.mts.gov.pt Hotels equipped for disabled travels include: Tivoli, Veneza, and Lapa Palace (see pp 127, 127 and 130 respectively).

Electricity
Portugal functions on a 220V mains supply.

Emergency numbers
Police, Ambulance and Fire: **T** 112.

Hospitals
Hospital de Santa Maria, Av Professor Egas Moniz, 1600, **T** 21 797 51 71. Main public hospital. Reciprocal EU cover is available at public hospital out-patient departments. Private hospitals recommended by UK embassy: **Clínica Médica Internacional de Lisboa**, Av António Augusto Aguiar, 40, **T** 21 351 33 10. **The British Hospital**, Rua Saraiva de Carvalho, 49, 1269-098, **T** 21 394 31 00 (general), **T** 21 394 31 33/ 21 394 31 15 (appointments/examinations). **Hospital da Cruz Vermelha**, Rua Duarte Galvão, 54, **T** 21 771 40 00 (general), **T** 21 771 40 02/3 (appointments/examinations).

Directory

Internet

Ask me Lisbon, Praça do Comércio, **T** 21 312 81 01. *0900-2000*. Fast and convenient, but expensive, €4 per hour. **Cyberbica**, Rua Duques de Bragança, 7, Chiado, **T** 21 322 50 04. *Mon-Sat 1100-2400*. Only €0.74 per quarter hour and one of the cheapest and friendliest places in the city. Also serves good cheap meals and snacks. **Webcafé**, Rua de Diário de Notícias, 126, Bairro Alto, **T** 21 342 11 81. *1600-0200*. Cavernous-style internet bar.

Language schools

Amerispan, www.amerispan.com **Cambridge School**, Av da Liberdade, 173, **T** 21 352 74 74. With schools across the city, and teaching multi-level intensive and part time classes in Portuguese, EFL and French, this school has the best reputation in the city. Also runs TEFL courses during the summer which are much cheaper than in the UK. **International House**, Rua Marquês Sá de Bandeira, 16, São Sebastião, **T** 21 315 14 96. Month-long intensive courses, flexible part time schedules and personal tuitition.

Left luggage

Lockers at Santa Apolónia and Cais do Sodré train stations, costing from €2-5 for 48 hours. Also at the baggage collection point in the Arrivals Hall of the airport, €2-6.

Libraries

Biblioteca Nacional de Lisboa, Rua Occidental Campo Grande, 83, **T** 21 797 47 41. *Mon-Fri 0900-1900*. ID and registration required to take out books. **Biblioteca Municipal Palácio Galveias**, Campo Pequeno, **T** 21 797 13 26. *Mon-Fri 1100-1900, Sat 1100-1700*.

Lost property

Governo Civil, next to Teatro São Carlos, Chiado. *Mon-Sat 0900-1200, 1400-1800*. **Municipal police station**, Palácio Foz, Praça dos Restauradores. *24 hours*.

Media

International newspapers and magazines are available from kiosks around Rossio, Praça dos Restauradores, along Rua Augusta, and in the more upmarket hotels. For good listings and cultural information the best local newspaper is *Diário de Notícias*. For football editorial and fixtures information, see *La Bola*.

Pharmacies (late night)

Pharmacies are open *0900-1900*. In case of emergency, each neighbourhood will have at least one which operates out of hours, indicated by rotas posted on each doorway.

Post offices

The **Correio Geral**, Lisbon's main post office, is on Praça do Comércio, **T** 21 322 09 00. *Mon-Fri 0830-1830*.

Public holidays

1 Jan; 6 Jan, Epiphany; 25 Apr, Revolution Day; 1 May, Labour Day; 6 Jun, Corpus Cristi; 10 Jun, Camões Day; 15 Aug, Assumption; 5 Oct, Republic Day; 1 Nov, All Saints Day; 1 Dec, Independence Day, 8 Dec, Immaculate Conception; 25 Dec, Christmas Day.

Telephone

Lisbon's international dialling code is 351. To call home from Portugal, dial 00 followed by your country's international dialling code; UK 44, US 1, AUS 61, followed by area code and local number.

Time

GMT in winter, GMT + 1 in summer – same as the UK. As in Britain, clocks move forward one hour on the last Sun in Mar and go back one hour on the last Sun in Oct.

Toilets

There are a few coin operated *casas de banho* dotted around Lisbon, signposted *homens/cabalheiros* (men) and *mulheres/ senhoras* (women), although most bar and café staff tend to be quite laissez faire about letting you use their facilities, provided you ask first.

Travel agents

Forum Travel, Rua dos Correeiros, 101-3°, 101-3°. **Rumos - Viagens e Turismo**, Av Almirante Reis, 113, Loja 316, **T** 21 317 24 90/99, agencia.rumos@rumosviagens.pt **Top Tours**, Av Duque de Ávila, 185-3°, **T** 21 316 98 00, www.toptours.pt

A sprint through history

218 BC	Roman army enters the Iberian Peninsula.
195 BC	Romans take Lisbon (Olisipo).
60 BC	Olisipo is established as the western capital of the Roman Empire.
409 AD	Northern Barbarians – Suevi, Visigoths, Alans – enter the Iberian Penisula and dominate Lisbon.
585	Visigoths conquer Olisipo and the city is renamed Olisibona.
711	Moors sweep across Iberia.
719	Moors occupy Lisbon.
737	Visigothic noble Pelayo defeats the Moors at Covadonga and becomes King of Asturias, later Asturias Leon. The territory known as Portucalense becomes a province of León, under the autonomous control of counts, following victories at Braga, Porto, Viseu and Guimaraes.
844	Normans arrive in Lisbon and Algarve.
1112	Warrior knight Afonso Henríques succeeds his father Henry of Burgundy as Count of Portugal.
1123	Afonso Henríques is declared sole ruler of Portugal when he wins independence from Spain by wresting power from his mother and her ally King Alfonso V of Leon and Castile.
1139	Afonso Henríques (1139-85), defeats the Moors at the battle of Campo do Ourique and is declared King by his soldiers. His claims are formally endorsed by the Pope at the Conference of Samara in 1143.

1147	Afonso Henríques, with the help of northern crusaders, diverted en route to Palestine, takes Lisbon from the Moors.
1279	King Dom Dinis (1279-1325) marries Isabel of Aragón.
1333	The Black Death enters Lisbon from the East, decimating the population. Years of hunger and disease ensue.
1356	First earthquake in Lisbon.
1385	The Spanish are defeated at Battle of Aljubarrota. João I of the House of Avis becomes King of Portugal.
1415	Portuguese Armada leaves for Ceuta, the western depot for the spice trade and a new crusade target.
1478	Treaty of Alcaçovas declares the Azores, Madeira, Cape Verde and Guinea as Portuguese territories.
1495	Reign of Dom Manuel I. Vasco da Gama sails from Belém and discovers the sea route to India.
1500	Pedro Álvares Cabral discovers Brazil.
1506	During Passover, violence breaks out against the *Conversos*, Lisbon's Jewish population who have been forced to convert to Christianity.
1536-1684	In 1537 king Dom Joao III petitions the Pope to bring the Inquisition to Portugal. Almost 1,400 people are burned alive.
1578	Attempts to take Morocco end in disaster, King Dom Sebastián is killed in Alcazarquivir.
1581	Philip II of Spain becomes Philip I of Portugal.
1630	Jews expelled.

1640	Dom João, the Duke of Bragança, accedes the throne. The discovery of diamonds in Brazil ushers in a period of great prosperity.
1755	The Great Earthquake devastates the capital on All Saints Day, 1 November, see box p39.
1761	Auto de fé: sentences are meted out by the Inquisition in Rossio. More than 70 heretics are condemned to death.
1807	French General Junot invades Portugal on 29 November. The royal family flee to Brazil.
1808	Peninsular wars.
1814	English help to force a French retreat.
1834	Abolition of the religious orders under the new constitutional monarchy following the defeat of Dom Manuel I.
1908	Dom Carlos and Prince Regent Dom Luis Felipe are assassinated in Praça do Comércio.
1910	Exile of Dom Manuel II. Establishment of Republic. Teófilo Braga presides over provincial government.
1932	António Salazar becomes Prime Minister. Fascist dictatorship lasts until 1968.
1933	'New State' ('Estado Novo') constitution.
1936	Salazar backs General Franco's nationalists in Spanish Civil War.
1939-45	During the Second World War, Portugal remains neutral but gives the UK permission to use its Azores airbases.
1949	Portugal becomes founding member of NATO.

1961	India annexes Portuguese Goa. Rebellion breaks out in other colonies: Angola, Guinea and Mozambique.
1970	Salazar dies.
1974	On 25 April, army officers overthrow the Caetano government. General Spinola is declared president.
1974-75	Portugal's colonies Guinea-Bissau, Cape Verde Islands, Mozambique, São Tome, Portuguese Timor and Angola gain independence.
1982	Civilian government restored. Military Council of the Revolution abolished.
1983	João Soares is declared prime minister.
1986	Portugal joins the EU.
1988	Fire devastates Lisbon's literary heartland, Chiado. The task of reconstruction is undertaken by renowned architect Álvaro de Siza Vieira.
1994	Lisbon is declared European Capital of Culture.
1996	Mayor of Lisbon, Jorge Sampaio wins the presidential elections, taking over from Soeres.
1998	Lisbon hosts Expo 98. Creation of Parque das Nações.
1999	Portugal's last overseas territory, Macau, handed over to Chinese adminstration.
Jan 2002	The end of the escudo. Lisbon joins the Euro.
Mar 2002	Social Democrat leader Jose Manuel Durão Barroso forms centre-right coalition government.
2003	Provision of aid and troops for the Iraq war proves polemical. Forest fires rage across the country. Lisbon is blanketed in smoke from fires in Mafra and Loures. Damage is estimated at €1 billion.

Architecture

1st century BC-3rd century AD	**Roman period** During the reign of Emperor Augusto, Roman Lisbon (Olispo) reaches its architectural zenith; construction of a theatre, baths, aqueduct and temple. All Roman vestiges are buried by the 1755 earthquake. A Roman theatre is built in AD 57 during the reign of Nero. Mosaic tiles from this period have been uncovered beneath Rua dos Correiros and Rua Augusta in the Baixa.
5th-7th century	**Visigothic period** Almost nothing remains. Capitals can be seen in Museo de Arqueologia.
8th-12th century	**Muslim period** In 719 Abdelaziz Ben Muza enters the city, initiating a period of urban and architectural splendour. Lisbon is renamed Al Usbuna. Alfama's construction conforms to a traditional Moorish layout. The construction of the Castelo de São Jorge is the highpoint.
12th-15th century	**Medieval period** A new urban plan is traced with palaces and fortress-style cathedrals, symbolic of the Reconquista, constructed on the sites of former mosques. The Convento de São Domingos is built in 1242 signalling the expansion of the city beyond the Roman walls of Cerca Moura, see p44. Dom Dinis (1279-1325) is instrumental in artistic development and pronouncing new concepts of urbanism. The Convento do Carmo (1384-1425) is one of the most ambitious projects of the Middle Ages.
16th century	**The Age of the Discoveries** Lisbon's architectural highpoint: development of the Manueline style, the final phase of Portuguese late-Gothic, characterized by maritime imagery and exotica and bearing the

King's seal. The purest form is the Torre de Belém, the most majestic example the Mosteiro dos Jerónimos.

17th-18th century	**Baroque period** João Antunes is heralded as one of the period's great architects. His Panteão Nacional de Santa Engrácia (1642), see p66, marks the transition from mannerism to baroque. During the reign of Dom João V (1706-50), the discovery of diamonds in Brazil finances extraordinary projects culminating in the lavish Palácio de Mafra and the chapel of the Igreja de São Roque. Some of Europe's greatest architects come to work in Portugal including Ludovice and Hungarian Carlos Mardel. The construction of the aqueduct (1731-48) was one the great engineering feats of its time.
19th century	**Neo-Manueline period** A romantic yearning for past glories is revealed in the most outlandish fashion at the Palácio de Pena and the horseshoe arches of Rossio railway station. The Gothic wrought-iron Elevador de Santa Justa marked the transition to more modernist tendencies.
20th century	**Modern period** Contemporary European architectural influences are apparent as the decorative takes precedence over the functional. The elegance of French art nouveau tendancies are revealed in the shop fronts of the Baixa, decorated with swirling arabesques, and in the pure belle époque of Hotel International. Norte Junior is one of the key architects of the period, his Casa Museu Malhoa (1904) wins El Premio Valmor, the ultimate architectural honour. Expo 98 transforms the squalid wastelands of the northeast into the glitzy glass and steel modernism of Parque das Nações.

Books

Birmingham, David, *A Concise History of Portugal* (1993)
Cambridge University Press. The best, and most succinct,
introduction to Portugal's history with particular reference to the
1755 earthquake, the declaration of the republic and Salazar years.

Camões, Luís Vaz, *As Lusiadas* (1572) Carcanet. This is Portugal's
national work, an epic poem which evokes Vasco da Gama's
triumphant 'discovery' of the sea route to India.

Kaplan, Marion, *The Portuguese: the land and its people* (1992,
updated 1998) Penguin. An excellent introduction to Portuguese
culture with insightful psychoanalysis within a well-framed historical
perspective. Despite a revision, it already feels rather dated.

Lopes Antunes, **António**, *Act of the Dammed* (1993) Secker and
Warburg. A humorous portrayal of the corrupt ruling class of the
Salazar dictatorship, as a rich family attempt to prevent their
valuable possessions from being seized by militant soldiers.

Lopes Antunes, **António**, *An Explanation of the Birds* (1992)
Secker and Warburg. In this bleakly funny novel Rui, a political
historian, takes his Marxist wife Marília away for a weekend in
order to break the news that their relationship is over. In the
middle of the novel is Rui's obituary which eulogises and at the
same time satirizes his life.

Pessoa, Fernando, *The Book of Disquiet* (1992) Serpent's Tail. Set
in Lisbon, this is the autobiography of Pessoa's pseudonym, or
heteronym, Bernardo Soeres, published posthumously, see p53.

Queiros, da Eça, *The Illustrious House of Remires* (1900) Penguin.
Eça da Queiros started his writing career as a disciple of Zola and

was considered one of the leading intellectuals of the 'Generation of 1870'. Protagonist Gonçalo Ramires is an allegory of Portugal; a aristocratic fantasist with mad-cap dreams of future success as novelist and politician.

Queiros, da Eça, *As Maias* (1946) Penguin. Eça's acknowledged masterpiece and, it is claimed, the novel with which the Portuguese most identify. The decline of three generations of a wealthy aristocratic family reflects the ideological, cultural and political developments in Portugal from the beginning of the 19th century.

Saramago, José, *The Year of the Death of Ricardo Reis* (1998) Harvill. Since winning the Nobel prize in 1998, Saramago has emerged as Portugal's most renowned contemporary writer. In this novel he unravels Fernando Pessoa's heteronym Reis who returns to Lisbon from Brazil to the insufferable straightjacket of Salazar's dictatorship.

Saramago, José, *Baltasar and Blimunda* (2001) Harvill. Set in Lisbon and Mafra, this engaging plot centres upon the construction of a flying machine and has a Latin-American magical realist style.

Vieira, Edite, *The Taste of Portugal* (2000) Grub Street. Recipe book of regional specialities, mouthwatering photography and cultural contexts.

Wilson, Robert, *A Small Death in Lisbon*, (2000) Harper Collins. Murder mystery providing a fascinating insight into Portuguese neutrality during Second World War and the Salazar dictatorship.

Zimler, Richard, *The Last Kabbalist of Lisbon* (2000) Overlook. American Zimler weaves an intricate detective yarn set in Lisbon during the massacre of the Jewish *conversos* in 1506. Based on fact, the novel follows the fortunes of a young Kabbalist attempting to discover the truth behind the death of his uncle.

Language

Basics

thank you *obrigado/a*
hi (informal) *olá*
goodbye *adeus*
see you later *até logo*
good morning *bom dia*
good evening (after lunch) *boa tarde*
goodnight *boa noite*
please *se faz favor/por favor*
I'm sorry/excuse me *desculpe/con liçenca*
yes/no *sim/não*

Numbers

one *um/uma,* two *dois/duas,* three *três,* four *quatro,* five *cinco,*
six *seis,* seven *sete,* eight *oito,* nine *nove,* 10 *dez,* 11 *onze,* 12 *doze,*
13 *treze,* 14 *catorze,* 15 *quinze,* 16 *dezasseis,* 17 *dezassete,*
18 *dezoito,* 19 *dezanove,* 20 *vint,* 21 *vint e um,* 22 *vint e dos,*
30 *trinta,* 40 *quarenta,* 50 *cinquenta,* 60 *sessenta,* 70 *setenta,*
80 *oitenta,* 90 *noventa,* 100 *cem,* 200 *duzentos,* 1000 *mil.*

Questions

how? *como?*
how much? *quanto?*
when? *quando?*
where? *onde?*
why? *por que?*
what? *o que?*

Problems

I don't understand *Não percebo*
I don't know *Non lo so*

I don't speak Italian *Não falo Português*
Do you speak English? *Fala inglês?*

Shopping

less/more *menos/mais*
How much is it/are they? *quanta custa?*
I would like... *Queria ...?*
What's this? *O que é isso?*
open/closed *aberto/cerrado*
I'll be right back *Volto já* (sign that could mean that shops have
closed up while someone popped out or for the month/holiday)
bank *banco*
post office *correio*
pharmacy *farmácia*
laundrette *lavanderia*

Eating and drinking

bill *a conta*
I'm a vegetarian *Sou vegetariano/a*
breakfast *pequeno almoço*
lunch *almoço*
dinner *jantar*

Travelling and directions

one ticket for... *um bilhete...*
single/return *simples/de ida/de ida e volta*
Does this train/bus go to...? *E este o combóio/autocarro para...?*
How long does it take? *Quanto tempo leva isso?*
What time does it leave/arrive? *A que horas parte/chega?*
How do I get to? *Como vou para?*
near/far *perto/longe*
Turn right/left *Vire à direita/esquerda*
Go straight ahead *Siga sempre en frente*
Where is the bus station? *Onde e o estação de autocarros?*

Hotels

a double/ twin/single room *um quarto de matrimonial/de duplo/individual*
bathroom *banho*
dirty/noisy *sujo/ruidoso*
expensive/cheap *caro/barato*
Is breakfast included? *Está incluído o pequeno almoço?*

Time

morning/afternoon/evening *manhã/tarde/noite*
What time? *A que horas?*
What time is it? *Que horas são?*
today/tonight *hoje/hoje a noite*
later *mais tarde*
tomorrow/yesterday *amanhã/ontem*

Menu reader

Peixe e mariscos (fish and seafood)

ameijoas clams
anchovas anchovies
atum tuna
bacalhau salted cod fish
bacalhau à bras salted cod fried with potato and scrambled egg
bacalhau à Gomes Sá salted cod
bacalhau com nata salted cod baked with cream and potato
caldeirada fish stew (onions, tomato, garlic, potato)
dourada sea bream
gambas/camarões prawns
langostinos king prawns
lulas squid
mexilhões mussels

pescada whitebait
polvo octopus
robalo sea bass
salmão salmon
vieira scallops

Carne, aves e caça (meat, poultry and game)
bife steak
bife à portuguesa/bitoque thin sliced beef topped with a fried egg
cabrito kid
coelho rabbit
costeleto chop
febras pork steak
frango chicken
leitão suckling pig
pato duck
perú turkey
porco à alentejana pork baked with clams
vitela veal

Frutas e legumes (fruit and vegetables)
alface lettuce
ameixa plum
ananás pineapple
berinjela aubergine
cebola onion
cenoura carrot
cogumelos mushrooms
couve cabbage
ervilhas beans
esparragado spinach purée
espinafres spinach
feijão beans (Brazilian stew)

framboesa raspberry
maça apple
melancia watermelon
morango strawberry
pêssego peach
toranja grapefruit

Gastro styles
açorda stale bread cooked with olive oil, garlic and egg
assado roast
bem passado well done
espetada skewered (kebab)
estufado braised
grelhado grilled
guisado braised
fumado smoked
mal passado rare
médio medium cooked
na brasa/no carvão charcoal grilled
no forno oven baked
petisco mini portion
recheado stuffed
sem sal without salt

Basics
aceite oil
açúcar sugar
alho garlic
caril curry
manteiga butter
pão bread
pimenta pepper
queijo/queijo fresco/requeijão cheese/cottage cheese/ricotta cheese

Index

Credits

Footprint credits

Editors: Claire Boobbyer,
Sarah Thorowgood
Publisher: Patrick Dawson
Series created by: Rachel Fielding
Proofreading: Stephanie Lambe
Cartography: Claire Benison, Kevin
Feeney, Robert Lunn, Sarah Sorensen
Design: Mytton Williams

Photography credits

Front cover: Alan Copson, Alamy
(Praça dom Pedro IV)
Inside: Adrian Lascom (p1 Padrão de
Descobrimentos, p5 Torre de Vasco
da Gama, p35 tram 28, p103 Cristo Rey)
Generic images: John Matchett
Back cover: Adrian Lascom,
(Praça da Figueira)

Print

Manufactured in Italy by LegoPrint.
Pulp from sustainable forests.

Footprint feedback

We try as hard as we can to make
each Footprint guide as up to date as
possible but, of course, things always
change. If you want to let us know
about your experiences – good, bad
or ugly – then don't delay, go to
www.footprintbooks.com and send
in your comments.

Publishing information

Footprint Lisbon
1st edition
Text and maps © Footprint
Handbooks Ltd Jan 2004

ISBN 1 903471 83 4
CIP DATA: a catalogue record for this
book is available from the British Library

Published by Footprint
6 Riverside Court
Lower Bristol Road
Bath, BA2 3DZ, UK
T +44 (0)1225 469141
F +44 (0)1225 469461
discover@footprintbooks.com
www.footprintbooks.com

Distributed in the USA by
Publishers Group West

For a different view…
choose a Footprint

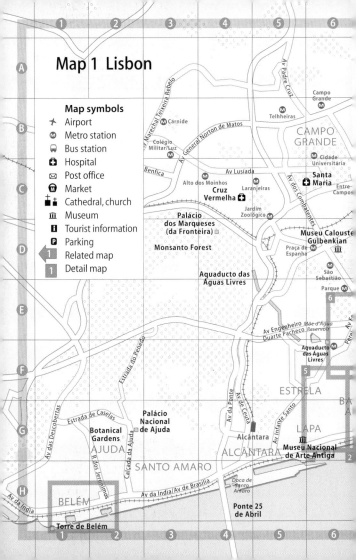

Map 1 Lisbon

Map symbols

✈ Airport
Ⓜ Metro station
🚍 Bus station
✚ Hospital
✉ Post office
🏪 Market
⛪ Cathedral, church
🏛 Museum
ℹ Tourist information
🅿 Parking
◀1 Related map
1 Detail map

Campo Grande
Telhheiras
CAMPO GRANDE
Cidade Universitária
Carnide
Colégio Militar/Luz
Santa Maria
Av Marechal Teixeira Rebelo
Av General Norton de Matos
Benfica
Av Lusiada
Alto dos Moinhos
Cruz Vermelha
Laranjeiras
Jardim Zoológico
Av dos Combatentes
Entre
Palácio dos Marqueses (da Fronteira)
Museu Calouste Gulbenkian
Monsanto Forest
Praça de Espanha
São Sebastião
Parque Ⓜ
Aquaducto das Águas Livres
6
Av Engenheiro Duarte Pacheco
Mãe d'Água Reservoir
Aquaducto das Águas Livres
5
Estrada do Penedo
ESTRELA
BA A
Estrada de Caselas
Palácio Nacional de Ajuda
Av da Ponte
Av de Ceuta
Av da Ponte
Alcântara
LAPA
Av Infante Santo
Botanical Gardens
AJUDA
Calçada da Ajuda
ALCÂNTARA
Museu Nacional de Arte Antiga
2
Av das Descobertas
R dos Jerónimos
SANTO AMARO
Av da India/Av de Brasília
Doca de Santo Amaro
BELÉM
Av da India
Ponte 25 de Abril
Torre de Belém

Map labels

LOURES

Sony Plaza

Torre Vasco da Gama

PARQUE DAS NAÇÕES

Av de Berlim

Oriente

Pavilhão de Portugal

Vasco da Gama Shopping Centre

Cabo Ruivo

Oceanário

Portela

Circular

Av Marechal Craveiro Lopes

Av Almirante Gago Coutinho

Av Marechal Gomes da Costa

Pavilhão do Conhecimento Ciência Viva

Olivais

Alameda dos Oceanos

Av do Santo Condestável

Dom Henrique

R da Cintura do Porto

Ⓜ Alvalade

Chelas

Ⓜ Roma

dos Estados Unidos da América

CAMPO PEQUENO

Ⓜ Areeiro

Bela Vista

Campo Pequeno

Av João XXI

SALDANHA

Av João Crisóstomo

Olaias

Ⓜ Alameda

Arco do Cego

Av Almirante Reis

Ⓜ Casa-Museu Dr Anastácio Gonçalves

Av Almirante Reis

Arroios

Museu Nacional do Azulejo Ⓜ

ANJOS

INTENDENTE

TOREL

Av Infante Dom Henrique

River Tagus

N

0 km 1
0 miles 1

Liberdade

GRAÇA

SANTA APOLÓNIA

OSSIO

ROSSIO

Castelo de São Jorge

Santa Apolónia

Belém detail

BAIXA

CHIADO

Sé

ALFAMA

4

R Dom Francisco de Almeida

Museu Marinha

Mosteiro dos Jerónimos

dos adre

3

R São Francisco Xavier

Santa Maria

R de Belém

Design Museum (Centro Cultural de Belém) Ⓜ

Praça do Império

R da Torre de Belém

R Bartolomeu Dias

BELÉM

Av da India/Av de Brasília

Padrão dos Descobrimentos

To Cacilhas

Torre de Belém

River Tagus

7 8 9 10 11 12

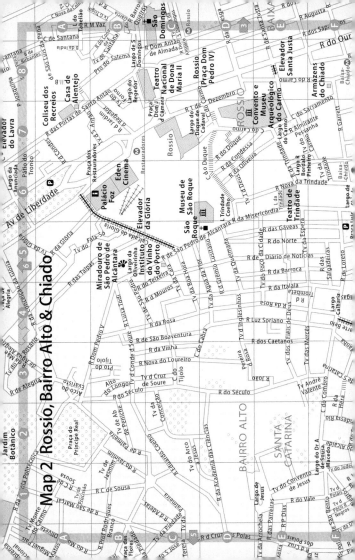

Map 2 Rossio, Bairro Alto & Chiado

BAIRRO ALTO

SANTA CATARINA

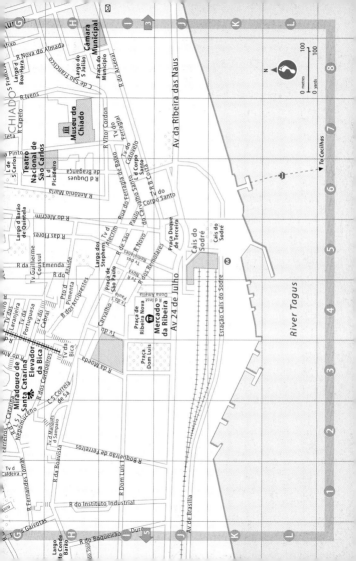

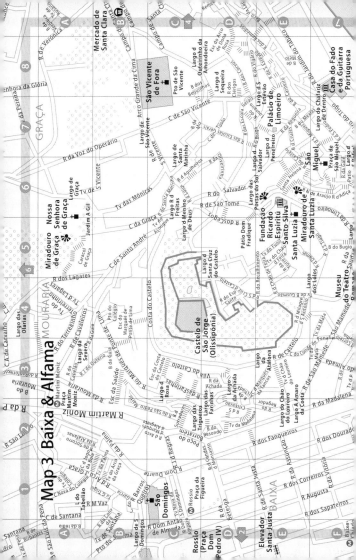

Map 4 Graça & Santa Apolónia

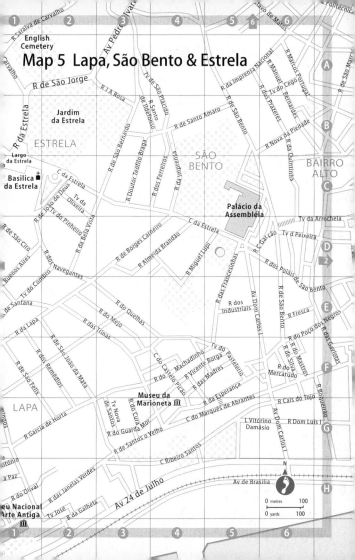

Map 5 Lapa, São Bento & Estrela

English Cemetery

R Saraiva de Carvalho

R de São Jorge

R J A Rosa

Av Pedro Álvares

Tv de São Tiago

R da Imprensa Nacional

R Marcos Portugal

R de São Marçal

Politécnica

R da Estrela

Jardim da Estrela

ESTRELA

R de São Bernardo

R Santo

de Ildefonso

R dos Ferreiros

R de Santo Amaro

R de São Bento

R Manuel Bernardes

Tv do Cego

R dos Prazeres

R Nova da Piedade

R da Quintinha

Largo da Estrela

Basílica da Estrela

C da Estrela

Tv da Oliveira

R de João de Deus

R Tv do Pinheiro

R da Bela Vista

R Doutor Teófilo Braga

SÃO BENTO

Palácio da Assembléia

C da Estrela

Tv da Arrochela

BAIRRO ALTO

R de São Ciro

Buenos Aires

R dos Navegantes

Tv do Combro

R de Santana

R de Borges Carneiro

R Almeida Brandão

R Miguel Lupi

R das Francesinhas

R dos Industriais

Av Dom Carlos I

R de São Bento

C Gaivão

Tv d Peixeira

R dos Poiais de São Bento

R Fresca

R do Poço dos Negros

R das Gaivotas

R da Lapa

R dos Remédios

R de São João da Mata

R do Mejo

R das Trinas

R do Quelhas

C do Castelo Picão

R Vicente Borga

R das Madres

Tv do Pateiro

R de Silva

Mercatudo

R do Mastros

LAPA

R de São Félix

R Garcia de Horta

R do Olival

Tv Nova de Santos

R da Cura

R do Guarda Mor

Museu da Marioneta

R da Esperança

C do Marquês de Abrantes

R Cais do Tojo

L Vitorino Damásio

R Boqueirão

R Dom Luís I

R de Santos o Velho

R das Janelas Verdes

Tv José

R da Galheta

C Ribeiro Santos

Av 24 de Julho

Av de Brasília

Av Dom Carlos I

Museu Nacional Arte Antiga

0 metres 100
0 yards 100

N

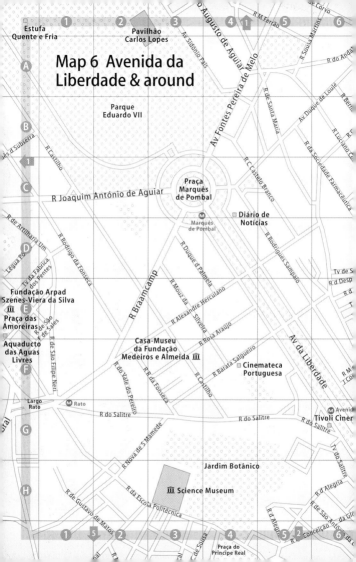

Map 6 Avenida da Liberdade & around

A

B

1

C

D

E

F

G

H

Estufa Quente e Fria

Pavilhão Carlos Lopes

Parque Eduardo VII

Praça Marquês de Pombal

Marquês de Pombal

Diário de Notícias

Fundação Arpad Szenes-Viera da Silva

Praça das Amoreiras

Aquaducto das Aguas Livres

Casa-Museu da Fundação Medeiros e Almeida

Cinemateca Portuguesa

Largo Rato

Rato

R do Salitre

R do Salitre

Tívoli Ciner

Avenid

Jardim Botânico

Science Museum

Praça do Principe Real

R Augusto de Aguiar

R M Ferrão

de Corvo

R de Santa Maria

Av Sidonio Pais

Av Fontes Pereira de Melo

R de Sousa Martins

R do Anda

Av Duque de Loulé

R Bern

R Luciano Co

R da Sociedade Farmacéutica

R Joaquim António de Aguiar

Castilho

R C Castelo Branco

R Rodrigues Sampaio

Tv de S

R d Desp

R de Artilharia Um

Légua Pó

R Rodrigo da Fonseca

Tv da Fábrica dos Pentes

R Braamcamp

R Duque d'Palmela

R Mouz da Silveira

R Alexandre Herculano

R Rosa Araújo

R de São Filipe Neri

R de São Sales

R do Vale do Pereiro

R da Fonseca

R Castilho

R Barata Salgueiro

Av da Liberdade

R M J Cor

R Nova de S Mamede

R de Gustavo de Matos

R da Escola Politécnica

R d Alegria

R de São Anto

R d' Conceição

da

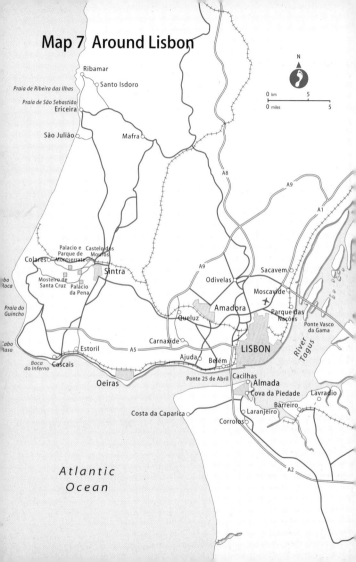